Haley De Korne
Language Activism

Contributions to the Sociology of Language

Edited by
Ofelia García
Francis M. Hult

Founding editor
Joshua A. Fishman

Volume 114

Haley De Korne
Language Activism

Imaginaries and Strategies of Minority Language Equality

DE GRUYTER
MOUTON

Author
Haley De Korne
University of Oslo
h.de.korne@iln.uio.no

The publication was financially supported by the University of Oslo and the Research Council of Norway through its Centers of Excellence funding scheme, project number 223265 (Center for Multilingualism in Society across the Lifespan-MultiLing)

ISBN 978-1-5015-2145-4
e-ISBN (PDF) 978-1-5015-1156-1
e-ISBN (EPUB) 978-1-5015-1142-4
ISSN 1861-0676
DOI https://doi.org/10.1515/9781501511561

This work is licensed under the Creative Commons Attribution-NonCommercial-NoDerivatives 4.0 International License. For details go to: https://creativecommons.org/licenses/by-nc-nd/4.0/.

Library of Congress Control Number: 2021930279

Bibliographic information published by the Deutsche Nationalbibliothek
The Deutsche Nationalbibliothek lists this publication in the Deutsche Nationalbibliografie; detailed bibliographic data are available on the Internet at http://dnb.dnb.de.

© 2023 Haley De Korne, published by Walter de Gruyter Inc., Boston/Berlin
This volume is text- and page-identical with the hardback published in 2021.
Cover image: sculpies/Shutterstock
Typesetting: Integra Software Services Pvt. Ltd.
Printing and binding: CPI books GmbH, Leck

www.degruyter.com

Acknowledgements

Thank you, *gracias, xquixepe'laatu, miigwech, merci, tusen hjertelig takk* to the many, many people who have contributed to making this book possible.

Estoy infinitamente agradecida con tod@s l@s istmeñ@s que me recibieron y compartieron su conocimiento y sus experiencias conmigo con una gracia infinita. Espero haber logrado reflejar en estas páginas un poco de lo importante de sus trabajos e iniciativas. Desafortunadamente no pude incluir todo lo compartido por cuestiones de espacio, y por eso pido perdón. Todo lo que aprendí de ustedes inspiró e impactó el marco teórico del activismo lingüístico propuesto en este libro. Xquixepe'laatu guiratu.

I am indebted to all the language activists who have shared their knowledge, experiences, and time with me– in particular in Oaxaca, but also in other parts of the world. I have tried to capture some of your inspiring work in these pages, however I am keenly aware of how much I have also had to leave out or failed to capture. For every person whose efforts are described in this book, there are many more whose valuable efforts are not. This book was inspired not just by those who are explicitly included in it, but also by all of the teachers, students, poets, musicians, scholars, and families who use and promote minoritized languages, and who I have been fortunate to cross paths with over the years.

Among the colleagues and friends in Oaxaca and Mexico to whom I owe great thanks are *bizana'* Víctor Cata and *benda'* Natalia Toledo for sharing their time, passion, and knowledge as language activists. *Muchísimas gracias* to Gabriela Pérez Báez and Mario López Gopar for invaluable mentorship and collaboration. Sincere thanks to Ximena Leon Fernández, Manuel David Ramírez Medina, Roselia Cha'ca, *bendahuiini'* Kiara Ríos Ríos, Kenia Velasco Gutiérrez, Gibrán Morales Carranza, Claudia Guerra, María Isabel García Rasgado, Vidal Ramírez Pineda, Rosario López Jimenez, María Soledad Pérez López, Mónica Esteva García, Reyna López López, Velma Orozco Trujillo, José López de la Cruz, Diana Lenia Toledo Rasgado, Janet Chávez Santiago, Ulises Hernández Luna, Aurelio Toledo Matus, Antonio Ortíz, Melanie McComsey, Kate Reistenberg, Pedro Cardona, Carlos Antonio Celaya Gómez, Didiert Hernández Martinez, Anaxhiely Osorio Sanchez, Leticia Gutierrez Pacheco, Margarito Vicente Santiago, Sergio Acevedo and the students and teachers of the Faculty of Languages, Universidad Autónoma Beníto Juárez de Oaxaca, among many more.

There are many mentors who have taught and encouraged me over the years. I thank Nancy Hornberger for her support during the conceptualization and first phase of this study, and for the example she sets of integrity, curiosity, and dedication as an educational linguist. I have been fortunate to be surrounded by wonderful colleagues at the MultiLing Center and the Department of Linguistics and

Scandinavian Studies at the University of Oslo during my subsequent data collection and the writing process of this book. *Takk* and *kiitos* to Pia Lane, Elizabeth Lanza, and Unn Røyneland for providing encouragement, advice, and inspiration as socially engaged scholars. I am grateful for critical discussions and input from the Multilingualism and Globalization group at MultiLing, including Toril Opsahl, Alastair Pennycook, Kellie Gonçalves, Jorunn Simonsen Thingnes, Rafael Lomeu Gomes, Olga Solovova, and Ingvild Badhwar Valen-Sendstad, for collaborations with Judith Purkarthofer, Kristin Vold Lexander, James Costa, and Anne Golden, and for the camaraderie of everyone at MultiLing. My work has also benefited greatly from conversations and collaborations with colleagues near and far, including Marilyn Martin-Jones, Ruth Rouvier, Wesley Leonard, Joke Dewilde, Ingrid Rodrick Beiler, Hilde Sollid, Åse Mette Johansen, Ana Deumert, and Guri Bordal Steien.

My former colleagues in the Educational Linguistics community at the University of Pennsylvania have motivated me to be more rigorous and humane as a scholar, including my committee members Nelson Flores, Robert Moore, and Sharon Ravitch, and compañer@s Catrice Barrett, Joanna Siegel, Miranda Weinberg, Sofía Chaparro, Frances Kvietok Dueñas, Coleman Donaldson, Aldo Anzures Tapia, Katie Murphy, Bridget Goodman, Jamie Schissel, Cécile Evers, Mariam Durrani, Holly Link, and Américo Mendoza Mori, among others. My work has also been supported and shaped by the generous mentorship of Leslie Saxon, Hossein Nassaji, Lorna Williams, Su Urbanczyk and colleagues at the University of Victoria; Jean-Jacques Weber and colleagues at the University of Luxembourg; and Michael Byram, Michael Fleming, Richard Smith and Stéphanie Pourcel at Durham University. *Miigwech* to George Trudeau, Kenny Pheasant, members of the Burt Lake Band of Ottawa and Chippewa Indians, and other teachers and participants in Anishinaabemowin programs in the Great Lakes region, and *wanishi* to Shelley DePaul and participants in the Lenape program in Pennsylvania for the inspiration of your work as teachers and activists, which has fed my motivation and thinking in this book.

Data for this book was collected between 2013 and 2019; I gratefully acknowledge the support of a pre-doctoral fellowship from the Smithonian Institution Department of Anthropology in 2014, a doctoral mobility fellowship with the Lacito Research Center through LabEx EFL in 2016, and the support of the Center for Multilingualism in Society across the Lifespan, University of Oslo (supported by the Research Council of Norway through its Centres of Excellence funding scheme, project number 223265) from 2016- present.

Thank you to the editors of the Contributions to the Sociology of Language series, Ofelia García and Francis M. Hult, for the honor of developing and publishing this volume in such esteemed company. I am also grateful for the editorial support, patience, and collegiality of everyone in the De Gruyter Mouton team. Any remaining mistakes in this volume are solely mine.

Last but not least, I am grateful for the constant encouragement and love of friends and family in different corners of the globe. Above all I thank my mother, Meg Littin, who is a role model of strength, perseverance, and compassion, and an avid supporter of even my most improbable dreams.

Contents

Acknowledgements —— V

List of Figures —— XIII

List of Tables —— XV

Chapter 1
Advocating for linguistic equality —— 1
1.1 Are all ways of communicating equal? Imaginaries of linguistic equality —— 3
1.2 Advocating for what? Approaches to 'language' —— 7
1.3 Advocating how? Approaches to equality and social change —— 11
1.4 A repertoire of activism strategies —— 17
1.5 Overview of book —— 22
1.6 Context and conduct of this study —— 25

Chapter 2
The moving target of activism: Changing language ecologies in the Isthmus of Tehuantepec —— 29
2.1 Indigenous multilingualisms: Pre-colonial language ecologies —— 32
2.2 From languages to *dialectos*: Colonial language ecologies —— 37
2.3 *Castellanización*: Nationalist language ecologies —— 38
2.4 Neoliberal 'multicultural' language ecologies —— 40
2.5 Traditions of Indigenous language activism —— 42
2.6 On-going change in the language ecology —— 44
2.7 Summary: Activism characteristics in changing times —— 52

Chapter 3
Creating knowledge and resources: Strategies in scholarship —— 56
3.1 Scholarly engagement with minoritized languages —— 62
3.1.1 Working as a scholar-activist across multiple disciplines —— 68
3.1.2 Methodological choices in support of language equality —— 70
3.2 Scholar-activist strategies in the Isthmus —— 75
3.2.1 Creating resources —— 75
3.2.2 Representing communication practices —— 78

3.2.3 Connecting people, spaces and resources —— 81
3.3 Summary: Characteristics of scholar activism —— 83

Chapter 4
Connecting community and school spaces: Strategies in primary and secondary education —— 86
4.1 Language (in)equality and education —— 90
4.1.1 Pro-diversity education: From strict immersion to plurilingual repertoires —— 91
4.2 Language and schooling in the Isthmus of Tehuantepec —— 94
4.3 Language activism in education in the Isthmus —— 99
4.3.1 Connecting school and community —— 99
4.3.2 Representing Diidxazá as a part of formal education —— 103
4.4 Summary: Characteristics of language activism in education —— 105

Chapter 5
Representing legitimate languages and identities: Strategies in higher education —— 109
5.1 Multilingualism and identities in the Isthmus —— 112
5.2 Language activism in the Tehuantepec Faculty of Languages —— 117
5.2.1 Representing legitimate languages and multilingual identities —— 120
5.2.2 Creating Isthmus Zapotec teachers —— 126
5.3 Summary: Characteristics of higher education activism —— 132

Chapter 6
Imagining convivial multilingual literacies: Strategies in community-based education —— 137
6.1 Indigenous literacies and community-based education —— 140
6.2 Isthmus Zapotec literacies —— 142
6.3 Imaginaries of literacy in the *Camino de la Iguana* —— 146
6.3.1 Our alphabet: Sharing sounds and symbols —— 148
6.3.2 We have a unique way to name the world: Diidxazá in the canon of universal literature —— 152
6.3.3 *Convivencia* in the *Camino de la Iguana* —— 158
6.4 Summary: Characteristics of community-based education activism —— 161

Chapter 7
Imagining future traditions: Strategies in popular culture spaces —— 165
7.1   Negotiating social meanings through popular culture activism —— 167
7.2   Popular culture activism in the Isthmus —— 169
7.2.1   Wake up! Hip-hop events and representations —— 170
7.2.2   The granddaughters of the *Binnigula'za*: Feminist events and representations —— 174
7.2.3   Creating virtual resources and spaces of negotiation —— 178
7.3   Summary: Characteristics of popular culture activism —— 184

Chapter 8
Developing a repertoire of activism strategies —— 188
8.1   Language activism strategies across contexts and scales —— 193
8.1.1   Strategic creating —— 194
8.1.2   Strategic connecting —— 196
8.1.3   Strategic representing —— 198
8.1.4   Characteristics across scales and activist positionality —— 199
8.2   Engaging in social change through language —— 203
8.2.1   Diidxazá as a deictic —— 205
8.2.2   'A grain of sand' theory of change —— 208
8.3   Summary: Convivial language activism —— 211

Appendix A: Language activism strategy framework —— 215

Appendix B: Transcription conventions —— 217

Appendix C: Glossary of common abbreviations, Diidxazá, and Spanish terms —— 219

References —— 221

Index —— 241

List of Figures

Figure 1 Actions and goals of language activism strategies —— 19
Figure 2 Characteristics of language activism strategies —— 20
Figure 3 The country of Mexico, highlighting the state of Oaxaca and the city of Juchitán —— 33
Figure 4 Map of Indigenous languages of Oaxaca —— 34
Figure 5 Geographic representation of Isthmus Zapotec use across the Isthmus —— 46
Figure 6 Geographic representation of Istmus Zapotec dialects —— 48
Figure 7 Sign displayed at the three main entrances to Juchitán —— 49
Figure 8 *Centro de desarrollo infantil "Ba'du-huini"* (Child development center "little child"), Juchitán —— 50
Figure 9 *Yu'Du' Lidxi Diuxi* (Church (sacred house) Home of God), La Ventosa —— 51
Figure 10 *Shunco* (Sweetheart, little one), San Blas Atempa —— 51
Figure 11 PowerPoint slide from primary school initiative —— 86
Figure 12 Pedagogical materials created by secondary school students —— 105
Figure 13 '*Aveces quisiera apantallar que se hablar zapoteco . . .* ' meme —— 115
Figure 14 Ximena Léon Fernández distributing flyers in a public park in Juchitán to promote UABJO courses —— 124
Figure 15 Students and teachers sharing a meal at the end of the semester —— 129
Figure 16 *Camino de la Iguana* poster 2014 (left); The Juchitán-based publication *Guchachi' Reza* 1982 (right) —— 138
Figure 17 Poster commemorating the 60th anniversary of the creation of the popular alphabet —— 144
Figure 18 Víctor teaching in the *Camino de la Iguana* —— 152
Figure 19 Natalia teaching in the *Camino de la Iguana* —— 156
Figure 20 Natalia and Víctor during a closing *convivio* —— 159
Figure 21 Poster for the '1st Festival of Female Artists in the Isthmus of Tehuantepec "*Gunaa Ruzaani*"' 3–5 April 2018 —— 175
Figure 22 Meme from the page *Memes Idiomas UABJO* —— 183
Figure 23 Lenia Toledo Rasgado and Reyna López López preparing a celebration for the end of their workshops in La Ventosa —— 191

List of Tables

Table 1 Key language activism strategies among scholars in the Isthmus —— 83
Table 2 Formal education institutions available to students in the Isthmus and Indigenous language inclusion —— 95
Table 3 Key language activism strateges in primary and secondary schooling —— 108
Table 4 Key language activism strategies in higher education in the Isthmus —— 133
Table 5 Key language activism strategies in a community-based literacy workshop —— 162
Table 6 Key language activism strategies in popular culture initiatives —— 185
Table 7 Examples of language activism strategies with contrasting characteristics —— 200

Chapter 1
Advocating for linguistic equality

Para mí es importantísimo difundirlo [zapoteco]. Pero siento que el gran error ha sido--- el gran error antes era enseñar español y se perdió el zapoteco. Y ahora el gran esfuerzo es rescatar el zapoteco. Pero el gran error está en querer forzar a las personas a hablar zapoteco. Ya no puedes recurrir a la barbarie de antes obviamente. Pero entonces ahora, ¿cómo le haces? Hasta que no crees una conciencia real en las personas, no va a haber eso.

For me it's extremely important to spread [Zapotec]. But I feel that the big mistake has been– The big mistake before was to teach Spanish, and Zapotec was lost. And now the big effort is to rescue Zapotec. But the big mistake is in wanting to force people to speak Zapotec. You can't return to the barbarity of before obviously. So now, how do you do it? Until you create a real awareness in people, it won't happen.[1]

(Mayoli García, Interview May 2014)

Language is one of the domains of social life where inequalities are pervasive; consequently, it is also a point of focus for those in pursuit of social justice and change. The *kind of change* which social actors envisage varies, however, and ideas about *how* positive change may be achieved are likewise diverse and sometimes in conflict. As the above comment by Mayoli García,[2] a student of Isthmus Zapotec language in Oaxaca, Mexico, notes, the obligatory teaching of one language (in this case Spanish) led to the displacement of Indigenous languages of Mexico such as Zapotec. She argues that current efforts to achieve a more equal status for Zapotec should not follow the same forceful approach to changing language practices, but should rather focus on creating awareness about this issue. Her concern about how to be an effective advocate for Zapotec, creating a positive change in the unequal, minoritized status of the language and the people who speak it, is also the driving question of this book. How to bring about positive social change in relation to language? Who participates, what kinds of change do they imagine, and what actions do they take?

As conceptualized in this book, *language activism* is a social project that aims to counter language-related inequalities, and may encompass many different actors, imaginaries, and actions. I view various forms of activism, advocacy, promotion and stance-taking as part of the same larger political project to resist inequalities and/ or imagine new avenues towards linguistic equality. The social

---

[1] All translations are mine. Please see appendix B on transcription, citation, and date conventions.
[2] I use a mixture of pseudonyms and real names in this study, following individual preferences.

Open Access. © 2021 Haley De Korne, published by De Gruyter. This work is licensed under the Creative Commons Attribution-NonCommercial-NoDerivatives 4.0 International License.
https://doi.org/10.1515/9781501511561-001

positioning of actors and the level and kind of activism they engage in vary widely; some social actors contributing to this project identify as language activists, advocates or promoters to various degrees, such as Mayoli. There are also many actors who identify neither as activists nor as language professionals, yet it is useful to consider their imaginaries and actions as part of this broader social domain, as will be examined in the chapters that follow. Language activism does not target language alone; rather its targets can include any of the many inequalities in which linguistic discrimination plays a role, including economic, political, gender, class and racialized forms of marginalization. The positioning of actors as members or non-members of minoritized language communities is complex, as is the positioning of actors as insiders or outsiders of certain social domains, such as public education. Rather than accept a simplifying distinction between community-insider activists and community-outsider advocates, or disruptive activists and system-internal advocates, I examine how actors participate in fluid forms of activism, advocacy, and language politics across multiple communities of practice. By adopting a broad understanding of language activism and advocacy in relation to who participates, the social coalitions that they participate in, and what actions can contribute to increasing linguistic equality, I aim to provide a fuller picture of the power dynamics of linguistic inequality and potential networks of support.

This book will tell the stories of a few of the language activists engaged in resisting the inequalities experienced by members of the Isthmus Zapotec language community. Isthmus Zapotec is an Indigenous language spoken primarily in the Isthmus of Tehuantepec, Oaxaca, Mexico, hereafter also referred to interchangeably by the auto-denomination Diidxazá and the common simplification Zapotec/ *Zapoteco*.[3] These stories provide insight into the imaginaries and strategies of language activism initiatives across several social domains, including academic research, public schooling, higher education, community education, and popular culture. Minority language activism can occur in many social domains and can be initiated from official political spaces, often called top-down initiatives, as well as personal, communal, and informal spaces, often called bottom-up initiatives. This is not a smooth nor linear process; positive linguistic change

---

[3] There are four branches of the Zapotec language family, with a debated number of language variants which are not mutually intelligible (Pérez Báez and Kaufman 2016). Many of these languages are locally called simply *Zapoteco*/ Zapotec. The terms Zapotec and *Zapoteco* in this book refer only to the Isthmus Zapotec variant; where other variants are mentioned this is explicitly indicated. At the time of writing this book there are on-going discussions about spelling norms for Isthmus Zapotec. I use the spelling 'Diidxazá', which is the spelling used by the 1956 popular alphabet and the accepted standard in use during my fieldwork.

holds different meanings or imaginaries for different actors from local to global levels, and is often a topic of intense debate. This book focuses primarily on language activism and advocacy at the local level, drawing attention to how diverse social actors imagine and enact strategies which aim to contest linguistic inequalities in a specific place and time. Through ethnographic description and analysis of multiple language activism initiatives, I sketch a repertoire of language activism strategies and aim to provide greater understanding of language activism as a negotiated social project which may inform and encourage activists, scholars, and educators working for change in other contexts of linguistic diversity and inequality.

1.1 Are all ways of communicating equal? Imaginaries of linguistic equality

Diversity is an inherent feature of the phenomenon of language. The range of linguistic families in the world, numerous dialects and registers within each community, and the variation of communication practices among different actors and contexts, and over time, are all part of the immense variation within human communication (Blommaert 2010). The Isthmus Zapotec language is no exception, as a part of the larger Zapotec language family which contains extensive variation and is spoken alongside other Indigenous languages and Spanish in southern Mexico (Pérez Báez and Kaufman 2016). These different ways of communicating are considered to be of equal value by linguists, who point out that each social group achieves their communication needs through a unique combination of features, including linguistic features (such as sounds, structures, and styles) as well as visual features (such as gestures and images). Diverse ways of communicating are of equal social value in that they are equally capable of fulfilling communicative functions within their unique time and place.

The equality of communication practices from this scholarly perspective quickly shifts when viewed from a socially, historically, and politically specific perspective, however. Humans– from social groups and scholarly disciplines to institutions and governments– have created a variety of ways of categorizing and valuing different language practices, so that language diversity is not neutral in most interactions, but is often deployed in the creation of power and hierarchy. Inherent diversity in sound, style, and so forth, is used to create social distinction and often social hierarchies (Bourdieu 1984; Agha 2007). In this sense, *minority language* should not be understood as an objective label relating to a low number of speakers or reduced territory, but rather a socio-political condition defined by a lower or minoritized status relative to other languages and subject to constant negotiation and shift. As discussed further in chapter two, in the Isthmus of Tehuantepec, Indigenous language speakers are often considered to have a lower social status than speakers of Spanish, with Indigenous languages typically being referred to as *dialectos*, popularly understood to be a rudimentary form of speech which is lesser-than-language. Many Indigenous languages around the world have been minoritized through similar processes of colonization and discrimination. Likewise a (minoritized) *speech community*, as explored in this volume, is neither a fixed nor homogenous entity, but refers to a social group whose members engage in shared meaning-making practices. Rather than being separate and contained, language or speech communities are often understood and defined in relation to other groups (Morgan 2004). Hierarchies also exist within speech communities, often among speakers of different varieties, generations, genders or social classes. For example, young adult speakers of Isthmus Zapotec are sometimes mocked by older speakers, as discussed in chapter 5. The social construction and negotiation of endangered or marginalized language communities is especially complex as these communities are often (re)defining themselves under conditions of discrimination and material inequality (Kroskrity 2014). Social difference and discrimination may be based on any feature of communication, and occur within as well as between speech communities.

This tendency to minoritize in contexts of language diversity has long posed a challenge for scholars and members of multilingual speech communities; as Haugen (1973) wrote, "language is not a problem unless it is used as a basis for discrimination, but it has in fact been so used as far back as we have records" (54). The role that language plays in the creation and reinforcement of social inequality may be subtle and overlooked, yet can lead to important social consequences. Within educational contexts, children from minoritized speech communities are often disadvantaged and evaluated poorly on the basis of their linguistic abilities, regardless of their content knowledge and general capacities (Heller and Martin-Jones 2001). Many residents of the Isthmus of Tehuantepec, or *Istmeños*, recount their negative experiences being punished and silenced in Spanish-only schooling (see chapters 2 and 4). The impacts of linguistic inequality are felt in many other areas of social life as well, from the legal and health systems to the employment market. With this in mind, Ingrid Piller has argued that "addressing linguistic disadvantage must be a central facet of the social justice agenda of our time" (2016: 6).

The notion that humans should not be disadvantaged on the basis of the language or dialect they speak was part of the broader ideology of human rights which received widespread acknowledgement in certain social and political circles following World War II. An influential position paper published by the education branch of the United Nations, UNESCO, in 1953, promoted the use of vernacular or mother-tongue education for children from minoritized communities, contrasting with the prevalent trend of educating children in majority, national languages only (UNESCO 1953). This position has been reinforced through numerous other declarations and policies at international and national levels, such as the UN Declaration on the Rights of Indigenous Peoples (United Nations 2007) and the Mexican national Law on the Linguistic Rights of Indigenous People (*Ley General de Derechos Lingüísticos de Los Pueblos Indígenas* 2003). Linguistic rights have become closely intertwined with discourses and initiatives promoting human rights and social justice in many parts of the world (Skutnabb-Kangas and Phillipson 1994). New forms of language activism on the international scale continue to emerge, such as the UN declaring 2019 as the year of Indigenous languages.[4]

Linguistic equality has therefore come to be an established ideal in many social domains, in addition to being a fundamental notion within linguistic science, although it is far from being achieved in social relations. In this sense, linguistic equality is a social imaginary rather than a social reality. The fact that numerous people share an orientation in favor of a pluralist (and plurilingual) way of life is evidence of what Charles Taylor (2002, 2004) describes as 'modern social imaginaries', expanding Anderson's (1991) imagined communities beyond a nation-state frame. Taylor (2002) describes the social imaginary as "the ways in which people imagine their social existence, how they fit together with others, how things go on between them and their fellows, the expectations that are normally met, and the deeper normative notions and images that underlie these expectations" (106). He discusses how normative social imaginaries shift over time, noting that notions of equality and mutual benevolence among individuals (including inherent human rights) have developed through a "long march" from governance by naturalized hierarchy towards the social imaginary of shared democratic control, a transition which is not complete. I situate the social project of contesting language inequalities within this overarching social imaginary, which projects a specific "moral order of society" (Taylor 2002: 92) in which all voices deserve equal value. Like human rights, linguistic equality is an imaginary which often remains a struggle to uphold in social practice due to conflicting norms and politico-economic structures which promote the wellbeing of some over that of others.

The variety of perspectives and beliefs held by different social actors in relation to language has been explored in the study of language ideologies, or

---

[4] https://en.iyil2019.org/

"the understandings, beliefs, and expectations that influence all choices made by language users . . . [and] speakers' sometimes-idealized evaluations and judgments of appropriate language forms" (McGroarty 2010:3). Complex and conflicting ideologies have been described in Indigenous language contexts in Mexico, where expectations of purism, tradition, adaptation and change overlap and clash (Hill and Hill 1986; Messing 2007). Kroskrity (2018) argues that although language ideologies have been studied individually, they usually exist in complex constellations which he terms 'language ideological assemblages' (Kroskrity 2018). Conflicting ideologies within a language activism initiative can prove challenging for those involved (Kroskrity and Field 2009; Kroskrity 2009), yet this multiplicity is largely inevitable, and worthy of consideration in and of itself. I view ideologies and imaginaries similarly, noting that diverse actors in the Isthmus hold different views of what is positive or desirable, and negative or undesirable in relation to the changing communication practices around them.

Further, a variety of discourses, or "particular ways of representing part of the world" (Fairclough 2003: 26) (see also Foucault 1980), contribute to strengthening or weakening different ideological positions. For example, a discourse that represents Indigenous Oaxacan languages as valuable and of equal status with Spanish, such as the *Todos se llaman lenguas* [They're all called languages] campaign, by the non-profit cultural center *Centro Académico y Cultural San Pablo* in Oaxaca City, is informed by and contributes to the imaginary of linguistic equality, while resisting language hierarchies. The discourses produced by the campaign through flyers and on-line publicity[5] reinforce and re-create this imaginary, attempting to spread it among members of the public. This imaginary also helps to motivate the *Centro Académico y Cultural San Pablo* to undertake practices which promote Indigenous languages in academic spheres, including hosting a bi-annual conference on Oto-manguean languages (the language family within which Zapotec is classified) and maintaining a large collection of Indigenous language books (among other languages and topics).[6] At the same time, the fact that many people refer to Indigenous languages as *dialectos*, not as languages, shows that the colonial-era ideology which places Spanish above all Indigenous forms of communication is widespread and present in daily discourses. The language ideological assemblage in Oaxaca thus includes imaginaries of linguistic equality, and on-going ideologies of linguistic inferiority.

---

5 Promotional video: https://www.youtube.com/watch?v=0Vck43KLPKc. Original campaign website: www.todas-lenguas.mx
6 http://bibliotecajuandecordova.mx

To claim that linguistic equality is a social imaginary is not to claim that it is a unanimously accepted norm, nor that all members of society embrace or pursue this imaginary in the same way. While arguing that linguistic equality represents a wide-spread ideal or imaginary around the world in the twenty-first century, I also note that there are different notions of what linguistic equality is in practice, and different notions of how it should be achieved. For some, the inequality experienced by Indigenous language speakers in Mexico is best addressed by imposing the use of Spanish in all contexts, so that equality is understood as a forced homogeneity. For others, equality is best addressed through changing social norms and services so that speakers of diverse languages will have equal access and opportunities while using their own language. These differences in ideologies surrounding Isthmus Zapotec and other minoritized languages contribute to the tense politics of language activism. In education contexts where choices about which languages and which linguistic varieties to teach must be made within the constraints of time and resources, there are often fraught considerations over what will contribute to social well-being and long-term equality for students. Understanding the imaginaries present in a specific context is a crucial first step towards ascertaining how these imaginaries might be advocated for and eventually brought closer to reality.

1.2 Advocating for what? Approaches to 'language'

Among the social actors who espouse imaginaries of linguistic equality, there is a great deal of variation in what is understood by 'language'. Perspectives or ideologies of language may be painted in broad brush strokes as ranging from viewing language as an object to viewing language as a social practice. The view that language is an object that can be considered autonomous from context is well-established within linguistics, where structuralist and positivist approaches to language have enjoyed considerable attention and prestige. Linguistic scholarship remains influenced by Saussures's *langue/ parole* and Chomsky's (1965) competence/performance dichotomies, both of which give higher status to the study of *langue*, competence, and linguistic form. The desire to standardize linguistic practices to conform to an idealized target or native speaker has motivated much applied linguistics scholarship, and in turn influenced many language classrooms. Although there are discussions about the need to go beyond simplistic notions of mother tongues and native speaker competence (Firth and Wagner 1997; Larsen-Freeman and Cameron 2008), these essentialist notions remain commonplace in much language education practice. Autonomous, objectified views of language have thus been taken up among actors outside of the ivory tower, in particular through schooling. Promoting an essentialized link between a (standard) language, a culture, and an identity has been a strategy of control among the founders of nation-states, in particular in Europe (Gal 2006). Political rhetoric, and language and education policy, continue to create a monolingual and monocultural norm in many parts of the world (Tollefson 1991; Piller 2016).

Heller (2007) discusses how research in the field of bilingualism has helped deconstruct autonomous notions of language, as well as static views of identity, culture and community. She argues for a shift "away from the whole bounded units of code and community, and towards a more processural and materialist approach which privileges language as social practice, speakers as social actors and boundaries as products of social action" (1). A social practice approach views language as something that is created within and by a specific sociocultural context, and that simultaneously impacts and shapes its context of use (Goffman 1981; Bakhtin 1986; Bhabha 1994; Makoni and Pennycook 2007). I refer to this perspective on language and community as constructivist, using this as an umbrella term for the constellation of perspectives that focus on context, process, and the co-construction of both language and social groups.

Constructivist perspectives on language have led to the promotion of integrated and fluid language use in multilingual contexts, building from additive bilingualism (Lambert 1975) towards flexible multilingualism (Blackledge and Creese 2010) and translanguaging (Williams 1994; García 2009a). These integrated approaches to multilingualism stand in contrast to 'parallel monolingualism', the ideology that multilinguals should use each language autonomously, rather than mixing and overlapping (Heller 1999). On a larger social scale, a constructivist perspective attends to the linguistic ecologies that emerge through interaction and contact among language communities, creating flows of influence and exchange, especially in multilingual territories (Haugen 1972; Fill and Muhlhausler 2001; Maffi 2001). Power and influence among speakers and speech communities is not understood as top-down nor unilateral, but rather as a dynamic relationship in constant negotiation as a result of numerous contextual factors from local to global scales (Ricento and Hornberger 1996; Hornberger and Hult 2008). Additionally social perspectives on language typically claim criticality, examining power relations and inequalities that may be established and perpetuated through language practices (Bourdieu 1991; Heller and Martin-Jones 2001; Pennycook 2001).

Social practice or constructivist perspectives on language are also reproduced within certain strands of education and popular culture that embrace the fluidity and co-construction of knowledge and meaning. For some educators language learning is understood as a social process that is co-constructed between the learner and those around them, rather than a linear trajectory towards a target norm. The learning process involves building on all available "funds of knowledge" (Moll et al. 1992) in order to develop a contextually appropriate communicative repertoire (Gumperz 1968; Rymes 2010) or a shared repertoire (Wenger 1998) that allows the learner to engage in a community. Recognizing the differing literacy and oral language use patterns of cultural groups, such as Native Americans in contrast to European Americans (Philips 1972; Street 1984; Eriks-Brophy and Crago 1994), is a result of constructivist ideologies of language and literacy. Furthermore, educators may confront inequalities which result from these differences through culturally responsive and sustaining pedagogy (Ladson-Billings 1995; Paris and Alim 2017). Writers, musicians and artists in minoritized communities also often align with a social perspective on meaning-making, contributing to discussions and discourses about fluid forms of language and culture in more or less explicit ways (Webster 2010; Moriarty and Pietikäinen 2011; Williams and Stroud 2013).

Such perspectives are often articulated against a variety of autonomous and essentializing views of language promoted in formal education, politics and the media, whereby a language is seen as autonomous, fixed, and governed by rules to which users must adhere, and is often closely fused with a place and a national identity (Makoni and Pennycook 2007; Blommaert 2010). The political discourse that all Mexicans should speak standard Spanish in order to preserve national unity and because it is superior to Indigenous ways of communicating, is an essentialist language ideology that promotes a homogenous and Eurocentric language ecology. Indigenous, minority languages in particular are often presented in simplistic or essentialized ways in the media and in some scholarly discourses; as exotic structures for linguists, as countable, diminishing resources, or as the channel to an authentic culture and place (Muehlmann 2008, 2012; Moore, Pietikainen, and Blommaert 2010). Many of these representations take place amidst discussions about the marginalization or decline in use of Indigenous languages around the world, generally called language endangerment (Hale et al. 1992). In the media, Indigenous languages of Mexico are often discussed as '*lenguas en riesgo*', languages at risk, and described as an authentic form of identity or a treasure that is – sometimes 'unfortunately', sometimes 'inevitably' – being lost. The discourses used to describe and draw attention to language endangerment may contribute to the ideology of language as an autonomous object, and an essentialized link to identity (Hill 2002).

The ideologies or perspectives of actors who advocate for a response to language endangerment are diverse, falling all along the continuum from autonomous to constructivist perspectives and exhibiting varying expectations and beliefs about Indigenous language use across social domains. For example, actors holding an objectifying view of language may feel that linguistic equality has been achieved when all languages are documented and archived, thus preserving them with some degree of accessibility for future generations. On the other hand, actors with a more constructivist perspective may feel that the creation of contexts for language use are essential for all language communities to experience equality, resulting in initiatives such as language nests and immersion schools (Kamanā and Wilson 2001; Hinton 2013). Indigenous language speakers and activists have long emphasized social and material understandings of language, as a form of identity, spirituality, connection to land, and relationality to the collective (Ferguson 2010; Meek 2010; Hermes, Bang, and Marin 2012). Henne-Ochoa et al. (2020) discuss Indigenous conceptions of "language-as-a-process-of-sustaining-relationality" (483) with a community and with a place. They note the crucial links between language, place, and identity, while highlighting that it is not a linguistic object that makes these links but rather communication as social action and as process. Consequently, they argue for an approach to language reclamation centered around social relations.

Constructivist and essentialist understandings of language are not necessarily opposed. Many would argue justifiably that language is *both* an object and an action. When limited resources and time are available for advocacy initiatives, however, one view may come to dominate the other, and efforts may be channeled one way over the other. Should funding and the limited time of Indigenous language speakers be devoted to the production of a dictionary or to a weekend class for children? Who gets to define what language is, and how it is represented, is a crucial concern. Myaamia linguist-activist Wesley Leonard argues that the definitions of linguists and others who have often claimed epistemological authority must not be taken uncritically; rather the definition of 'language' must be decolonized so that the understandings and priorities of Indigenous speakers and community members guide Indigenous language initiatives (2017). At the same time, Leonard and others acknowledge that there are likely to be multiple definitions and understandings of 'language' within a community (Messing 2007; Kroskrity 2009; McKenzie 2020), necessitating an open approach to the question 'what is language?'

With this in mind, my conceptualization of language is fundamentally constructivist and social as I seek to illuminate the relationship of communication practices and social well-being – language and inequalities. As Pennycook (2010) articulates it, "To look at language as a practice is to view language as an activity rather than a structure, as something we do rather than a system we draw on, as a material part of social and cultural life rather than an abstract entity" (2). However, I regularly participate in essentialist language discourses as

I interact with different disciplines and actors and engage in various aspects of language education. This is common of many social actors, who may understand language in multiple ways, and develop their priorities for language activism accordingly. All of the ways that different actors perceive and consequently engage with minoritized Indigenous languages are a central concern of this volume, in particular when these forms of engagement become institutionalized and codified within political systems, social projects and intellectual disciplines.

1.3 Advocating how? Approaches to equality and social change

Different actors aim to rectify inequalities experienced by minoritized language speakers in diverse and sometimes conflicting ways, ranging from promoting linguistic homogeneity to promoting equal status for diverse languages. If everyone speaks the same language, this might be considered equity – the same resources given to all. Equality or justice, however, is not so context-independent, and must be considered in relation to the experiences and opportunities of social actors *in situ*. Just as it is important to grasp the multiple ways that language is understood and made meaningful in human life, so it is equally important to be aware that equality, justice and positive social change mean different things to different people. There are complex ideological assemblages and shifting material conditions which inform peoples' understandings and priorities of what change should occur. For parents in the Isthmus of Tehuantepec it is generally viewed as a positive change that children are growing up as confident speakers of Spanish, a capacity that will allow them more social opportunity and equality in present-day Mexican society. At the same time, some parents also lament that many children are not confident speakers of Diidxazá, while young adults express regret that they are not able to communicate with their grandparents as comfortably as they would like. From a linguistic perspective, speaking Spanish and Diidxazá do not need to be opposed, and yet in the current social context one is often viewed as a detriment to the other.

Minority language activism can thus have many goals: advocating for the rights and opportunities of members of minoritized communities (including the right to learn socially-powerful languages), revitalizing endangered languages, and promoting Indigenous language education, among others. As stated in section 1, I also define the practice of activism in a broad and flexible way, including strategic actions by insiders and outsiders, as well as stance-taking in relation to social issues. In the pages that follow, some of the diverse imaginaries and strategies within the domain of minority language activism will be illustrated through cases of language activists in Oaxaca. My goal is to present language activism as a social domain with inherent internal diversity, where different understandings of positive social change and the subjective nature of equality need to be taken seriously. This diversity can sometimes result in conflict and disagreement about the goals, processes and outcomes of initiatives; however, it can also lead to new insights when language activists are aware of this diversity and find ways to work with it.

Taking action while adhering to a constructivist paradigm is not straightforward, due to acknowledgement of the validity of multiple points of view, and the inability of any individual to consider a context in its entirety. This predicament has been considered by numerous scholars, who question whether and how to take action and avoid a postmodern paralysis when multiple approaches are considered valid. Although a post-modern or constructivist approach embraces the deconstruction of social categories, including right and wrong, a relativized morality can still be established within individual contexts. Pennycook (2006) advises that post-modern activists should attempt to address difference, dominion, disparity and desire among stakeholders, while Janks (2000) proposes attention to diversity, domination, access and design. Attending to and addressing forms of inequality are key in both of these approaches. Action research practitioners Greenwood and Levin (1998) argue for a "pragmatic" approach, informed by "a strong commitment to the democratization of knowledge, learning, and self-managed social change" (10–11). As scholar-activists they do not aim to guide or impose change, but are "participants in change processes where democratic rules guide decision making" (11). A pragmatist paradigm such as this edges closer to the possibility of objectivity via democratic consensus, and as such may be preferred by some activists. A constructivist or post-modern paradigm will generally require a willingness to repeatedly question and deconstruct one's own assumptions, including assumptions about what constitutes knowledge, learning, and participation. Both constructivist and pragmatist or democratic approaches offer the possiblity to avoid essentialist or positivist paradigms while engaging in social change.

In contrast, there are many approaches to achieving language equality which have not adopted a constructivist nor pragmatist perspective. Official approaches to linguistic equality have consisted of policies at international and national levels, often drawing on an objectifying or essentialist paradigm of language. Language has come to be viewed as part of broader human rights, as mentioned above, and United Nations declarations such as the Declaration on the Rights of the Child (1959) and the Declaration on the Rights of Indigenous Peoples (2007) have created rhetorical support for language activism in national and local spheres. The recognition of linguistic human rights has not lead to the establishment of linguistic equality in practice however, leading to arguments that top-down solutions are insufficient (Stroud and Heugh 2004; Lim, Stroud, and Wee 2018). As Wee (2018) argues, "Neither groups and their members nor their cultural practices are ontologically fixed and homogenous entities, though a rights discourse treats them as such" (53). He points out that an essentialist approach to language rights runs the risk of defining language and community in a narrow way, and creating new exclusions. At the same time, the collective, communal nature of language use, and the co-substantiation of language and identity have been emphasized by many Indigenous language activists, as discussed above, lending weight to arguments for collective rights. Declarations of linguistic rights on international and national levels have offered a path towards some improvements, even if they continue to fall short in practice (Skutnabb-Kangas 2018).

In line with the critiques leveled at linguistic rights, scholars' attempts to support marginalized groups have similarly been taken to task for leading to disappointing results, in particular when they draw on a positivist discourse of correcting the misinformation and 'myths' about language(s). Lewis (2018) discusses the limitations of 'error correction', or the attempt to prove that a form of communicating that is widely viewed to be inferior is in fact equally complex and as efficient as more respected forms of communication. He points out that although sociolinguist William Labov famously illustrated the equality of Black English in both research and in a high-profile court case, this has not eradicated widespread prejudices against speakers of Black English. This further highlights the need to go beyond legal and academic declarations of equality. Scholars have often engaged in what Chickasaw anthropologist-linguist-activist Jenny Davis calls "linguistic extraction" or "defining, analysing, and representing languages and the people connected to them separately from the complex socio-historical, political, and deeply personal contexts in which they actually occur" (Davis 2017: 40). She argues that this practice distracts from socio-historical and material inequalities, and distances speakers from authority over their own ways of speaking. The political and material conditions which serve to perpetuate linguistic inequalities also need to be challenged by scholar-activists in order to bring about positive change (Flores and Chaparro 2018). As Tuck and Yang (2012) point out, efforts to change or 'decolonize' perspectives and ideologies, while laudable, are not the same as actually changing power structures and access to resources.

Investigation into language and education policies at national levels has highlighted the key role of local actors in interpreting and putting policies into practice (Ricento and Hornberger 1996; Canagarajah 2005; Menken and García 2010). Sociolinguists also argue that we are increasingly in a post-national era

(Blommaert 2010; Heller 2011), and as such it is appropriate that the strategies of engaged political actors orient to units of social organization other than the state, as well as to discourses and influences that circulate across social scales. Language and education scholar Christopher Stroud has argued that not only do local actors play a role in language politics, but that positive social change is more likely to occur through actions of bottom-up 'linguistic citizenship' than through top-down linguistic human rights. He notes that linguistic human rights "tends toward a privileging of official values and perceptions of what might constitute the language in question, and can only entertain the legitimacy of alternative language practices as part of the 'language' with difficulty" (Stroud 2018: 7). In contrast, he focuses on linguistic citizenship, or "what people do with and around language(s) in order to position themselves agentively, and to craft new, emergent subjectivities of political speakerhood, often outside of those prescribed or legitimated in institutional frameworks of the state" (2018: 5). When intended to confront linguistic inequalities (as is often the case in the examples explored by Stroud), these acts of linguistic citizenship are synonymous with language activism; conversely, all forms of language activism can also be viewed as linguistic citizenship. Along with Stroud and other ethnographers of language policy, I maintain that these individuals have significant power in language politics (Hornberger and Johnson 2007; Hult 2010).

Minority language activists, as conceptualized and explored in this book, are engaging in diverse acts of linguistic citizenship. Importantly, however, they are engaging not just as individuals, but also as parts of networks, communities or social projects. Social groups are significant contexts of socialization and thus also key sites for the negotiation of social change. Taylor (2002) suggests that "what start off as theories held by a few people may come to infiltrate the social imaginary, first that of elites perhaps, and then that of society as a whole" (106). When we consider linguistic citizens or language activists as parts of groups, we can better understand how their "emergent subjectivities of political speakerhood" (Stroud 2018: 5) may come to gain wider traction and bring about ripples of change – and certainly not only from a so-called 'elite' source as Taylor suggests. Organized forms of activism which build into social movements have played a significant role in political life in Latin America in particular, and are more likely to bring about social change than individual, indirect actions (Escobar and Alvarez 1992). While the goals and actions of those who identify as activists and engage in stereotypical efforts such as public demonstrations and targeted outreach are an important part of language activism (and are most likely what is readily conjured to mind by the term), I am also interested in quieter voices and subtler actions, including certain choices and stances which reach outward only in indirect ways, yet which also contribute to this domain. In this way, I locate language activism as part of language politics more broadly, and recognize that all social actors play a role in creating this political space (Canagarajah 2005; Davis and Phyak 2017).

One framework for examining collaborative social change is Jean Lave and Etienne Wenger's (1991; Wenger, 1998) theory of learning through which individuals are socialized into specific ideologies as well as communicative norms through participation in a *community of practice*. Communities of practice are characterized by shared discourses, goals, and collaboration. Literacy scholars David Barton and Karin Tusting (2005) have pointed out the crucial impact of context-specific communication norms and power dynamics within communities of practice, providing further nuance to this framework. Whether the community of practice shares an ideology that is accepting of language diversity and speaker agency, or views other communities' norms as inferior, or something in-between, it has a significant impact on the perceptions and practices of its members. For example Mayoli, the Zapotec student quoted in the introduction to this chapter, expresses her desire for the current community of people promoting the use of Zapotec to avoid taking up the same ideologies through which Spanish was promoted in the past, noting that they were barbarous and forceful; *"el gran error está en querer forzar a las personas a hablar zapoteco. Ya no puedes recurrir a la barbarie de antes"* [the big mistake is in wanting to force people to speak Zapotec. You can't return to the barbarity of before] she warns. As Wenger (2000) comments, "Communities of practice cannot be romanticized. They are born of learning, but they can also learn not to learn. They are cradles of the human spirit, but they can also be its cages. After all, witch-hunts were also community practices" (230).

The socialization that occurs within a community of practice can build towards greater linguistic agency, democracy and equality– or the opposite. Likewise, minority language activism can inadvertently lead to new forms of marginalization and disempowerment in the effort to change existing power relations (Cameron 2007; Leonard 2012). Numerous Indigenous language activists have argued the need for self-determination and local control in language advocacy initiatives as a way of avoiding imposed language ideologies and potential exclusionary outcomes (Leonard 2017; Hermes and Engman 2017; Henne-Ochoa et al. 2020). Similarly, social theorist Ivan Illich argued that top-down *manipulation* is the factor which undermines the potential of social institutions as sites of learning and well-being, while *conviviality* is the factor which, he proposes, supports and enables this potential (Illich 1970). He analyzes social institutions on a scale from manipulative to convivial, with the latter being his ideal social learning environment. Dynamics of manipulation and conviviality provide a useful analytic lens through which to consider participation in language activism initiatives, as illustrated further throughout the volume. Language activism initiatives can be viewed as communities of practice, each with their own internally-negotiated norms, goals, and dynamics of participation.

Additionally, the socio-political-historic context in which the community operates, and to which it must respond, is also significant. I examine language advocacy initiatives as socio-historically located communities of practice or *social projects*, following anthropologist Elizabeth Povinelli (2011). Povinelli describes a social project as "a metadiscourse that aggregates aspects of the social world" (11), and a space for social change similar to "counterpublics" (Fraser 1992; Warner 2002). Povinelli notes that social projects "extend beyond simple human sociality or human beings. [. . .] a social project is dependent on a host of interlocking concepts, materials, and forces that include human and nonhuman agencies and organisms" (7). The specific social projects that interest her are "spaces of otherwise" such as Aboriginal Australian ways of being, and how these can "endure" in hostile environments (29). Current social projects and imaginaries in favor of Diidxazá use emerge from and contend with contexts characterized by the presence of colonialism, nationalism, economic inequality and universalized formal schooling. The social project of colonialism in Mexico and elsewhere in the world created enduring linguistic and racial hierarchies, or forms of coloniality where Eurocentric logics dominate (Quijano 2000). The post-colonial projects of nationalist assimilation followed by neoliberal cultural recognition shifted public discourses about Indigenous languages to some degree, although the hierarchies remain largely intact with obligatory Spanish schooling playing an important role (as discussed further in chapter 2).

Against the bleak post-colonial and settler-colonial setting, Povinelli singles out social projects (separate from smaller "individuated projects" and larger "social worlds") as spaces of potentiality for new ways of being. She asks "How do new forms of social life maintain the force of existing in specific social spacings of life?" (Povinelli 2011: 9). In other words, how does a non-imposed, non-hierarchical Diidxazá speech community develop in today's post-colonial, neoliberal Mexico? As Mayoli goes on to ask, after rejecting forceful approaches to language promotion, *"entonces ahora, ¿cómo le haces? Hasta que no crees una conciencia real en las personas, no va a haber eso"* [So now, how do you do it? Until you create a real awareness in people, it won't happen]. Understanding language activism and potential social change requires attention to *conciencia* and the subjectivities of linguistic citizens; it also requires attention to the socialization and negotiation of power dynamics within communities of practice; and it requires consideration of the historical and material conditions in which these communities pursue their social projects. Social change can occur through official processes, such as policy declarations and curriculum reform, as well as through personal and social group practices, such as how a teacher chooses to interpret the curriculum and how students ultimately engage with it. Changing the unequal social realities experienced by Zapotec and other Indigenous communities is indeed a project in need of "new social imaginaries", new potentiality, the ability to think and behave "otherwise", as explored by Povinelli (2011) and Taylor (2004). So now, how are minority language activists doing it?

1.4 A repertoire of activism strategies

There are numerous ways that stakeholders in the Isthmus are working to counteract the processes of denigration that have linked local ways of speaking and being with poverty and ignorance, and excluded them from prestigious spaces such as education. Between 2013 and 2018 I observed many different practices related to the teaching, learning and promotion of Diidxazá, and engaged in some activism practices as an educator, linguist and researcher within a methodological framework of ethnographic monitoring (Hornberger 2013b; De Korne and Hornberger 2017). The socio-historic context of my observations is examined in chapter 2, and further methodological details are discussed in relation to academic research as a domain of activism in chapter 3. My research was guided by several questions: Who is engaging in language activism in the Isthmus, in particular in relation to Isthmus Zapotec? What imaginaries of language and social change do they express? What are their strategies of engagement? I noted that communities of educators, families, writers, artists, scholars, civil society organizations, missionaries, politicians and more were engaging in Diidxazá advocacy in some way. Taylor (2002) discusses the "repertoire" of political actions that different societies exhibit, from organized protest to democratic elections. In line with a constructivist perspective of language politics, I consider the range of language activism practices in the Isthmus to constitute a repertoire of language activism strategies.

I also observed how language activists' social projects encompass various conceptions of Diidxazá and of positive social change. The different understandings of Diidxazá among the communities of practice that I consider range from a conceptualization of language as an object (among descriptive linguists for example), to a socio-political practice (among literacy advocates for example), to mobile symbolic capital (among some educated youth for example), and many others. My use of the term Diidxazá activism includes this understanding of the multiplicity of meanings that are attached to Diidxazá, without intending to reinforce any one meaning. Diidxazá activism is thus not a homogenous nor teleological social project; it is motivated by valorization of objectified languages, by certain social ways of being, by global opportunities, and by other desires associated with Diidxazá, and does not project a unified outcome. I explore this issue further in chapters 3 and 8 where I summarize the deictic and indexical nature of 'Diidxazá'. Recognizing that what is viewed as success or improvement will vary from community to community, and context to context, necessitates a post-structuralist or constructivist approach to activism. This is in line with scholars who have signaled the primacy of "community", "local", or "speaker" choices in endangered language initiatives (Cameron et al. 1992; Hornberger and King 1996; Czaykowska-Higgins 2009; Leonard and Haynes 2010), urging that choices about language be made by community actors so that it is their imaginary of positive change which guides action. Adopting a constructivist conception of activism also addresses the fact that multiple imaginaries can exist within communities, and that multiple choices may be viewed as legitimate.

Not surprisingly, Diidxazá language activists also engage in a wide range of strategies in pursuit of their varying imaginaries. While many of the activism strategies that are taken up in the pages that follow do not conform to stereotypes of loud, public, targeted activism, they do incorporate a fundamental degree of intentionality which sets them apart from social practices which are not strategic. *Practices* may reproduce or challenge structures of inequality in ways that are not intentional. *Strategies*, on the other hand, are practices which orient to an imaginary of social change and are carried out with the intention to influence social life in some way, large or small. As Wenger (1998) discusses, social and personal imagination may "conceive of new developments, explore alternatives, and envision possible futures", but alignment of imagination with action or engagement is necessary in order to bring about change (178–180). Intentional or reflective forms of engagement are a distinct form of social practice in that they involve some degree of conscious choice, a dialogic relationship between reflection and action constituting what educational and social theorist Paolo Freire termed praxis (Freire 1969, 1970). Language activism strategies can be intentional in subtle and private ways, such as a grandparent's choice of language when interacting with their grandchild. They can also be intentional is more stereotypical ways, such as a teacher organizing public events in support of Diidxazá. Whether in public or private spaces, intentional strategies are a form of political participation and linguistic citizenship. The range of strategic practices exemplified by these actors constitute a repertoire of potential language activism strategies, as illustrated further below. I observed and compared the strategies of diverse actors in part to inform my own strategies as a language activist; with time and analysis these observations informed the following attempt to sketch out some of the local politics of Isthmus Zapotec activism and language activism more broadly.

Through analysis of my ethnographic data I developed a framework to categorize the strategic practices that I observed and participated in across local advocacy initiatives. The aim of this framework is descriptive; it is neither prescriptive nor comprehensive. Any and all strategies can be of use (or not), depending on the unique features of each context. There is no magic cure, no universal best strategy, no 'good' or 'bad' activism. The framework is sketched out starkly here and examples that fill out each aspect of it are presented throughout subsequent chapters.[7] I organize strategies in terms of 1) a fundamental action; 2) the target of the action; and 3) significant characteristics of the strategy. The fundamental actions are forms of *representing* (representing something through discursive means), *connecting* (creating a connection among existing people, things, or spaces), and/ or *creating* (producing something new). These actions are most saliently targeted at the goals of *resources, events, spaces or structures, people or identities*, and *communication practices*, as represented in Figure 1.

Actions	Goals
– Creating	– Resources
– Connecting	– Events
– Representing	– Spaces/Structures
	– People/Identities
	– Communication practices

Figure 1: Actions and goals of language activism strategies.

Resources refers to non-human materials, such as texts, recordings, videos, or other scholastic or educational products. *Events* refers to limited-term or one-off occurrences that bring people together, such as a conference on Indigenous languages, a bilingual hip-hop concert, or a linguistic workshop. *Spaces and structures* refers to more durable social spaces such as schools or long-term education programs, including cultural centers and organizations. A one-time event may eventually become a space or structure if it reoccurs regularly. *People and identities* refers to people in their potential social roles as speakers, teachers, learners, experts, etc. *Communication practices* refers to any communicative practice, including all forms of reception and production, whether written, visual, or audio, mediated or face to face. A strategy may involve primarily one action and

---

[7] A succinct representation of the framework is presented in Appendix A.

one goal (such as the creation of didactic resources), however there are often multiple actions and goals overlapping and pursued simultaneously (such as the creation of successful learners and increased communication practices in the target language through the use of the didactic resources) as illustrated in the pages that follow. In chapters 3–7 I offer examples of these strategies in diverse activism initiatives, and discuss further aspects of the imaginaries and strategies of language equality in practice. While some strategies are driven by resistance to aspects of existing conditions, at the same time they are almost always also a form of reimaging conditions or imagining new realities, as explored in chapters 6 and 7 in particular.

In addition to these core actions and goals (the *what* of language activism strategies) there are several common characteristics which shape *how* strategies are carried out. These characteristics are represented as scales in Figure 2. The *location* or geographic affiliation of the people or actions involved may range from local to regional, national, and international. The *timeframe* within which a strategy takes place and reverberates can vary from a momentary choice, such as an individual choosing to post on social media in Zapotec rather than Spanish, to medium term and long-term endeavors, such as creating an app for language learning which will be used for a few years or a new educational space which will be used for a decade. The *visibility and mobility* of a strategy may be low, such as a conference event attended by a private, elite audience, or higher in the case of a public event and very high in the case of on-line resources which can be transmitted digitally. Strategies make use of different *socio-historical orientations* or indexes through which they align with aspects of a community's past, present or future. For example, some teacher-activists may

Characteristic	Scale		
Location:	Local	←→	International
Timeframe:	Slow	←→	Rapid
Visibility & mobility:	Low	←→	High
Socio-historical orientation:	Future	←→	Past
Diversity orientation:	Syncretic	←→	Purist
Participation:	Open participation	←→	Controlled participation

Figure 2: Characteristics of language activism strategies.

choose to focus on concepts related to Zapotec history, such as the pre-colonial base-20 numerical system, while others may focus on neologisms and using language in present or imagined future settings. A related characteristic is the *orientation towards diversity*, whereby some activists will promote linguistic or cultural features perceived to be pure, unitary and authentic, such as writer-activists who strive to avoid all influence of Spanish in their texts. In contrast, other activists promote a more flexible or syncretic (Hill and Hill 1986) understanding of languages and cultures in contact, such as musician-activists who intentionally draw from their multilingual repertoires in their songs. Finally, the dynamics of *participation or control* can vary from an open, emergent collaboration, to something more tightly controlled and hierarchical. I link this characteristic to the scale Illich established between convivial and manipulative learning environments (Illich 1970), mentioned in section 1.3 above.

Although some of these characteristics may align and impact each other, there is no inherent relationship among them, nor any preferred points on the scales. A strategy may be local, rapid, mobile, purist and with open participation, such as a social media post which corrects or critiques the spelling of another person's post, which then incites further debate for a day or two. A strategy can be international, slow, low-mobility, historically-oriented, and with controlled participation, such as a dictionary of words elicited by a foreign researcher from elder speakers and produced in print version only, which eventually sits in a place of honor in libraries and schools for decades. Maybe the on-line interaction leads someone to feel entitled to write in the minoritized language more often – or maybe it does not. Maybe the impressive dictionary inspires a student to learn more about their heritage language – or maybe it does not. A strategy, in short, can be any combination of these characteristics, and any combination can lead to a good strategy, depending on the circumstances. These characteristics are further exemplified throughout the volume (see also chapter 8 for a summary and comparative discussion).

As mentioned above, this framework is intended to describe a range of strategic actions, and does not imply the superiority of strategies with certain targets or characteristics. Strategies do not emerge nor are they carried out in a vacuum; each strategy is embedded in a specific language ecology which shapes and informs the who, what, and how of language activism, and enables or constrains the outcomes (as explored further in chapter 2). Different strategies will thus be more or less possible and desirable depending on the context and the positionality of the activist. For example, high-visibility strategies may appear universally desirable to activists, but low-visibility strategies may in fact be highly effective if carried out by key actors over time. By focusing on language activism strategies within a local context, the Isthmus of Tehuantepec, I hope to draw attention to less-visible, local strategies which I argue deserve more attention and value than they sometimes receive. Future studies of other language activism initiatives could, and hopefully will, extend this framework and repertoire of strategies further than I have developed it here. Considering that the social project of linguistic equality must respond to constantly shifting socio-political conditions, I have no doubt that language activists will continue to develop new strategies. We can and we will.

1.5 Overview of book

The chapters that follow will illustrate the actions, goals, and characteristics of the repertoire of language activism strategies that is presented in the framework above (Figures 1 and 2). Each chapter focuses on a different social domain which I argue plays an important role in the layered politics of language activism: research; public education; higher education; community-based education; and popular culture. These domains are interrelated in important ways however, as some actors engage in multiple domains (such as education and research), and some strategies involve connecting different domains (such as popular culture and education). These networks of influence and potential support across domains are also crucial to this story and its unfolding outcomes.

Following on from the presentation of language activism strategies in this chapter, chapter 2 shows how language activism is embedded in and influenced by specific language ecologies which are subject to change over time. The sociopolitical history of the Isthmus of Tehuantepec has made this a multilingual region for many centuries, and the shifts in the political, economic, and linguistic ecology provide an important backdrop for language activism in this context. The current linguistic ecology consists of Indigenous languages which arrived at different points in time and European languages which have arrived in subsequent waves as well. I give a brief overview of the linguistic ecology in the pre-colonial, colonial, nation-building, and neoliberal eras, including some of the historical reference points that are drawn upon strategically by language activists today. Cultural and linguistically-oriented activism has a long history in the Isthmus, and continues in a variety of forms, as illustrated in more detail in chapters 3–7.

Multiple domains of scholarship have engaged with minority language advocacy in general, and several scholars have been influential language activists in the Isthmus in particular, including people from the Isthmus and from abroad. Chapter 3 gives an overview of academic engagements with language advocacy and activism, describing scholarly disciplines as communities of practice with varying priorities and concerns. I situate myself as an activist and scholar working across several disciplines, noting that most scholars are members of multiple communities of practice and take a variety of insider-outsider stances in relation to the contexts in which they work. I examine the legacy of exploitative research that today's activist scholars attempt to overcome and discuss several ethical and methodological considerations for engaging in language activism. I illustrate the activism strategies taken up by scholars in the Isthmus, in particular a focus on the creation of knowledge and resources, positive representations of Indigenous languages, and supporting connections among people and resources. The colonial history of scholarly activities in the Americas casts a long and influential shadow, and as such, vigilance against exploitation and problematizing hierarchies of knowledge remain crucial. At the same time, the social status of research and the resources which researchers may mobilize can be effective supports to language activism initiatives.

Another social space that enjoys high social status is schooling. Public school communities of practice have immense impact on language socialization. The role of schooling in linguistic equality is explored in chapter 4, including different approaches to language diversity in education. I describe language use in public schooling in the Isthmus and illustrate how Zapotec is largely excluded. I then highlight several groups of teachers who engage in language activism through strategies of connecting students' home life with the school and representing Zapotec as a part of the high-status school environment. Educator-activists often struggle with the rigidity of the institutions they work in, however, limiting the extent or length of some of their efforts. Additionally, not all stakeholders in school communities share the same imaginary of positive social change; while some parents and educators continue to view Indigenous languages as a problem, educator-activists in favor of Zapotec have both ideological and pedagogical challenges to address.

The gate-keeping and legitimation power of higher education is also crucial in shaping language politics and in some cases in supporting the capacity building of language activists. Chapter 5 analyses a small branch campus of the state university, the Tehuantepec campus of the Faculty of Languages at the Autonomous Benito Juarez University of Oaxaca, which began teaching Isthmus Zapotec for the first time in 2013. In a context where foreign languages have held unquestioned dominance and students at the Faculty who spoke Indigenous languages avoided using them, this represented a significant change. It is also a contrast to the discourses and critiques which young adult speakers of Isthmus Zapotec often experience in their daily lives as multilinguals in this shifting language ecology. I consider the imaginaries of several of the teachers and administrators who have been involved in supporting the program, and the experiences of some participating students. I highlight the significance of higher education in representing Indigenous languages and multilingual identities as legitimate, and in creating the new identity category of Isthmus Zapotec teacher. The slow nature of change within an institutional environment is evident, but the impacts are also clearly positive and hopefully sustainable over a longer timeframe.

Literacy and literature have been prominent in Isthmus Zapotec activism at the regional level, and the visibility and popularity of Zapotec writers is an important characteristic of this community. Chapter 6 analyzes the imaginaries and strategies of a community-based literacy workshop, the *Camino de la Iguana* [Path of the Iguana], which aims to create Zapotec readers and writers. In a social space that they have created, the teachers have the opportunity, and necessity, of imagining what it means to be literate in Diidxazá, and supporting learners of different backgrounds to achieve this goal. The teachers' strategies include promoting an appreciation of Indigenous language and literary heritage, while supporting the multilingual repertoires of emergent speakers and the dialect diversity within the region. Additionally, the political nature of writing is emphasized, with participants encouraged to view themselves as emerging writers who are part of a global community in which Isthmus Zapotec literature is on a par with literature from any country, in any language. The activism strategies within the workshop are characterized by drawing on both historical and contemporary references, as well as both local and international references. The teachers strike a fine balance in their orientation towards diversity, between the inevitable push towards purism in writing practices, and acceptance of language change and variation. The convivial interactions which they prioritize are additionally crucial to the workshop's success.

Chapter 7 describes spaces of cultural production and activism in the Isthmus of Tehuantepec, including the bilingual rap and hip-hop movement, feminist collectives, and on-line activism. Popular culture activists also have a wide scope to imagine new ways of being, and to negotiate what language and identity means to them. Through creative appropriation and reimagining of tradition, as well as engagement with contemporary socio-economic issues, cultural activists strategically bridge the local and global, and the past and the present. The strategies of creating events, representing identities, and connecting people are common among musicians and collectives in the Isthmus. These collectives draw on support and references from outside of the region, but are fundamentally run through voluntary collaboration and local support. They also achieve a high degree of visibility and mobility through their participation in social media and broadcasting. The role of digital spaces in supporting language activism is explored, with attention to initiatives that aim to create resources, as well as those that serve to connect and engage members of the community to discuss issues of language and identity. Here diversity orientations are also present, as popular culture initiatives often spark debates over what is viewed as appropriate or correct linguistic or cultural forms. Popular culture activism occurs in a rapid timeframe, and as such may be harder to trace than slower, institutional forms. However, it also has a wider reach in terms of audience and potential impact.

Engaging in different forms of activism or advocacy requires a range of context-sensitive strategies, as illustrated throughout the volume. Chapter 8 summarizes and discusses the actions, goals and characteristics of the language activism strategies framework, drawing on examples from throughout the book. I argue that strategies which occur in local spaces, over a brief span of time and which are not highly visible are still significant in combating inequalities and influencing language politics. I reflect on the challenges of a social constructivist approach to language activism, including shifts in my own strategies over time. Some of the lessons that I have learned from Isthmus Zapotec language activists include accepting the deictic nature of 'language', and the varying theories of change which inform different activism initiatives. Considering activism strategies across initiatives and scales, it is clear that there are no ideal nor one-size-fits-all strategies, but that activists employing a repertoire of adaptable strategies have the potential to resist inequalities and imagine new linguistic futures.

1.6 Context and conduct of this study

I was introduced to the Isthmus in 2012 through the generous invitation of Mexican linguist-activist, Gabriela Pérez Báez, and Isthmus Zapotec linguist-writer-activist, Víctor Cata. Gabriela Pérez Báez had been working on documentation and a dictionary of Isthmus Zapotec for over 10 years. She was looking for an applied linguist to assist with education outreach in an ethnobotany documentation project that began as part of the dictionary project, and for which she had received funding from the Smithsonian Institution, where she worked as Curator of Linguistics. Víctor Cata had moved back to his hometown in the Isthmus, Juchitán, a few years before, where he was pursuing his writing and teaching of Diidxazá literacy, as well as collaborating in research projects with scholars like Gabriela. Prior to returning to the Isthmus he had spent two decades in Mexico City, first earning a BA in History and a MA in Amerindian Linguistics, as well as working in the library of the National Anthropological Museum for 10 years. Both of these colleagues were (and are) eager to encourage scholarship on language in the Isthmus, noting that the current legal climate has created opportunities for changing the discriminatory norms surrounding Indigenous languages. Both Víctor and Gabriela approach Indigenous language revitalization and reclamation with passion, transdisciplinary partnerships, and a crucial dose of humor;

the opportunity to work with and learn from them was far too good to pass up. I was especially interested in the convergence of different actors (linguists, educators, writers) around language issues and the historic multilingualism present in the Isthmus. After a month of pilot research in the Isthmus (April 2013), I returned to live in Juchitán from the beginning of August 2013 through the end of November 2014, and later lived in the state capitol of Oaxaca City from March-July 2015, making regular visits to the Isthmus. I returned for shorter visits to the Isthmus in January 2016, October 2016, April-May 2017, and January 2018. The data that I present here was collected during this timeframe, with some additional on-line data collected in 2018, 2019, and 2020.

With the goal of mapping who was engaged in promoting or teaching Isthmus Zapotec across the region and what they were doing, I visited numerous education and cultural centers, as well as attending civic and cultural events such as poetry readings and hip-hop performances. Wherever possible I followed up to conduct interviews with key individuals. In addition to shorter visits to a variety of sites across the region, I spent extended time as a participant observer in three sites in particular: a community-based literacy initiative (the *Camino de la Iguana*, see chapter 6); a university campus (the Tehuantepec branch of the Faculty of Languages of the Autonomous Benito Juárez University of Oaxaca, see chapter 5); and the collaborative outreach workshops which emerged out of Gabriela Pérez Báez's ethnobotany project with community members and researchers (see chapters 3 and 8). As a participant observer in these sites, I was regularly present during Zapotec classes, casual conversations before and after class, and in social interactions with participants. When approved by participants, I conducted audio recordings and took pictures. I also conducted audio-recorded interviews with participants in these sites, in most cases after getting to know them as a co-participant over time. I made field notes while observing, and often after coming home.

I am a settler European-American, and therefor a physical and cultural outsider in the Isthmus. Tourism remains rare there and the only notable white residents during the time of my residence were (primarily Spanish) men locally called *eolicos*, after the *parques eolicos*, or wind farm developments where they work. When I first arrived in spring of 2013 there had recently been a fight between some *Juchitecos*, Juchitán residents, and some *eolicos*, and a few people advised me to be cautious, in case I was mistaken for a wind farm worker, or more probably, one of their wives. I was occasionally asked if my work was related to the *eolicos*, but when I then said that I was a researcher interested in language and education, this explanation was always accepted positively or at least neutrally. I often came across people who had had contact with a linguist or researcher in the past due to the residence of (primarily female, American) scholars, including missionary-linguist Velma Pickett, and more recently anthropologists Anya Royce, Deborah Augsburger, and Melanie McComsey who had conducted long-term ethnographic research and established close personal ties in Juchitán (Royce 1975; 2011; Augsburger 2004; McComsey 2015). That another American would arrive with an interest in language seemed to be a source of pride, and generally not a surprise.

I conducted my research primarily in Spanish, while continuing to learn Diidxazá and use it frequently in observations and to a more limited degree in conversations. I attempted to adopt a neutral stance with regard to Diidxazá practices in my conversations and interviews (i.e. not taking a stance on standardization, child rearing, etc.). From the beginning, however, I was associated with well-known pro-Diidxazá activists such as Víctor Cata, and people would often associate my work with efforts to *rescatar*, rescue or recuperate the language, even though I avoided describing my work with these terms. As I began to collaborate in several programs, this identification increased. What people knew about me influenced my subsequent interactions and interviews, and I was frequently told primarily positive comments about Diidxazá use, which were not always reflected in my observations of the social practices of the commenter. Unable to invent a neutral identity, I accepted that my identity created a bias through which I was often told what people thought they *should* say to an outsider who likes the local language, which is interesting in its own right. Fortunately, the extended nature of my study also allowed for closer acquaintances leading to more candid discussions, as well as observation of everyday communicative practices.

Over time I developed an insider-outsider identity in the three focal contexts mentioned above, eventually participating in lesson and curriculum planning, co-organizing educational events, and speaking at public outreach functions. This insider-outsider status was illustrated in a conversation with several friends and collaborators where I was asked if I preferred to be called *huada* Haley, a fairly neutral Zapotec word for foreign women, or *Teca* Haley, a female resident of Juchitán. It seemed that both were acceptable labels to describe me, and I said either one would be fine with me. On another occasion in a group conversation when a visiting Mexican researcher made a negative comment about foreign researchers (not directed at me, although I was present), a teacher whose classes I had been observing quickly excluded me from the comment, saying to the group 'Haley isn't a foreigner, she's a *Teca*'. Although I remained visibly, audibly, and behaviorally distinct from most of the people around me, I almost always felt that people reacted positively to my presence and to my interest in Diidxazá.

The generous welcome and kindness of *Istmeños* aside however, my position as a relative newcomer to the Isthmus inevitably had an influence on what I was able to observe and understand, and on my interpretations of this context. I cannot offer an objective account of language activism in the Isthmus (and I do not believe an objective account is possible); instead I have endeavored to offer a multi-perspectival account, and to draw attention to some of the ways that my own understandings have changed over time through my engagement with language activists in the Isthmus. I discussed my observations with stakeholders throughout the study, getting formal and informal feedback on my ideas and perspectives, and using this feedback to shape the questions I have asked, the ways I have engaged, and how I am presenting the stories here. For example, I was initially interested in spoken communication and not particularly interested in literacy practices, but observations and interviews showed me the clear status of Isthmus Zapotec writing and writers, and led me to consider its significance within the language ecology to a greater degree.

The corpus of notes, interviews, photos, and documents I collected in various sites has been compiled and analysed through rounds of thematic coding, open coding, and memo-writing with the help of the qualitative analysis software Atlas.ti. Throughout this book I draw on data from interviews, field notes, photographs and documents to illustrate my analyses and interpretations (see appendix B for transcription and citation conventions). The specific interviews and field notes that I cite to support discussion or generalizations in the text are representative of things that I heard or observed multiple times. I attempt to relate both the general trends that I observed in relation to language activism in the Isthmus of Tehuantepec, and some of the individual stories of the people who make up this dynamic language ecology. It has been a privilege to observe and learn from language activists in the Isthmus, and to be able to share what I have learned as best I can here and elsewhere. I am all too aware that the trends and stories that I share here are but a glimpse of a much more complex reality, containing many more people and stories than I am able to do justice to. I believe that a glimpse can still be enlightening, however, and I hope that others will find inspiration in the stories in the following chapters, as I have done.

Chapter 2
The moving target of activism: Changing language ecologies in the Isthmus of Tehuantepec

In 2013 the Mexican Law on the Linguistic Rights of Indigenous People, which officially recognizes Indigenous languages like Isthmus Zapotec as "national languages", turned 10 years old. When a 2-week Diidxazá literacy workshop, *Camino de la Iguana*, was taught that spring by Juchitán-based language activists Natalia Toledo and Víctor Cata in *Gui'xhi' ro'* (Big mountain/ hill in Zapotec, also known officially as Álvaro Obregon), a rural town about 40 minutes outside of Juchitán de Zaragoza in the Isthmus of Tehuantepec, Oaxaca, most of the children who attended were the same age as the law, some a few years older or younger, and all of them spoke Isthmus Zapotec as their preferred form of communication. When it came to writing it was another story however; when told to write a poem or an autobiography, students repeatedly asked the Diidxazá-speaking teachers if they should write in *diidxazá* [Zapotec] or *diidxastia* [Spanish]. Some wrote in Spanish even when told several times to write in Zapotec. After years in a Spanish-only education system, for many students writing seemed to be synonymous with Spanish, while the new vowels and consonants being taught by the Zapotec-speaking, yet cosmopolitan-looking teachers who arrived in a taxi from the urban hub of Juchitán (with an unusual foreigner in tow), were unfamiliar. Some students took to Zapotec writing and reading more than others, and the teachers encouraged them to follow in the footsteps of past and present Isthmus Zapotec literary figures, giving them booklets with some well-known Diidxazá poetry. They reminded the students that a man from their town, in fact the father of 2 of the students, was one of the winners of a competition for Zapotec writers hosted by a non-governmental arts foundation in the state capitol a few years previously, and that writers from the Isthmus Zapotec community have won this award more often than writers from other Zapotec communities. Several public school teachers also participated in the workshop on their own initiative (and their own time), telling me in conversation after the workshop that they would like to include Isthmus Zapotec in their classes more, but that they were not confident in writing it.

The challenging learning curve for Isthmus Zapotec speakers being taught a written norm for the first time was visible in every iteration of the literacy

Open Access. © 2021 Haley De Korne, published by De Gruyter. This work is licensed under the Creative Commons Attribution-NonCommercial-NoDerivatives 4.0 International License.
https://doi.org/10.1515/9781501511561-002

workshop that I observed over the following year and a half, with Isthmus Zapotec speakers consistently more comfortable reading and writing in Spanish due to the predominance of Spanish in schooling and the linguistic landscape. The age of the speakers in the workshops changed, however; in some parts of the Isthmus the youngest speakers participating in the workshop were in their 20s; in other areas in their 30s or 40s; and in others in their 50s and 60s. I learned that *Gui'xhi' ro'* was one of only a few towns where a majority of children spoke Zapotec. Children always showed up to participate in the literacy workshops, often with more gusto than the adults, but in many locations the children were speakers of Spanish who understood a few Isthmus Zapotec words or phrases, if any. Some came from families who had immigrated to the region, with parents who were also speakers of Spanish or of another Indigenous language, while the majority came from *Istmeño* families and had been raised in Spanish by Zapotec-speaking parents and grandparents.

I was told time and again that Diidxazá is not being passed on in the Isthmus because many people think it is a *dialecto* (a lesser form of communication) and that if children grow up speaking it they will not speak Spanish well, or have a hard time learning Spanish. Through observation it became clear that raising children predominantly in Spanish was currently the practice among a majority of the population. As one mother commented,

> Mis hijos, la niña de 12 años y el niño de 9, no hablan el zapoteco. Ya hace como 10 años que los niños que vienen naciendo, a partir de 10 años atrás, ya no están hablando, ya no están aprendiendo el zapoteco, ya nosotros los papás como que les hablamos más en el español, para no confundirlos con el zapoteco. Porque a veces cuando nosotros, en mi caso no, que desde niña hable el zapoteco, y aprender el español sí fue un poco complicado, porque, aquí en Juchitán decíamos, en La Ventosa es. . ., por el tono del zapoteco, siempre teníamos mal entre el español y zapoteco, la mezcla del español y zapoteco, era muy difícil. Pues la gente que según esto ya sabía mucho, se le parecía como naco, pues hablar así, sí, sí daba un poco de vergüenza.
>
> My children, the 12-year-old girl and 9-year-old boy, don't speak Zapotec. Now for about 10 years the children who are being born, since 10 years ago, now they're not speaking, now they're not learning Zapotec, now we, the parents, it's like we speak to them more in Spanish, so as not to confuse them with Zapotec. Because sometimes when we, in my case, that since childhood I spoke Zapotec and learning Spanish was a bit complicated, because here in Juchitán we said, in La Ventosa um. . . because of the tone of Zapotec we always had trouble between Spanish and Zapotec, the mix of Spanish and Zapotec, it was really difficult. Well the people who apparently already knew a lot, it appeared to them like *naco* [uncouth, low class], to speak like that, yes, yes it gave some shame.
>
> (Interview November 2013)

Although this mother brought her daughter to one of the Zapotec literacy workshops, I observed her interacting only in Spanish with her daughter. The girl only attended a few days of the workshop however, and her mother told me she stopped coming because she had too much homework. When I visited their home a month later the girl was indeed busy with her homework, in particular her English homework (on that occasion she was struggling to understand a decontextualized paragraph about Amelia Earhart) which she said was always challenging and time consuming. In contrast, the girl told me that she does understand everything her parents say in Zapotec, she just does not speak it herself. Again and again I observed this practice of using only Spanish with children, as well as the willingness to invest more time in learning English than learning Isthmus Zapotec.

Through this glimpse of language practices, and others to follow, I will attempt to illustrate the language ecology (Haugen 1972; Fill and Muhlhausler 2001) of the Isthmus of Tehuantepec. There are multiple agents, contexts, and processes across different social scales which make up a language ecology (Hornberger and Johnson 2007). For example, echoes of international, national, regional and local efforts to promote Indigenous languages– such as the global imperialism of English, the 2013 Mexican law, the Oaxaca state-level writing competition, and the non-formal literacy workshop created by local actors– are all present in the Isthmus. However, a well-established trend away from Indigenous language use and towards greater valuing of Spanish in public, and increasingly in private spaces, is also very apparent, as is pressure to learn English for future schooling and employment opportunities. The communicative repertoires of children in the Isthmus in the early 21st century range from preferring Isthmus Zapotec to preferring Spanish to varying degrees, and the aspirations of members of the speech community likewise vary. These paradoxes are not new: the language ecology of the Isthmus of Tehuantepec has long been multilingual and fraught with political tensions.

Taking a historically embedded and contextualized view of such a language ecology, it becomes clear that linguistic equality must be interpreted in relation to each historical moment, and that forms of exclusion and inequality may be produced through different mechanisms and actors. From the dominance of certain varieties of Zapotec over others to the imposition of Spanish, and more recently English, in Mexican schools, language hierarchies have continued to shift over time. Advocating for linguistic equality is consequently a historically-contingent endeavor, with a moving target that must be understood in relation to the prevailing power dynamics and the communicative repertoires and aspirations of people at a given time. The political environment in Mexico and in the Isthmus has shifted in recent decades to promote Indigenous language use in more ways, while in other ways it has remained discriminatory, as discussed further below. With numerous Indigenous languages and a history of local resistance to colonial imposition, it can be challenging to tease out the interwoven stories around language use, language politics and education in the Isthmus, and to determine appropriate activism strategies. At the same time, it also makes the region of especial interest in studies of Indigenous education, language activism and politics. In this chapter I give a brief background to language use in the Isthmus of Tehuantepec from the pre-colonial period through the present, highlighting shifting patterns of inequality and exclusion (2.1–2.5). I further analyze language practices in the Isthmus and the linguistic landscape in order to sketch the regional language ecology at the time of my study (2.6). Understanding this context is a pre-requisite for insight into both the characteristics of diverse activism initiatives, and the place and people who constitute them. In conclusion, I discuss the challenges and affordances of understanding linguistic equality as a moving target embedded within a changing language ecology (2.7).

2.1 Indigenous multilingualisms: Pre-colonial language ecologies

The territory that is now Mexico has been inhabited by numerous sociolinguistic groups, who have come into contact and sometimes conflict over many centuries. A common way of identifying and dividing social groups in Mexico is through classifying their communicative practices into categories of language families and languages– the essentialist paradigms of enumeration and categorization discussed in chapter 1. Following this dominant perspective, there are 11 language families and a debated number of languages spoken in Mexico today (the current official estimate being 68 languages with 364 variants (*Instituto Nacional de Lenguas Indígenas* (INALI) 2008)). Oaxaca state is one of the regions of Mexico with the greatest linguistic and cultural diversity, with 16 ethnic groups and a debated number of languages (Barabas and Bartolomé 1999). Figure 3 illustrates Mexico, the state of Oaxaca, the state capital Oaxaca city, and the city of Juchitán. Juchitán is in the Isthmus of Tehuantepec, the region of land where the distance between the Gulf of Mexico and the Pacific Ocean is the shortest.

2.1 Indigenous multilingualisms: Pre-colonial language ecologies — 33

Figure 3: The country of Mexico, highlighting the state of Oaxaca and the city of Juchitán.[8]

Five languages are present in the Isthmus, hailing from 4 different families: Ayuuk (Mixe) and Zoque (both from the Mixe-Zoque family), Zapotec (Oto-manguean family), Ombeayiüts (Huave) (isolate) and Chontal (isolate).[9] The rough geographic distribution of these languages, as well as the other Indigenous languages of Oaxaca is illustrated in more detail in Figure 4. Zapotec languages or variants cover the largest section of the state. After Nahuatl and Yucatec Maya, Zapotec is considered the Indigenous language with most speakers in Mexico (441,769 according to the Ethnologue (Lewis, Simons, and Fennig 2015)), although these figures overlook the internal diversity and lack of intelligibility between some varieties of Zapotec. Zapotec is considered a language group with four main sub-divisions and roughly 62 variants, many of which are not mutually intelligible (Pérez Báez 2011; Pérez Báez and Kaufman 2016). The

---

8 Map reprinted with permission from *Encyclopædia Britannica*, © 2007 by Encyclopædia Britannica, Inc.
9 I attempt to use auto-determinations of Indigenous groups in addition to the names used in Spanish as much as possible, although I acknowledge that preferences for these names can vary within each group. Here I use the auto-determinations which I heard most frequently during my study.

Figure 4: Map of Indigenous languages of Oaxaca.[10]

four varieties are Isthmus Zapotec across the coastal plain of the Isthmus, Sierra Sur Zapotec in the southern mountains, Valley Zapotec in the central valleys where the state capital Oaxaca City is located, and Sierra Juárez Zapotec in the northern mountains (Barabas and Bartolomé 1999). In Figure 4 the position of Isthmus Zapotec is visible in between the Huave or Ombeayiüts zone along the coast, the Chontal zone along the coast to the west, the Ayuuk/ Mixe zone in the mountains to the north, and the Zoque zone in the mountains to the northeast.

The geographical spread and relatively large number of speakers of Zapotec today is an echo of the presence and power of the Zapotec empire in pre-colonial Mesoamerica. Zapotecs developed a wealthy and hierarchical empire, governing much of what is now Oaxaca from around 500 BCE to 900 CE. The oldest signs of habitation in the central valleys of Oaxaca date from 950 BCE, where density and social organization continued to develop, partially through contact with Olmec civilization between 1200–900 BCE. Around 400 BCE what would become the imperial city of Monte Alban was founded on a mountaintop at the intersection of several valleys (Barabas and Bartolomé 1999: 62–63) overlooking the site of the state capital today. The auto-denomination *Binnizá,* "cloud people" (*binni* [people] *zá* [cloud]), now used in the Isthmus, as well as the auto-

---

10 Map by Felipe H. Lopéz. Reproduced with permission from Munro, Pamela, Brook Danielle Lillehaugen, and Felipe H Lopez. 2007. *Cali Chiu? A Course in Valley Zapotec*. Lulu.com.

denomination of the Isthmus Zapotec language Diidxazá (*diidxa* [word/ language] *zá* [cloud]) could have been inspired by the dramatic clouds that form a striking part of the landscape in the Oaxacan mountains. Covarrubias (1946) in his classic study of southern Oaxaca notes that Zapotecs in particular have no origin or migration story, but claim to originate in the region. He quotes an early historian, who wrote "I have found no reference, with semblance of truth, of the first arrival of this nation, nor of the origin of their lords, from which it may be deduced they were very ancient . . . To boast of bravery they claimed to be sons of jaguars and other wild beasts; if they were great chiefs of ancient lineage they considered themselves descendants of old and shady trees; those that were proud of being untamable and stubborn, said they were born of rocks and cliffs . . ." (174).

The Zapotec empire produced significant achievements in architecture, astronomy, medicine, and writing, with up to 30,000 people residing in Monte Alban at its peak (Barabas and Bartolomé 1999: 63). Like the Aztec and Mayan empires, the Zapotecs had a sophisticated calendar, a base-20 numerical system, advanced architecture, and writing which was used in elite circles (de la Cruz 2008). The first phase of Zapotec writing is dated from 600 BCE to 800 CE, and included semi-phonetic writing as well as logographic or hieroglyphic writing (de la Cruz 2008:12). A second phase is identified from 800 CE to the Spanish invasion in 1521 CE, consisting of symbolic or pictographic representations (de la Cruz 2008:13). De la Cruz questions why Zapotec writing seemingly regressed from more sophisticated phonetic representations to pictographic representations, and proposes the hypothesis that it was due to:

> la multiplicidad lingüística existente en el territorio dominado por los binnigulaa'sa': sacrificaron el apego a la gramática de su lengua, para usar una forma de escritura que pasaba directamente del signo visual– sin referencia a los sonidos de una sola lengua– a la imagen mental que generaban los pictogramas o ideogramas
>
> the linguistic multiplicity existing in the territory dominated by the ancient Zapotecs: they sacrificed the attachment to the grammar of their language in order to use a form of writing that passed directly from the visual sign– without reference to the sounds of a single language– to the mental image that generated the pictographs or ideographs.
>
> (2008: 13)

Whatever the motivations for change, Romero Frizzi (2003) notes that the Zapotecs were among the first Mesoamerican civilizations to develop writing, and almost certainly influenced other civilizations whose writing systems are now better known. The pre-colonial Zapotec writing system is not fully understood at present, there being fewer remnants than there are of Maya (Urcid 2005).

Monte Alban began to decline for reasons that probably included political conflict and environmental stress, resulting in a shift to networks of smaller city-states throughout the valleys. Zapotecs from the valley city-state of Zaachila migrated down to the Isthmus around 1400 CE as the Aztec influence was strengthening in the region (de la Cruz 2008: 56–57). They displaced the Ikoots or Huave who were believed to have been living there, took over the fertile plain, and began to dominate economic trade in the region. The Ikoots territory was reduced to a narrow strip of land by the ocean and they were subject to general discrimination by many Zapotec. The Zapotecs who settled in the Isthmus ruled from a city-state based in Tehuantepec and maintained contact with other Zapotec seats of power in the mountains and central valleys. Their power was not unilateral and they were not the only Indigenous group to expert dominance over other groups however; by 1486 CE the Aztec had founded the garrison of Huaxyacac (now Oaxaca City) in the central valleys and were extracting tributes from Zapotecs, Mixtecs, and others throughout the greater Oaxaca region (Barabas and Bartolomé 1999: 64). Already in 1484 the Aztec recorded the towns of Tehuantepec and Juchitán in the Mendocino codex as places where they extracted tribute (Ruíz Martínez 2013). Juchitán was represented with the symbol of a flower that has been interpreted as *guie' xhuuba*, a fragrant flowering tree unique to the region, and given the Nahuatl name *Ixtcxochitlán* (place of white flowers) (Ruíz Martínez 2013: 17–18), which is the presumed origin of the name Juchitán.[11] Tehuantepec means Jaguar Hill in Nahuatl, and a large hill that borders the town still bears the same Zapotec name today (*Dani Beedxe*), indicating the likely bilingualism of at least some of the residents at the time. Despite the military dominance of the Aztec, the regional Zapotec rulers still wielded considerable power in the Isthmus, where the king Cosijoeza banded with the Ñuu Savi (Mixtec) and successfully resisted an attack from the Aztec army in the *Guie' Ngoola* fortress near Tehuantepec, brought on by the Zapotecs' refusal to pay tribute. Nonetheless, it was primarily the names given through the process of internal colonization by the Aztec that were recorded and are in use today, an enduring symbol of the waves of displacement and dominance among Indigenous groups in the region. These struggles amidst Mesoamerican powers took an unpredictable turn a few decades later however with the beginning of the Spanish invasion in 1519 (Miano Borruso 2002).

---

11 One of the current names for the city is *Guidxi Guie'*, town of flowers, along with *Lahuiguidxi*, central town, and *Xavizende*, a zapotecization of San Vincente, the patron saint of the city.

2.2 From languages to *dialectos*: Colonial language ecologies

Under Spanish colonization the Isthmus became part of the *Marquesado del Valle*, and was developed for cattle ranching, as well as trans-oceanic trade. Although records of Zapotec life under colonial rule are sparse, it was generally a time of hardship, including heavy tolls from new diseases and hard labor to pay tributes to the Spanish overlords. In 1521 there were 24,000 Indigenous residents of the Isthmus paying tribute; in 1550 there were 6,000, and only 60 years after the invasion in 1580 the population paying tribute had dropped over 80% to 4,000 (Acuña 1984, in Barabas and Bartolomé 1999: 71), a dramatic drop in the overall population due to harsh conditions (Tutino 1993). There were rebellions against Spanish exploitation throughout the 16th and 17th centuries, with the most famous being the 1660 rebellion of Tehuantepec, where the Zapotecs succeeded in governing the city for one year before the colonial government retook the city (Miano Borruso 2002). Numerous subsequent rebellions occurred in Juchitán as well, leading to the stereotype that *Istmeños*, and in particular *Juchitecos*, are "*rebeldes, rudos, y laboriosos*" [rebellious, rough, and hard-working] (Barabas and Bartolomé 1999: 72).

While the Spanish began instructing some Indigenous elites in Latin literacy during the colonial period (Heath 1972; Montemayor 2004), there was a general erasure of existing literacy and numeracy practices. "The Spanish conquest obliterated every manifestation of high Indian culture" (Covarrubias 1946: 292) through burning manuscripts and killing people in possession of traditional religious items, contributing to the limited understanding of pre-colonial Zapotec writing today. At the same time, already in the 1500s missionaries in Oaxaca were studying and recording spoken Indigenous languages and using this knowledge in pursuit of evangelization. Fray Juan de Córdova, a Spanish-born Dominican monk who arrived in Oaxaca around 1547, is the best-known of numerous missionaries who produced extensive documentation and linguistic description of the Zapotec then spoken around Oaxaca City (Jiménez Moreno 1942). Of all the varieties of Zapotec, modern-day Isthmus Zapotec is the closest to what Córdova recorded, and his 1578 dictionary is still considered a valuable reference by Zapotec scholars today.

The Latin-based (re)education provided by missionaries to some Indigenous people was not the norm, however; the majority of the population was not engaging in formal education under colonial rule. As Robles (1977) comments, "*Una organización predominantemente feudal colocaba a la gran mayoría de aborígenes en posición explotada y marginada de los favores del gran desarrollo de los servicios educativos de entonces*" (17). [A predominantly feudal organization placed the vast majority of Indigenous people in an exploited position, marginalized from the favors of the great development of educational services of the time]. While excluded from Eurocentric education, Indigenous groups were perpetuating their own education through oral and communal forms of teaching and socializing youth, however. Maldonado Alvarado (2002) argues that

> Aunque los zapotecos fueron una cultura dominante en tiempos prehispánicos, la mayoría de su población organizaba la vida de manera oral mientras que las minorías en el poder desarrollaban un sistema de escritura elitista que murió con ellas. Siete siglos después, [. . .] los zapotecos siguieron organizando su vida de manera oral, aunque sufriendo el peso de la dominación en español por escrito
>
> Although the Zapotecs were a dominating culture in prehispanic times, the majority of the population organized life in an oral way while the minorities in power developed an elitist system of writing that died with them. Seven centuries later [. . .] the Zapotecs continued organizing their life in an oral way, although suffering the weight of the Spanish domination through writing. (2002: 45)

He goes on to state that the development of Spanish-origin, text-based education did more than exclude the Indigenous population, it created a form of symbolic domination because "*lo escrito descalifica lo oral, o más concretamente una cultura con escritura descalifica a las sociedades orales*" [writing discredits orality, or more concretely a culture with writing discredits oral societies] (40–41). The devaluing of Indigenous communication practices was thus pervasive throughout the colonial period, with Indigenous languages viewed as inferior forms of communication, without writing or literature. The devaluing of Indigenous so-called *dialectos* intensified when the political tides turned to postcolonial nation-building.

2.3 *Castellanización*: Nationalist language ecologies

Following independence from Spain in 1810, a Spanish-dominant nation-building ideology prevailed in Mexico, with political leaders no longer ignoring the Indigenous population, but instead attempting to include and assimilate them through linguistic as well as economic means (Heath 1972). The first law establishing free primary education was passed in 1867, and in 1883 the first public primary classes were held in Juchitán, with *Escuela Primaria Oficial numero 1* opening in 1890 where the *Casa de la Cultura* is today (Ruíz Martínez 2013). By 1895 – 376 years after the Spanish invasion – Spanish had become the language spoken by a majority of people in Mexico, a process often called *castellanización*, Spanish-ization (Hamel 2008a). This was not yet true of Juchitán or the

Isthmus, however; despite the trends in the urban areas of the Mexican nation-state, many Indigenous languages remained dominant in their own regional and local spheres throughout this period.

The era of mandatory public schooling in Mexico officially began with the 1867 *Ley de Instrucción Pública*, although it did not become truly established until the founding and subsequent expansion of the *Secretaria de Educación Pública* in 1921 (Robles 1977). The Mexican revolution in 1910–1920 resulted in a further centralist, assimilationist political environment, for which the national *Secretaría de Educación Pública* became a tool and support (Martínez Vásquez 2004). The first regional teacher training college in the Isthmus, the *Escuela Normal Regional de Juchitán*, opened in 1926 and numerous primary and secondary schools followed (Ruíz Martínez 2013). It was as a result of this aggressive national campaign for school construction and Spanish-language literacy that use of Spanish began to spread in Oaxaca in the 1940s (Hamel 2008b; Sicoli 2011). Juchitán politician Heliodoro Charis Castro, one of numerous rebel-turned-politician icons who was elected mayor in 1935 and later congressman and senator, was instrumental in the creation of schools (and other public and infrastructure works) in his municipality. He was known for speaking Spanish with a heavy Zapotec accent, and is supposed to have said *"niños y jovenes, estudien, porque en la vida se ganan más batallas con las letras que con las armas"* [children and young people, study, because in life you win more battles with letters than with weapons]. At this time, studying was synonymous with learning Spanish. Charis Castro and other Zapotec elites were well-attuned to the power dynamics of the time, and saw the acquisition of Spanish (in addition to the locally-dominant Zapotec) as a possible resource for their community.

Despite the high hopes of political leaders like Charis Castro, mandatory public schooling perpetuated social inequalities and has largely been a space that excludes Indigenous languages and ways of knowing and being (Maldonado Alvarado 2002; Hamel 2008b). The results of Spanish-only schooling in Indigenous communities were largely poor, with many drop-outs. Alternative inclusive approaches to Indigenous education also had a presence in Mexico through pilot studies since the 1930s (Hamel 2008b) and numerous initiatives by teachers and communities. In 1978 diverse programs for Indigenous students were centralized under the *Dirección General de Educación Indígena* (DGEI), a branch of primary education responsible for running bilingual schools. In comparison with mainstream Spanish monolingual schools, bilingual programs typically lack resources and focus on transitioning students to Spanish rather than developing bilingualism (Hamel 2008a, 2008b; Coronado Suzán 1992) as discussed further in chapter 4. Through both so-called bilingual and mainstream monolingual schools, the priority of the Mexican nation-state was to spread standard Spanish and a centralized curriculum.

2.4 Neoliberal 'multicultural' language ecologies

The influences of economic globalization, including the effects of the North American Free Trade Agreement of 1994, which weakened the livelihoods of farmers in Oaxaca and elsewhere, have led to increased political tension and migration (López Bárecenas 2009). Residents of the Isthmus of Tehuantepec have continued their long heritage of political activism, and have organized in various social movements in response to national and international development projects (Doane 2005; Tutino 1993). These socio-economic changes are also leading to challenging shifts in the linguistic and educational landscape, including the presence of youth who speak English due to increased migration from Indigenous communities to the US and back again (Pérez Báez 2005; Zúñiga and Hamann 2015), and a growing interest in learning English. US-origin businesses, such as Wal-mart and its derivatives Sam's Club and Aurera Bodega, take business away from locally-run markets and small stores; the 4th Wal-mart-owned store in the Isthmus opened in 2014 in a part of Tehuantepec that was previously a public market. Destabilized local economies also lead to internal migration away from rural regions and towards urban centers. Extensive internal migration within Mexico and Oaxaca is resulting in mixed urban schools where students who speak Indigenous languages often do not want to admit it, and instead attempt to blend in with the Spanish mainstream (López Gopar 2009).

The effect of economic migration in the Isthmus is not as stark as in some parts of Oaxaca, however there is a different process underway, that of the arrival and rapid development of wind farms by international corporations. Since around 2007 this process is leading to land disputes (Huesca-Pérez, Sheinbaum-Pardo, and Köppel 2016), a visible presence of foreign (largely Spanish) workers, and increased stratification of *Istmeño* society as some landowners benefit from the developments while others resist it (Dunlap 2019). In the development of a new project in 2014, a "community consultation" between the *Comisión Federal de Electricidad* (CFE), the investor (a large Mexican company), and citizens of Juchitán took place as a result of Mexico's ratification of the International Labor Organization's convention 169 (International Labour Organization 1989), guaranteeing the right of previous consultation for projects on Indigenous lands. While many saw this as a farcical "consultation" with no benefits (Friede and Lehmann 2016), it is evidence of the influence of global politics on local realities in the Isthmus.

At the national level the past few decades have seen increased rights for Indigenous communities. Beginning with the recognition of Indigenous cultural rights in the constitution in 1992, the 1996 San Andres accords achieved as a result of the Zapatista movement in Chiapas gained important ground in raising awareness of cultural and linguistic diversity in Mexico, and demanding education that is based in Indigenous cultures, rather than including them as "intercultural" tokens (Rebolledo 2010). The *Coordinación General de Educación Intercultural Bilingüe* (CGEIB) founded in 2001, followed by the Law on the Linguistic Rights of Indigenous Peoples in 2003 and the founding of the *Instituto Nacional de Lenguas Indígenas* (INALI) in 2005, are all "fruits" of the "*discurso intercultural bilingüe sembrado por el zapatismo y el movimiento indígena*" [intercultural bilingual discourse sown by Zapatistas and the indigenous movement] (Rebolledo 2010: 147). INALI has been engaged in training interpreters, among other language documentation and education projects, helping to make at least some changes in the way that Indigenous language speakers are treated in some public spaces. The presence of multiple languages and cultures is often lauded as a key characteristic of Oaxaca in government and tourism discourse, in particular in promotion of the yearly *Guelaguetza* dance festival which some view as important revenue for the state, while others view it as further exploitation of Indigenous communities.

Efforts to make "interculturalism" part of public schooling in Mexico have been deemed superficial, characterized by celebrating cultural difference without considering the hierarchies and power dynamics among groups (Velasco Cruz 2010). Even programs that might appear to have an inclusive or multiculturalist agenda, such as the recruitment and training of *promotores bilingües* (Indigenous bilingual classroom assistants) have followed an assimilationist agenda. Julia Noriega Sánchez, a Zapotec teacher, recounts her experience being trained as a *promotora bilingüe* by the *Instituto de Investigación y Integración Social del Estado de Oaxaca* (Institute of Research and Social Integration for the State of Oaxaca, IIISEO) as follows: "*nos mandó a acabar con nuestras lenguas porque la meta era castellanizar. Al IIISEO veníamos de todo el estado de Oaxaca y teníamos la misión de acabar con nuestra cultura, con nuestra lengua*" [We were told to finish off our languages, because the goal was to castillianize [spread use of Spanish]. At IIIESO we came from everywhere in the state of Oaxaca, and we had the mission to finish off our culture, our language] (Noriega Sánchez 2012: 26).

Indigenous speech communities have thus received more recognition and rights in recent decades, resulting in changes to some of the discourses that characterize language ecologies in Oaxaca, but fewer changes to the material inequalities experienced by members of these communities. Multicultural rights and recognition policies have been critiqued throughout Latin America for resulting in commodifying and patronizing marginalized communities, who find it impossible to claim their so-called rights in practice (Hale 2005; García 2005; Speed 2005; Overmyer-Velázquez 2010). In general there is great distrust of the government authorities among residents of the Isthmus, in particular the federal government, although the state and local government officials are often the targets of critique for corruption and the system of *caciques*, or powerful families who dominate political parties and regional elections. The government is assumed not to have the peoples' interest at heart, whether through a greater focus on corrupt business and trade negotiations (locally and regionally) or through prioritizing the wealthier northern regions of Mexico (nationally). In light of this it is common to turn to social networks for support (including the traditional practice of *trueque*, *tequio*, *guendaruchaa* or *guendalisaa*; communal labor and reciprocity), and for civil society groups to self-organize to attempt to provide services, including cultural and educational opportunities, which they see as lacking (see chapters 6 and 7).

This practice was in full evidence following a series of significant earthquakes that took a heavy toll in the Isthmus in September 2017, causing the collapse of many public and private buildings, and dozens of casualties. Although supplies and some support eventually arrived from government entities, an important response came from members of the community working to house and feed their neighbors, as well as private individuals from all over Mexico and internationally sending supplies to the Isthmus. Many schools were closed as a result of earthquake damage, and in addition to workshops supported by INALI and Save the Children, several local groups organized to offer workshops for children during this time. The slow reconstruction of the buildings and economy of the region is still underway as I write this book, and the long-term impacts this natural disaster may have on the region remain to be seen.

2.5 Traditions of Indigenous language activism

Against the backdrop of different assimilationist and multiculturalist national and regional policies, Isthmus Zapotec language advocacy initiatives have been going on within the Zapotec community since at least the late 19th century, alongside identity-based political activism that has been going on for centuries (Tutino 1993). The language activism initiatives which are best recorded in available history are those related to writing and publishing. A group of students from Juchitán began publishing a pro-Zapotec newsletter (*Neza* [Path]) in Mexico City in 1935, which, albeit published largely in Spanish, included some Zapotec poetry and strongly pro-Zapotec rhetoric, characterized as *"ferviente nacionalismo étnico de los intelectuales zapotecos"* [fervent ethnic nationalism of the Zapotec intellectuals] (Miano Borruso 2002: 108). For example, an article entitled *"Zapotequización"* [Zapotecization] defines this term as *". . . el entrometimiento de caracteres zapotecos en el alma de las cosas o de las personas extrañas que con sólo situarse o vivir en los pueblos del Istmo juchiteco, adquieren un revestimiento peculiarmente zapoteco"* [. . . the intermingling of Zapotec characteristics in the soul of the foreign things or people that, by merely situating themselves or living in the cities of the Juchitán[12] Isthmus, acquire a peculiarly Zapotec covering] (Morales Henestrosa 1935). Further publications followed, and a standard orthography called the *alfabeto popular* [popular alphabet] was developed in 1956, spearheaded by Isthmus Zapotec writers based in Mexico City and adopted in collaboration with linguists (Pérez Báez, Cata, and Bueno Holle 2015; De Korne 2017b). The *alfabeto popular* was further promoted by the *Casa de la Cultura*, an organization in Juchitán which has been printing Zapotec poetry and other literature since being co-founded by painter and activist Francisco Toledo in 1972. The journal *Guchachi' Reza* [*Iguana Rajada*, Sliced Iguana] was published under the direction of several different Isthmus Zapotec writers and scholars between the 1970s and 1990s, containing historical and political articles (in Spanish), art, photography, and poetry (primarily in Diidxazá) (see chapters 3 and 6 for further discussion of Zapotec literary initiatives).

While Oaxaca is among the poorest states of Mexico, the region of the Isthmus has enjoyed greater wealth and perhaps less political marginalization than other Indigenous communities. The Isthmus Zapotec have remained economically dominant in comparison with other Indigenous groups such as the Ikoots (Huave), and are demographically more numerous than any of the Zapotec communities in the mountains or central valleys of Oaxaca. They have consistently promoted their language and culture in regional and national arenas; Tehuantepec is known for the embroidered *huipil* (blouse), long skirts, and extravagant gold jewelry that were made famous when Frida Kahlo adopted them into her wardrobe and paintings. Juchitán is known for the election of the independent, left-wing *Coalición Obrero-Campesino-Estundiantil del Istmo* (COCEI, Laborer-peasant-student coalition of the Isthmus) party in 1981 at a time when the rest of the country was run by the *Partido Revolucionario Institucional* (Institutional Revolutionary Party, PRI), drawing the attention of political anthropologists and the

---

[12] Referring to the *Istmo juchiteco*, instead of the more common Isthmus of Tehuantepec, gestures towards the long-time rivalry between the cities of Tehuantepec and Juchitán, a complex topic that will not be taken up here.

wrath of the national government (Campbell 1989, 1994; Rubin 1994). A discourse of pride for *Istmeño* history, bravery, and beauty pervades much of the music and poetry composed and made popular by *Istmeños*. Juchitán in particular has generally received more attention from media and researchers than other parts of the Isthmus, as the base of the COCEI and a large *muxe* (third gender) community which has been the subject of several documentaries and numerous studies (e.g. Stephen 2002; Gosling and Osborne 2000).

Providing a backdrop and support to language and culture activities in the Isthmus, the state of Oaxaca has been home to a variety of Indigenous language advocacy organizations, including the *Coordinación de Maestros y Promotores Indígenas de Oaxaca* (Coordination of Indigenous Teachers and Aides of Oaxaca, CMPIO), founded in 1974, the *Centro Editorial en Literatura Indígena, A.C.* (Indigenous Literature Publishing Center, CELIAC), founded in 1988, and the *Centro de Estudios y Desarrollo de las Lenguas Indígenas de Oaxaca* (Center for studies and development of the Indigenous languages of Oaxaca, CEDELIO). There are numerous Indigenous language and culture initiatives elsewhere in the state, each with their own local particularities (Faudree 2013, 2015; Suslak 2009).

2.6 On-going change in the language ecology

> *No, yo no lo hablo tanto porque, este, mi papá siempre nos hablaba en español pero como mi abuelita siempre hablaba el zapoteco entonces al escucharlo lo entendí y lo puedo, este, pronunciar. Pero así platicarlo mucho, este, sí– Hay personas que no pueden hablar acá español y es forzosamente hablar con ellos zapoteco y ahí es donde lo hablo [. . .]– pero sí le entiendo, sí puedo.*

> No, I don't speak it much because, um, my dad always spoke to us in Spanish but since my granny always spoke Zapotec so through listening to it I understood it and I can, um pronounce it. But like that to speak it a lot, um, yes– there are people here that can't speak Spanish and it's necessary to speak Zapotec with them and that is where I speak it [. . .] – but yes I understand it, yes I can.   (Interview November 2013)

This 25-year-old woman lives in La Ventosa, a village of almost 5,000 people inside the district and municipality of Juchitán, located near the center of the windswept coastal plain of the Isthmus. There are a wide range of language practices within what is generally considered the geographic and linguistic region of Isthmus Zapotec, ranging from agriculture-dependent villages where Zapotec is the dominant form of communication (such as *Gui'xhi' ro'*, Álvaro Obregon, described in the opening of this chapter) to middle class urban centers where residents have some degree of affiliation with Isthmus Zapotec music, clothing, food, and history, but have almost no contact with Zapotec language use (such as Salina Cruz). As the young woman above notes, there are people who do not speak much Spanish, as well as people who do not speak Diidxazá, and people like herself in between. The presence of other Indigenous languages is also a part of the regional ecology, with Spanish as the undisputed lingua franca. The political boundaries do not follow cultural or linguistic boundaries; the sprawling municipality of Juchitán, for example, includes part of the Ombeayiüts (Huave) speaking zone; the town of Álvaro Obregon, where Isthmus Zapotec is dominant among all ages; the town of La Ventosa where most people around 30 and older speak Isthmus Zapotec; and the city of Juchitán where in the wealthier northern neighborhoods very little Zapotec is spoken, while in the poorer southern neighborhoods (in particular the "7th section") Isthmus Zapotec is used frequently and some children are acquiring it. The differing communicative repertoires, socio-economic conditions, and dialects or varieties of Isthmus Zapotec present in the Isthmus are all significant factors which inform and impact language activism in this context.

The varied communicative repertoires, described also in the opening of this chapter, are the result of shifting language socialization practices among families, influenced by the centuries of discrimination discussed in sections 2.1–2.4. *Istmeño* linguist Vincente Marcial Cerqueda calculates that Isthmus Zapotec is being learned by children as a first language in 2 out of 24 towns in the Isthmus (Marcial Cerqueda 2014), a result which is supported by my observations and interviews throughout the region. The map in Figure 5 represents my analysis of approximate levels of Diidxazá use by town based on observations and interviews. As I did not focus my research on the question of language vitality; this is intended as an indication of the varying levels of language use, not a precise measurement. These levels of use are nonetheless important to note because they come to have a significant effect on the language activism initiatives that are discussed in the following chapters due to the diverse repertoires of the people participating in these initiatives. The towns underlined in green in Figure 5 (San Blas Atempa, Santa Rosa, Álvaro Obergon (*Gui'xhi' ro'*), Santa María Xadani, and the 7th section of Juchitán) are the areas of most dominant Isthmus Zapotec use, located primarily in the countryside and along the coast in between Juchitán and Tehuantepec. Isthmus Zapotec is spoken to varying degrees in the towns underlined in yellow (Juchitán de Zaragoza, El Espinal, Union Hidalgo, Chicapa de Castro, La Ventosa, La Mata, Asunción Ixtaltepec, Ixtepec, and San Pedro Comitancillo), but I observed generally little transmission to children. In some of these towns the youngest speakers are mature adults or older, and the town is moving towards minimal use of Diidxazá, indicated by yellow and brown underlining. The towns underlined in brown (Tehuantepec and Salina Cruz) have a cultural affinity but minimal Isthmus Zapotec use at present.

46 —— Chapter 2 The moving target of activism: Changing language ecologies

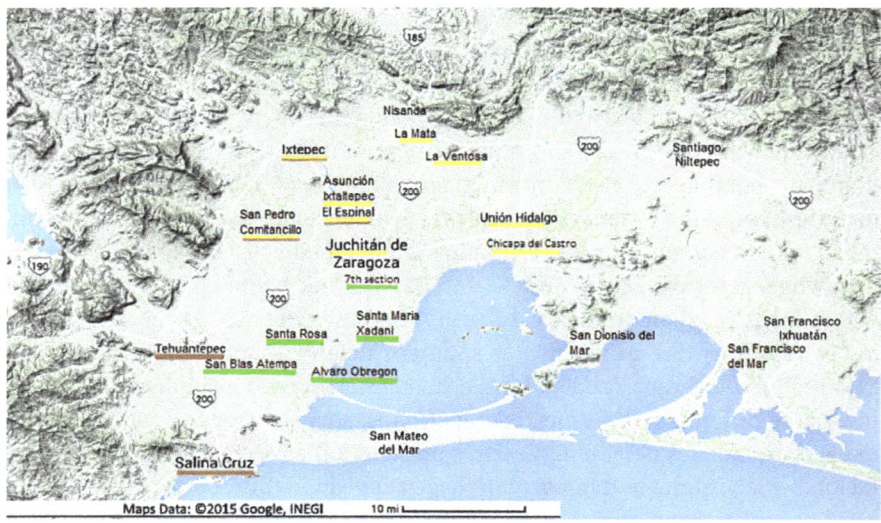

Figure 5: Geographic representation of Isthmus Zapotec use across the Isthmus.

Salina Cruz is included as a city with historical connection because they practice Isthmus Zapotec traditions such as *velas*, and affiliate with Isthmus Zapotec clothing, food and music, however the city grew up with a mixed populace around the development of the oil refinery in the 1970s, and has never been a Zapotec-speaking city. Tehuantepec on the other hand was a Zapotec city prior to colonization by the Aztecs in the 15th century and the Spanish in the 16th century, and continues to affiliate strongly with Zapotec culture, but only elderly people speak Diidxazá there today. Figure 5 also shows the three Ikoots (Huave) towns of San Mateo del Mar, San Dionisio del Mar and San Francisco del Mar, along the coast.

During my study I lived in the north of the city of Juchitán, a zone where Isthmus Zapotec is used among adults, but is generally not being transmitted to children. A study of Isthmus Zapotec home language socialization in Juchitán in the late 1990s found that wealthier families, while continuing to state that they wished their children to be bilingual, were raising their children mainly in Spanish (Augsburger 2004). More recent research has documented the increasing use of Spanish among children in the southern 7th section of the city, still popularly viewed as Zapotec dominant despite these ongoing changes (McComsey 2015). During my study I travelled to towns across the region in order to observe education programs and events and to conduct interviews. In almost every locale I observed adults conversing in Isthmus Zapotec amongst themselves and using Spanish to address children. Many interviewees and acquaintances told me that their father in particular forbade the use of Isthmus Zapotec in the home, although some eventually learned it from their mothers, grandparents, or peers in the street. Spending time with grandparents, who in many cases live with their extended families or act as primary caregivers when parents travel or live away for work, is a common way through which younger generations are acquiring at least passive comprehension abilities, as noted in the comments of the young woman above. This same phenomenon has been noted elsewhere in Mexico as the "grandparent effect" (Hill 1998; Suslak 2009). Many of the families I came to know followed a three-generation shift pattern, where the current grandparent generation speaks primarily Diidxazá, the current parents are often bilingual in Diidxazá and Spanish, and the children are dominant in Spanish, although some eventually acquire abilities as adolescents or young adults due to extended exposure to the language over time and in some cases personal motivation.

The trends of increasing socialization through Spanish documented in Juchitán are clearly present in most other towns, and correlate roughly with economic class and proximity to the railway, roads and trade routes. In Tehuantepec, the former colonial capital and commercial hub, the youngest speakers are in their 70s and 80s (Cata 2003). Ixtepec, San Pedro Comitancillo, Asunción Ixtaltepec, and El Espinal are all in proximity of railway lines, and appear to have mainly adult and senior adult speakers.[13] Juchitán, La Ventosa, Union Hidalgo and La Mata are towns with a mix of economic levels, have speakers in their 20s and 30s, and older. Finally, in the rural communities of Santa María Xadani, Álvaro Obregon, and Santa Rosa, and to a lesser extent in the suburban communities of San Blas Atempa and the southern sections of Juchitán, children arrive in school speaking Zapotec, and acquire Spanish in school. As in many other minoritized language communities, the more a family is involved in economic and eventually social relations outside of the region, the more the imposed language (in this case Spanish) has come to be used (Fishman 1989).

A further important distinction to be made is that speakers of Isthmus Zapotec recognize dialect differences within the speech community, although they note that these dialects are mutually intelligible. The people who I worked with readily recognize three significant dialects which vary primarily as to vowel phonation and tone, as well as some lexical differences; the dialects of 1)

---

[13] I spent much less time in these northern towns and interviewed fewer people from them, so my observations on this northern area of the Isthmus are more tentative than in the southern region where I spent extended time.

Juchitán and surroundings ("*los tecos*"), 2) of San Blas/ Tehuantepec ("*los blaseños*" and "*los tehuanos*"), and 3) of Asunción Ixtaltepec/ La Mata ("*los binni guiati*"). *Istmeño* linguist Víctor Cata (unpublished manuscript) notes a 4th dialect in Ixtepec and San Pedro Comitancillo. Indeed, the creators of the popular alphabet in 1956 took these dialect variants into account and noted that the alphabet should be adapted to each of the regional dialects, not imposed as a monoglossic standard (see also chapters 3 and 6). These 4 dialect variants are indicated on the map in Figure 6.

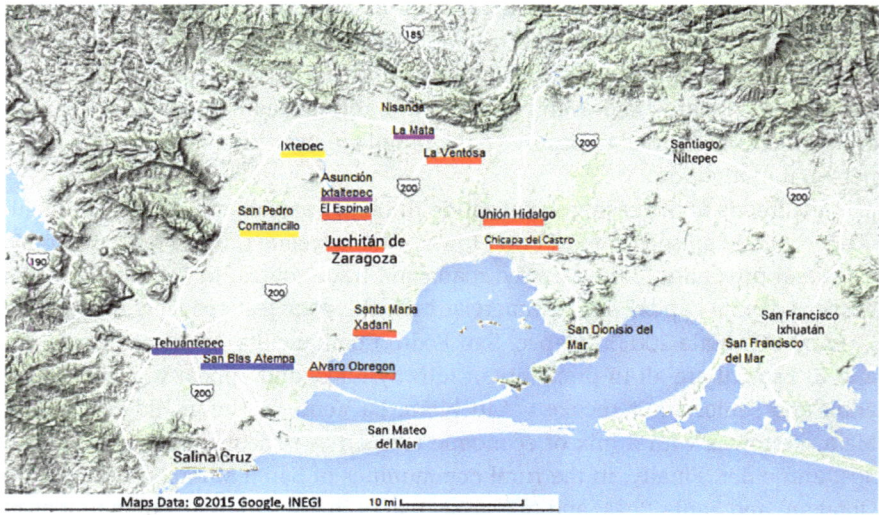

Figure 6: Geographic representation of Istmus Zapotec dialects.

Most speakers also comment that there are further differences from one town to another. Dialect variety was not a focus of my research, however I soon noted that these differences become significant in the teaching and learning of Diidxazá, as speakers from one dialect often wind up as teachers in another dialect zone, and the Juchitán dialect is the most represented in Isthmus Zapotec documentation and publications (see chapters 5 and 6).

When comparing the maps in Figures 5 and 6, it is interesting to note that what appears to most readily define the towns within the zone of greatest active Diidxazá use (around Santa María Xadani, Álvaro Obregon, Santa Rosa and San Blas Atempa) is not a political or dialect affiliation. They are split between dialects and between the municipalities of Tehuantepec and Juchitán. Rather, geographic isolation from the highway (where access roads are only partially paved and public transit is intermittent), participation in agriculture and fishing subsistence, and low income relative to the rest of the region are common across this area. Locally, this area is also often viewed as *brava* [fierce, brave], politically volatile, and an area where "good" or "pure" Diidxazá is spoken. While many people who I interacted with are aware that Isthmus Zapotec is used more in some of those towns "over there", they do not conceptualize an area or zone of active Diidxazá use as I am suggesting here; I came to view this area as a zone over time, after observing literacy workshops taught in Xadani and Álvaro Obregon, interviewing people from Xadani, San Blas, and the southern 7th section of Juchitán, and visiting schools in Xadani, Santa Rosa, Álvaro Obregon, and the 7th section.

The linguistic diversity of the Isthmus is visible on the streets and in homes. Although Spanish text predominates in public spaces, Diidxazá is used in commercial signage and a smaller amount of official signage, as well as some public art. When entering Juchitán on any of the three main highways, visitors are greeted by a sign (see Figure 7 below) which welcomes bilingually in Spanish and Diidxazá, and shows a famous photograph by Graciela Iturbide of an *Istmeña* with iguanas on her head (as many women continue to carry the products that they will sell in the market). The Isthmus Zapotec translation uses one of the three common Diidxazá names for Juchitán, *Lahuiguidxi* (central town).

Figure 7: Sign displayed at the three main entrances to Juchitán (photo January 2014).[14]

Less permanent official signs, such as banners produced by the mayor's office to commemorate an event, also often include a few words or small translation of Diidxazá, although they are not usually fully bilingual. Zapotec use in commercial

---

14 All photos are by the author unless otherwise noted.

signs is often limited to nouns, specifically proper nouns that give the locale (business, school, etc.) a name, rather than words which explain the function of the locale. They are thus not intended for monolingual Zapotec readers. For example, Figure 8 uses a noun to name the locale (*"Ba'du-huini"*, little child), and provides information as to the purpose of the locale, a *Centro de Desarrollo Infantil*, child development center, in Spanish.

Figure 8: *Centro de desarrollo infantil "Ba'du-huini"* (Child development center "little child"), Juchitán (photo January 2014).

Aside from official and commercial signage, Zapotec can be observed on a sizable number of Evangelical Churches (such as Figure 9), and a smaller amount of graffiti (such as Figure 10, in an alley).

In the more private linguistic landscapes of peoples' homes, the most common texts in Diidxazá are pamphlets produced by the Jehovah's Witnesses. Invitations to parties are another common text, some of which also use Isthmus Zapotec, but are usually largely in Spanish. Finally, the popularity of social media across generations in the Isthmus is resulting in regular use of written Diidxazá on facebook and other virtual media. Isthmus Zapotec circulates on peoples' screens through memes and reproduced images, as well as through comments and direct communication (see chapter 7 for further discussion). Written use of Diidxazá in

Figure 9: *Yu'Du' Lidxi Diuxi* (Church (sacred house) Home of God), La Ventosa (photo May 2014).

Figure 10: *Shunco* (Sweetheart, little one), San Blas Atempa (photo December 2013).

both the tangible and virtual linguistic landscapes varies considerably as to orthography practices. As discussed further in chapter 6, the recognized 1956 alphabet remains unfamiliar to many people. Writing on store fronts and official signs often does conform more or less to the spelling norms of the 1956 alphabet; however writing in on-line forums does so less frequently. Diidxazá is thus a regular part of the textual lives of people in the Isthmus, alongside the de facto dominance of Spanish and the presence of English and other national and international referents.

The perspectives or ideologies which people hold in relation to both spoken and written Isthmus Zapotec vary, often in paradoxical ways. While the language and other manifestations of traditional culture such as music, folk dance and the various kinds of embroidery which characterize formal clothing are generally held in high esteem, the language in particular can also be a stereotype of lower class, a lack of education, or poverty. As the mother quoted in the opening of this chapter stated, speaking with a Zapotec accent is not well-regarded and can make people feel ashamed, so that they aspire to have their children speak like monolingual Spanish speakers. The language ideological assemblage (Kroskrity 2018) in the Isthmus thus includes discourses which value and praise Diidxazá, as well as those which link Diidxazá to problems and barriers to social mobility and well-being. Beyond the broad orientations that value or devalue Diidxazá, there are also a variety of discourses about the quality of language use. Critiques of current language use and interest in a pure or pre-colonial variety of Zapotec often arise in talk and practices around the language. A pure, uncontaminated imaginary of Zapotec is popular, in spite of the centuries of evolution, including unequal contact with Spanish, that have created "syncretic" (or fluid) language practices like those observed in Nahuatl communities in central Mexico (Hill and Hill 1986; Messing 2007). The internal diversity of Diidxazá dialects is also a topic of discussion in education settings in particular, as people question which variety is "correct" and thus the most appropriate to be taught (De Korne 2017c). These ideological currents inform different imaginaries of the future Isthmus Zapotec speech community, as well as language activism initiatives as examined further in the chapters that follow.

2.7 Summary: Activism characteristics in changing times

The potential supports and barriers that language activists may encounter in the Isthmus have changed over time and will continue to shift. Whether or not the increased policy support at national and international levels will eventually result in local improvements in the disappointing education and political systems discussed above remains to be seen. Pride for *Istmeño* heritage, including language, is evident historically and in public spaces today, although the influence of centuries of *castellanización* and discrimination remains all-too-present as well. Indigenous language speakers have won official recognition, but many of them remain economically marginalized. The current education system, where young *Istmeños* spend many obligatory hours, does not promote anything more than transitional bilingualism in the majority of cases. Spanish, and increasingly English, are now added to the multilingual ecology of the Isthmus alongside the enduring use of Diidxazá and other Indigenous languages.

Like any social endeavor, language activism initiatives can only hope to succeed if they are contextually appropriate and address issues in a way which makes sense to local stakeholders. The linguistic aspirations of members of the Isthmus Zapotec community are shaped by the context described here, and include the acquisition of Spanish and English for social mobility, as well as the acquisition of Isthmus Zapotec for family communication and identity (see also De Korne 2017a). As discussed in chapter 1, linguistic equality can mean different things to different members of the speech community, who may prioritize different languages and varieties at different times. Understanding linguistic equality as a multiple and moving target may feel like a challenge to language activism, and indeed any activism, which often adopts absolute or at least explicit discourses of right and wrong in pursuit of specified goals. However, it can also be a source of strength in that goals must be justified in relation to contextualized rights and wrongs. Rather than arguing with an absolutist discourse that Indigenous languages are a treasure for all of humanity, for example, language advocates can argue with a constructivist discourse that a certain group is currently disadvantaged on the basis of language, or that they experience the lack of opportunities to use or learn their heritage language as a problem.

This gives a clear advantage to activists with a deep, personal knowledge of the local context on one hand. On the other hand, local activists may choose to collaborate with regional, national or international actors who have access to resources that they do not have, as discussed further in chapter 3. Many activism initiatives are in some way informed or supported by actors from different scales of the language ecology. For example, the *Camino de la Iguana* literacy workshop described in the opening of the chapter (and further discussed in chapter 6) was funded by a non-governmental foundation at the Oaxaca-state level, but developed and taught by two Juchitán-based activists. The workshops offered by INALI and Save the Children following the 2017 earthquakes employed some local people as teachers and facilitators, while the oversight and funding came from national and international sources. In relation to the strategy framework laid out in chapter 1, the literacy workshop had ties to both local and regional actors, although the primary location of the majority of people involved was at the local level. The INALI and Save the Children workshops also involved local actors and occurred locally, although there were links nationally and internationally which influenced the nature of the workshops.

As the language ecology of the Isthmus has shifted over time there is more influence and evidence of regional, national and international scales, and the possibility for visibility and circulation through digital platforms has increased radically. The locally-based strategies of Isthmus Zapotec writer-activists throughout the 20th century arguably achieved strong visibility throughout the Isthmus, as the names and works of Isthmus Zapotec writers and musicians are still widely known and praised. However, there are increasing opportunities for strategies which are faster (a social media post rather than an article in a literary journal) and potentially have greater visibility (circulating on-line rather than in print). Additionally, initiatives with national or international links may achieve a higher degree of visibility in certain circles, for example through attracting the attention of the news media or publishing information on their own web platforms. However, as examined further in the chapters that follow, the characteristics of speed, visibility, and international affiliation are not always desirable; important strategies that are slow, local, and relatively private may be well-suited to certain spaces and times.

The language ecology of the Isthmus, where multiple Indigenous languages and Spanish overlap, remains a site where multilingualism is common, as it has been for centuries. This multilingualism is clearly unequal, with speakers of Indigenous languages– and furthermore certain varieties of Indigenous languages– experiencing relatively more prejudice and disadvantage than speakers of Spanish do. In the chapters that follow, I illustrate some of the imaginaries and strategies through which activists in several domains have been resisting and disrupting this inequality. Beginning with the domain of scholarly research (chapter 3), I then turn to public schooling (chapter 4), higher education (chapter 5), community-based education (chapter 6), and popular culture (chapter 7) to show how activists and advocates with local, national and international affiliations are engaging in language politics in the Isthmus. These activists are imagining and implementing strategies which draw on resources both locally and globally, over rapid and slow timescales, and in private and public ways. Some activists orient towards Isthmus Zapotec history and traditions, while others orient towards current changes and future innovations; some orient towards a unitary, 'pure' imaginary of language and culture, while others promote hybrid or syncretic imaginaries. Finally, most of these activists aim for open and participatory initiatives, although some degree of control or limitation is also employed as a resource in certain contexts. The initiatives of the language activists who I highlight in each domain – and many others who are not mentioned for reasons of space – show clearly that the long tradition of resistance and activism is alive and well in the Isthmus Zapotec region.

Chapter 3
Creating knowledge and resources: Strategies in scholarship

> El lenguaje [es . . .] el ánfora cristalina que permite eternizar los conceptos y las vivencias de los hombres. Por eso es el más fiel reflejo de su mentalidad y la más fecunda manifestación de su cultura. Podrán desaparecer las razas y las naciones, pero si se conservan sus idiomas, el hombre de ciencia, físico, químico, fisiólogo, psicólogo o filósofo podrá retirar del acervo intelectual contenido en el lenguaje, la parte que le interese, para analizarla, clasificarla a fin de reconstruir, como un naturalista, con un solo dato, el organismo completo, en sistema científico que le parezca.
>
> Language [is . . .] the crystal vial that permits the eternalization of the concepts and lived experiences of man. Because of this it is the most loyal reflection of man's mentality and the most fecund manifestation of his culture. Races and nations can disappear, but if their languages are conserved, the man of science, physics, chemistry, physiology or philosophy, will be able to retrieve from the intellectual archive contained in language the part that interests him, in order to analyze it, classify it in order to reconstruct, like a natural scientist, with a single data point, the complete organism in the scientific system that he chooses. (Crúz 1935: 8–9)

The value of language as an "intellectual archive" that accurately reflects thought and culture and lends itself to later classification and analysis, elegantly articulated by Wilfrido C. Crúz in the above citation, should sound familiar to anyone who has participated in the field of linguistics, and in documentary linguistics in particular. Many other language scholars and activists have made the argument that language has enduring value as a scientific object, drawing on a paradigm in which language is essentialized or understood as a structure (rather than a socially constructed practice), as discussed in section 1.2. Linguistic anthropologist Jane Hill (2002) discussed both the potential usefulness and risks of rhetoric that presents language as an object of incalculable and universal value. She noted that "hyperbolic valorization" and "universal ownership" of language are common themes in the arguments made by scholars and some advocates in the field of language endangerment, such as the above descriptions of language as a "crystal vial" that can be accessed by any and all disciplines of science at some future point when the speakers of the language may have "disappeared". Although these arguments may be effective for their intended audience of policy makers, other scholars, and people outside of endangered language communities, Hill (2002) was concerned that they may have an unintended result of delegitimizing everyday speech and the knowledge of speakers within minoritized communities.

Scholars play a political role through their actions and through their discourses and imaginaries, as Hill and others have pointed out. There are multiple paradigms and practices across the academic disciplines that engage in minoritized language issues, each with potential advantages and disadvantages in specific contexts. Although there are trends and stereotypes among scholarly practices – such as documentary linguists focusing on linguistic structure and sociolinguists focusing on language use and meaning (Moore, Pietikainen, and Blommaert 2010) – an ethnographic examination of language promotion in the Isthmus of Tehuantepec reveals a wide variety of imaginaries and strategies employed among scholar-activists. The citation that opens this chapter is one such example of scholar-activism which does not fall into one category alone. While it contains discursive styles that are typically attributed to linguistic researchers, it was written by an Isthmus Zapotec speaker and self-trained scholar of Zapotec language and culture.

Wilfrido C. Crúz (1898–1948), a native of the town of Espinal, engaged in various forms of linguistic and cultural research and scholarly publishing on the side of his primary occupation as a lawyer and later a politician in Oaxaca City. The passage above comes from his *El Tonalamatl Zapoteco: Ensayo sobre su interpretación lingüística* [The Zapotec Tonalamatl [Almanac]: Essay on its linguistic interpretation], an analysis of the Zapotec ritual calendar and a linguistic analysis of the terms therein, as well as a retelling of some Zapotec legends. Published in 1935, it was a product of research he had engaged in and presented over several decades (Hernández Ruiz, forthcoming). In the above passage, and throughout his work, Crúz argued for the importance of linguistic analysis as an aid in scientific research of all kinds. He critiqued the lack of Indigenous language comprehension among historical and anthropological scholars working in Mexico, arguing that linguistic analysis was necessary for cultural comprehension and scientific discovery. He later worked on a vocabulary of Zapotec comparing different varieties (Isthmus, Sierra, Valley) and was especially interested in recording words that were going out of use. He also lamented the lack of purity in the Zapotec of his day due to the "*acción corrosiva de la cultura europea en los diversos dialectos del zapoteco*" [corrosive action/ effect of European culture on the diverse dialects of Zapotec], in particular the use of Spanish words (Crúz 1935: 6–7). Although Crúz's work did not gain wide circulation, it has been preserved and is valued among historians and language enthusiasts in the Isthmus, due to both its content and pride in Zapotec autochthonous scholarship.

Crúz was not alone in studying and writing about his language; as early as the late 19th century *Istmeños* such as Arcadio G. Molino, a native of San Blas Atempa, were writing in and about Isthmus Zapotec (Pérez Báez, Cata, and Bueno Holle 2015). At the time Crúz was producing scholarship in the 1920s-40s, a younger generation of Isthmus Zapotec intellectuals was emerging, in particular a community of youth who had moved to Mexico City to study. One of the key promoters of this endeavor was Andrés Henestrosa (1906–2008), a native of Ixhuatán, who heard Crúz talk about his research into Zapotec legends in the 1920s, and published his own version of some of these myths and several of his own stories in his 1929 book *Los hombres que dispersó la danza* [The men who were dispersed by dance]. Henestrosa went on to have a career as a writer, scholar, and eventually a politician. While Crúz worked to uncover words and traditions he viewed as endangered in order to document them for posterity, Henestrosa viewed his work as part of an ongoing cultural practice. Henestrosa (2009 [1929]) wrote in the forward to the 1945 second edition of *Los hombres que dispersó la danza* that Crúz's work *"tiene un alcance científico, arqueológico, se preocupa por la verdad histórica: el mío busca la verdad poética, que es otra cosa"* [has a scientific, archeological reach, it is concerned with historical truth: mine looks for poetic truth, which is another thing] (22). The group of young intellectuals of which Henestrosa was a part began to publish the journal *Neza* [Path] beginning in 1935, containing articles in Spanish on Isthmus history, culture and language, as well as poetry in Isthmus Zapotec. This journal gave a venue for the multiple *Istmeños* who were interested in studying their history, language, and culture, as well as those engaged in literary production in both Spanish and Zapotec.

When the American missionary and linguist Velma Pickett (1912–2008) began researching Isthmus Zapotec in the 1940s she noted that there were people writing in – as well as about – Diidxazá. In reflecting on the trajectory of her work she wrote *"Cuando llegué a Juchitán en diciembre de 1943, encontré que ya había escritores y que usaban varias ortografías de acuerdo al gusto del escritor. [. . .] Antes de llegar al campo, mi conocimiento en la lingüística me dirigía hacia la regla de usar un símbolo fonético por cada fonema. Sin embargo, en la práctica [. . .]"* [When I arrived in Juchitán in December 1943, I found that there were already writers and that they used various orthographies following the taste of the writer. [. . .] Before arriving in the field, my knowledge of linguistics directed me towards the rule of using one phonetic symbol for each phoneme. However, in practice [. . .]] (Pickett 1993:27). Pickett went on to describe how the linguistic principles she brought with her were impractical in several ways, and she eventually adopted more flexible strategies. Pickett was among the first wave of missionary linguists sent by the Summer Institute of Linguistics (SIL), a Christian missionary organization founded in the United States in 1934. SIL missionaries have engaged in extensive linguistic documentation and literacy work as a part of their missionary goals. From their initial work in Mexico, SIL expanded around the world and maintains an active presence

Chapter 3 Creating knowledge and resources: Strategies in scholarship — 59

in language documentation, Indigenous literacy initiatives and linguistic research. While some of their work is framed as scholarship first and foremost, the ultimate goal is to evangelize the communities whose languages are documented, a colonial paradigm which harks back to the abusive practices of multiple Christian sects during the colonization of the Americas. Pickett was neither the first foreign linguist nor missionary to be interested in Zapotec; Fray Juan de Córdova (1503–1595), a Dominican missionary who arrived among the first waves of Spanish colonization, recorded the Zapotec spoken in the central valleys of Oaxaca and published an extensive vocabulary list and linguistic analysis in 1578 (see also chapter 2).

Pickett aimed to go beyond documentation to the promotion of literacy, although her initial attempts to develop a phonetically transparent orthography met with various critiques from her would-be public. She was eventually invited to participate in the 1956 round table initiated by Zapotec writers which resulted in the creation of the popular alphabet (see chapter 6, also Pérez Báez, Cata, and Bueno Holle 2015; De Korne 2017b), and she subsequently abandoned the orthography that she had developed and promoted the popular alphabet through her publications. Over her many decades of involvement with Diidxazá, Pickett collaborated with numerous Zapotec writers and was instrumental in the creation of a Diidxazá grammar (Pickett, Black, and Cerqueda 2001), a Spanish-Diidxazá glossary, and literacy books published using the popular alphabet. Her 1993 reflection on her participation in the development of the Isthmus Zapotec popular alphabet quoted above was written at the invitation of *Istmeño* scholar Víctor de la Cruz and published in the journal *Guchachi' Reza* [*Iguana Rajada*, Sliced Iguana] of which he was then the editor.[15] She concludes the piece noting that certain aspects of the popular alphabet may not have been well chosen from a linguistic perspective, *"Pero seguimos el clima politico del tiempo y las decisiones de la mesa redonda, y me parece que los escritores del Istmo en la actualidad están contentos con las decisiones"* [But we followed the political climate of the time and the decisions of the round table, and it appears to me that the writers in the Isthmus today are happy with the decisions] (Pickett 1993:30). Pickett noted the contrast between the norms of her academic field and the social practices that she encountered, ultimately choosing the social norms as the most appropriate way to produce the desired resource of a recognized orthography. Juggling different paradigms and priorities in activism is common, whether one is working to create both linguistic

---

[15] *Guchachi' Reza* was a Zapotec-run magazine published by the *Casa de la Cultura* in Juchitán beginning in 1975. See also chapters 2 and 6.

description and tools for evangelism, or scholarly texts and accessible learning materials.

While many linguists and anti-colonial scholars (including myself) profoundly disagree with the evangelical aims of missionary linguists such as Pickett, it is clear that some missionary linguists developed positive relationships and collaborations in the communities where they worked. In Juchitán, where Pickett lived, people I met remembered her as a linguist (not as a missionary) and talked about her with great affection and respect, along with several other linguists who worked in the region later in the 20th century. During the decades Pickett conducted her work, all of the linguistic documentation and literacy materials produced by SIL-affiliated linguists were made freely available and dissemination was encouraged, first in paper and eventually in the on-line database *Ethnologue*. When I arrived in Juchitán in 2013 (70 years after Pickett) I observed that her vocabulary and grammar materials were in use by university students who had found them on-line and shared them amongst themselves in pdf formats, sometimes consulting them on their phones. In 2015, SIL put up a pay-wall and made *Ethnologue* a subscription-based resource, however, a choice that has disappointed and angered many linguists and activists, as evidenced by responses on *Ethnologue*'s twitter profile and linguistic blogs and list-serve conversations. Pickett was not alive to see or comment on this. Her collaborative work has been widely circulated and referenced among scholars and learners of Isthmus Zapotec in the 20th and 21st centuries; however, this may change as SIL attempts to monetize and sell the results of this research.

Wilfrido C. Crúz, Andrés Henestrosa and Velma B. Pickett are some of the people viewed as scholars or researchers of Isthmus Zapotec by *Istmeños*. Together, they illustrate something of the range of aims and actions within the domain of language research and the diverse forms of language advocacy and activism that can be linked to research. Each pursued an imagined outcome of collecting, curating and ultimately sharing knowledge about Isthmus Zapotec, however the form of knowledge they prioritized and what they produced varied. Crúz prioritized documentation and purism, producing texts aimed at a scholarly audience, but which have also attracted interest among *Istmeños* of various professions. Henestrosa attempted to capture a cultural aesthetic and collective memory, creating stories which helped establish his renown as a writer and literary figure, and which are well known both in and beyond the Isthmus Zapotec community. He successfully straddled or deconstructed the line between art and scholarship, and is recognized for cultural, historical, and linguistic contributions. Pickett adapted her priorities as a linguist in favor of the greater priority of a socially acceptable writing norm and didactic materials aimed at increasing literacy among the Isthmus Zapotec community (and eventually, increased reading of her preferred version of the Bible). Through collaboration with Zapotec writers she gained insights and strategies to support literacy, in addition to her descriptive linguistics training. The social position of these actors varies in important ways; while Crúz and Henestrosa were scholars of the community in which they were born, Pickett was a foreigner researching a community of which she was not an organic member. As is often the case among language activists, all of them were part of multiple communities of practice. In addition to engaging in language scholarship, Crúz and Henestrosa were both politicians, Henestrosa was also in literary circles, and Pickett was an evangelist. I choose to highlight these scholars partially because they do not fit the scientific stereotype of an 'objective', 'outside' scientist working diligently to uncover truth and knowledge. In this chapter I examine research as a socio-political practice, and aim to highlight the partiality, subjectivity, and inside-outside positioning of researchers which influences minority language research.

I first learned about the work of all these scholars from people engaged in language activism in the Isthmus during my study. The varied results of their research continue to be part of the resources and influences which are present in advocacy initiatives many decades after their work was conducted. While they may not have articulated their diverse aims as part of a social project in pursuit of linguistic equality, aspects of their work have been taken up by language activists and thus form part of this social project. In this chapter I discuss several of the scholarly communities of practice which engage most prominently with language activism, including the diverse ideological orientations and resulting priorities which they typically adopt. I understand scholarly communities or scholarly actors as those who engage in research and attempt to produce and share authoritative knowledge. Most often they are part of research institutions or universities, however they can also be based in non-government organizations, missionary organizations or other organizations which engage in research as part of their activities. As characterized by Lave and Wenger (Lave and Wenger 1991; Wenger 1998), each of these communities of practice is typically structured around *mutual engagement* towards a *joint enterprise*, making use of a *shared repertoire* to achieve their common goal(s). The norms of the community may change over time, and individual members may vary in the ways in which they participate. Additionally, the overlapping memberships of individual social actors influence their goals and choices. For example, although many linguists would aim for a transparent and detailed linguistic description, as Pickett did, many linguists do not have evangelical goals and might have less motivation to use a popular writing norm instead of the linguistics community-internal repertoire of the International Phonetic Alphabet.

The significance of language research as a socio-political practice has been well established, with scholars emphasizing both the potential positive and negative social impacts brought about through the pursuit of language research (Cameron et al. 1992; Errington 2001; Leonard and Haynes 2010; Lewis 2018). The ability to produce knowledge which is generally viewed as legitimate and authoritative gives research, and researchers, immense potential as social actors. At the same time, the political and ideological biases of academic institutions color and limit the kind of knowledge that is pursued and produced. I am especially interested in academic disciplines as communities of practice that engage in language advocacy because they act in particularly public and visible ways, and because I am a participant in several of them, as described further in section 3.1.1 below. Some scholars embrace the political nature and potential of research, and identify as both researchers and social agents, if not activists. Others maintain a more positivist orientation, aspiring towards objectivity and impartiality. All researchers wishing to share their work beyond narrow disciplinary boundaries are likely to face differing paradigms within their institutions, in popular media, and in society.

In the following section I illustrate how different domains of scholarship (also referred to as disciplines or communities of practice) have engaged in minoritized language research (3.1). While still on the margins of academic respectability in many ways, paradigms and frameworks for socially-engaged, action research are numerous. I then situate myself as a scholar and activist participating in multiple disciplinary communities and discuss the balancing act of working among different paradigms and methods (3.1.1), highlighting some of the methodological considerations that are important in language activism research (3.1.2). I offer an analysis of the activism strategies I observed among scholars in the Isthmus (3.2). Analyzing the strategies that I observed among other scholar-activists and reflecting on my own strategies, I illustrate the salient strategies of *creating* a variety of *resources* (from databases to cellphone apps, to didactic games), *representing* the value of local *communication practices,* and *connecting people, spaces* and *resources*. In summary I review some of the possibilities and tensions of scholar activism (3.3).

3.1 Scholarly engagement with minoritized languages

Scholars have engaged with minoritized language issues from a variety of perspectives, orienting towards language use at different social scales and carving out corresponding units of analysis, as shown in the cases of Crúz, Henestrosa and Pickett. Like all social actors, scholar-activists are informed by their moment in time and the communities of practice (academic and otherwise) that they are a part of. I draw on the notion of social scales to help tease out different forms of scholarly engagement across time and space. As Blommaert (2010) notes, "scales organize different patterns of normativity, of what counts as language" (37). Academic disciplines have developed many useful lenses for understanding language and social relations (ranging from essentialist to constructivist, and combinations in between, as discussed in section 1.2), and their practices and priorities can be linked with different social scales, including international, national, or regional territories, languages, ethnic groups, school systems, classrooms, individual learners, and instances of language use. Likewise, some disciplines focus on processes of power negotiation and legal regulations, while others focus on processes of language learning and socialization, cultural contact, and/ or production of discourses. Most disciplines consider more than one scale, process, or unit of analysis, and as in all communities of practice, they engage in constant negotiation of their shared assumptions and undertakings.

While some scholars work in multiple disciplines or transcend disciplines all together, many of us are heavily influenced by the norms of the discipline(s) we participate in. In order to lay the groundwork for discussion of strategies across scales and across disciplines, in this section I describe scholarly disciplines with special relevance to language activism, including language planning and policy, sociolinguistics, linguistic anthropology, documentary linguistics, applied linguistics, (multilingual) education, and international development. Each community of practice that I describe is ultimately more diverse than the description and consists of evolving practices that I do not capture here; I attempt to map out only the most salient conceptual paths that have been demarcating the social project of minoritized language research.

Traditional language policy and planning (LPP) research considers the shift or maintenance of a specific language at the scale of a territory or political unit as influenced by political regulations, such as official language status and corpus or standardization planning (Cooper 1989; Fishman 1991). Language ecology scholars discuss the organic interplay of multiple languages within a territory (Haugen 1972; Fill and Muhlhausler 2001; Maffi 2001), noting that languages thrive or become threatened in complex linguistic ecologies many of which are undergoing dramatic shifts worldwide (Calvet 1974; Hornberger and Hult 2008). More recently, LPP research has attended to political processes at local scales such as the classroom or the family (Canagarajah 2005; Shohamy 2006; Menken and García 2010), and across scales (Hornberger and Johnson 2007). Achieving a balance between different language varieties in society or redressing past imbalances is often the goal, in addition to describing how political processes and regulations influence language use. As more and more countries, including Mexico, have given legal recognition to Indigenous languages, scholars have pointed out that national-level recognition has not been powerful enough to change social prejudices in society, as discussed in chapter 2 (Stroud and Heugh 2004; Hamel 2008b). This has led to greater interest in bottom-up politics and the agency of local actors within LPP (Johnson and Johnson 2015; Lim, Stroud, and Wee 2018).

At the intersection of language and society on the meso and micro scale, interactional sociolinguistics has examined language politics at regional and local scales, including discursive and interactional forms of inequality such as diglossia and prejudice among speech communities (Ferguson 1959; Goffman 1967; Haugen 1973). Variationist sociolinguistics has illuminated patterns in language use that relate to social inequalities, providing further insight into the social differences constructed through language (Labov 1970; 2008). Linguistic anthropology has also examined patterns in language use, socialization, and the social meanings or ideologies associated with different ways of speaking in diverse cultural contexts, from schools, to families, to political arenas (Philips 1972; Ochs and Schieffelin 1984; Gal and Woolard 2001). More recent work drawing on both the interactionist sociolinguistics tradition and linguistic anthropology continues to make visible the social dynamics at play through and around minoritized and endangered languages in particular (Nevins 2004; Meek 2010; Webster 2010; Moore 2012; Urla 2012; Davis 2019).

Some scholars have also focused on the discourses and ideologies that circulate around minoritized languages in the wider society, including the media, policy, and popular discourse, as well as activist discourses. Beginning with Richard Ruiz's (1984) classic typology of orientations to language as a problem, a right, or a resource, numerous critical discourse analysis studies have illuminated language ideologies in different contexts, on different scales (Schieffelin, Woolard, and Kroskrity 1998; Fairclough 2003; Jaffe 2009; Reisigl and Wodak 2009). Discourses that have come to be stereotypical of language endangerment media and scholarship have been examined and critiqued, in particular the tendency to essentialize and enumerate languages, cultures and communities (Hill 2002; Suslak 2009; Moore, Pietikainen, and Blommaert 2010), and to resist what may be considered to be natural changes in language practice (Duchêne and Heller 2007; Blommaert 2010). Discourse analysis studies thus often deconstruct ideologies of language endangerment and point out potential harms, such as Cameron's (2007) analysis of language preservation discourse as qualitatively similar to discourses underlying the formation of nation-states and supremacist movements.

The field of documentary and descriptive linguistics has expanded exponentially in recent decades, aiming to record and archive as many language varieties as possible, as they are declining in use, or as frequently expressed, before they 'die' or 'go extinct' (Hale et al. 1992; Hagège 2000; Harrison 2010; Grinevald and Bert 2012). Taking discrete languages or dialects (and often specifically their structural properties) as units of analysis, the goal is to conserve the oldest variety of a language, with minimal interference from other varieties. Young linguists are taught that "as fieldworkers, we study language and culture from the outside by objectifying it, analyzing it, and quantifying it" (Bowern 2015: 177). Although the focus on endangered languages is more recent, this discipline has conceptual roots that go back to the 'salvage linguistics' of early American linguists (Moore 2000) such as Franz Boas, Leonard Bloomfield, Edward Sapir, and Morris Swadesh (e.g. Boaz 1911). The process of recording a language is considered to save the language from 'extinction', as it will be conserved in archival format whether or not it continues to be used, similar to Wilfrid Crúz's vision of the "intellectual archive contained in language" which can advance science after "races" and "nations" have disappeared, as quoted in the opening of this chapter. The quantitative and archive-focused practices of this discipline have been critiqued by linguists interested in the goal of supporting threatened language communities (Dobrin, Austin, and Nathan 2009), bringing new forms of reflexivity and an emphasis on collaborative models (Yamada 2007; Stebbins 2012; Pérez Báez 2018) as the field continues to expand with its own graduate programs, conferences and journals.[16]

Applied linguistics and second language acquisition research has developed quasi-experimental approaches to understanding the linguistic, cognitive, and social variables and processes of language acquisition and education, with the goal to ultimately improve language education practice (Pica 1997). Many applied linguistic studies have focused on individual learners as units of analysis which are studied under the influence of controlled contextual variables, such as age, additional languages spoken (especially first language or L1) (Lado 1959), and different forms and amounts of language input (Krashen 1982). The errors or "interlanguage" produced were seen as part of the learner's unidirectional trajectory towards native or monolingual-like mastery of a language (Selinker 1971), creating a paradigm of "native speakerism" which remains ingrained despite efforts to challenge it (Rampton 1990; Kumaravadivelu 2014). Although applied linguistics scholarship has considered mainly learners and

---

16 For example: http://icldc4.weebly.com; http://nflrc.hawaii.edu/ldc; http://www.elpublishing.org

speakers of national languages and ignored marginalized languages, attention to minoritized languages has increased in the past decade, and there are many common interests between applied linguistics scholars and minoritized language activists and educators (Valdés 2005; Cope and Penfield 2011; King 2016). A 'social turn' in applied linguistics has supported increased use of qualitative methodologies and consideration of additional influences and concerns in the language learning process (Firth and Wagner 1997), including understandings of self, others, and cross-cultural communication in language education (Byram 1997; Norton 2000). Current trends in applied linguistics recognize the multiplicity of factors that influence language learning, not all of which fit into experimental designs, and many of which exist on scales beyond the individual learner (Larsen-Freeman and Cameron 2008; Pennycook 2001, 2018) and beyond individual languages (May 2013; Douglas Fir Group 2016).

Consideration of multilingual learners' processes of language development has led to a more flexible view of language acquisition and use among scholars in education, with attention to the agency that individuals use to move between different language resources and registers and the interrelation of competencies across languages (Heller and Martin-Jones 2001; Lüdi 2004; García 2009a). Applied linguistic and education scholars' engagement with minoritized languages has expanded through attempts to teach threatened languages and/or develop learning materials in collaboration with language communities (Hinton and Hale 2001; De Korne et al. 2009), and to promote endangered languages in schools (Hornberger and King 1996). As the promotion of Indigenous languages in schools gains traction, Indigenous education practitioners and researchers have encouraged the use of "indigenous frameworks for thinking about schooling" (Smith 2005: 94), in line with the call for culturally responsive forms of education (Ladson-Billings 1995; Osborne 1996; Paris 2012) (discussed further in chapter 4). Literacy education scholars have likewise moved towards a more fluid and locally-informed approach to reading and writing education, aiming to better understand how biliteracy is developed (Hornberger 2003) and to support multimodal and critical literacies (Cazden et al. 1996; Kress 2000; Martin-Jones and Jones 2001). Andrés Henestrosa's adaptation of Zapotec oral myths into Spanish prose with frequent use of Diidxazá terms, and his support of contemporary Zapotec literature through the journal *Neza* and other projects throughout his career, is an example of the kinds of translingual and transcultural expression which literacy educators encourage as a way to give voice to multilingual people who have been marginalized by would-be monolingual nation states (Hornberger and Link 2012).

In contexts in which minoritized languages are used by children entering formal education, "mother tongue" or "vernacular" education has been officially endorsed by UNESCO (UNESCO 1953; 2003) and argued for by the recent field of linguistic human rights (Skutnabb-Kangas and Phillipson 1994). It has been incorporated as a strategy in the efforts of numerous aid and development organizations (such as MTB-MLE network, www.mlenetwork.org); Save the Children (Pinnock 2011); UNICEF (Ingram 2010); USAID (Carolyn Adger, p.c. July 2012) and many smaller NGOs and missionary organizations, including the organization of which Velma Pickett was a member, SIL. These civil society and faith-based organizations may have a significant impact on actual education practices through funding schools and collaborating with national governments.[17] Their programs tend to focus on the scale of ethnic or linguistic groups, assuming that one mother tongue can be attributed to each group, and that these groups will prefer to receive education in their vernacular language (Benson 2004; Dekker and Young 2005; Ball 2010). The aim is to improve the educational outcomes of children in specific groups or schools (although how "improvement" is understood can vary, and is often measured by standardized tests). The goal of literacy in the minoritized language is also a common goal, but often included only as a secondary measurement of program success, with transition to literacy in the majority language receiving greater emphasis in NGO programs (Guzman 2005; Premsrirat and Samoh 2012). Missionary linguists, SIL in particular, have generally invested more time in local language literacy than NGOs, creating first alphabets and then primers and workbooks alongside translated religious texts (as noted above, in the case of Isthmus Zapotec this includes a "pedagogical grammar" and other workbooks as well as translation of the new testament).

In summary, while linguists orient to languages and applied linguists orient to learners, sociolinguists orient to the ideologies and social meanings around languages and learners– which, they sometimes argue, are responsible for creating languages, learners, speakers, etc. as recognizable social phenomena in the first place. Education development researchers and practitioners orient to overall education outcomes (however they choose to conceptualize and measure those), as well as alphabets, literacy materials and text production. The scholarly communities of practice that contribute to the production of knowledge and resources on Indigenous or minoritized communication practices are thus made up of different paradigms, epistemological traditions, and a wide range of actors, with differing imaginaries, goals, and forms of engagement. Each of these disciplines has something to offer to scholar-activism projects, although none of them is

---

[17] For example, the Philippines DepEd Orders 74 of 2009 and 16 of 2012 (establishing mother tongue education as national policy) were directly influenced by the research and reporting of SIL members (Walter and Dekker 2008).

sufficient to solve issues of language inequality. In the following sections, I describe how I have studied and worked within several communities of practice as a scholar-activist (3.1.1) and some of the methodological considerations which I consider to be important in this endeavor (3.1.2).

3.1.1 Working as a scholar-activist across multiple disciplines

While some of the scholars in the academic communities described here are members of minoritized language communities (in any of the many ways which 'membership' can be understood), many are not, and all have multiple identities and motivations which inform their work, as described in relation to Crúz, Henestrosa and Pickett in the opening of this chapter. I am a white, female, settler-European American who has chosen to become an interdisciplinary scholar, educator and activist. Throughout my involvement in Indigenous language education and advocacy I have worked in different ways and come to talk about my work relative to the communities of practice I have participated in. When I first studied Anishinaabemowin or Ojibwe in tribally-run classes and worked on materials development and documentation for the Burt Lake Band of Ottawa and Chippewa Indians in my home region of northern Michigan, I adopted the habit of writing about 'the Language' with a capital 'L. I did this because of the ways my teachers and colleagues talked about their heritage way of speaking, often discussing its uniqueness, spiritual significance, and intimate connection with their identity. As a student of applied linguistics in British Columbia, Canada, I was socialized to learn the auto-denominations of First Nations' languages and to use them wherever possible, respecting Indigenous names as part of separate systems of meaning making, and signaling my respect for the equality and individuality of these systems. I also learned about language acquisition within the native-speaker, quasi-experimental paradigm that has dominated much of applied linguistics, although I chose to focus in my own research on the issue of "community control" within official language education policies (De Korne 2010).

When I learned about multilingualism and minority languages in Europe within a critical and interactionist sociolinguistics framework as a research fellow in Luxembourg, for the first time I was exposed to scholarship which questioned the moral superiority of minority groups and linguistic rights movements. I began to learn conceptual frameworks that captured the fluid and constructed nature of language, social groups, and power hierarchies; issues which I had already observed in practice but not named as such. This constructivist perspective gained new nuances as I participated in education scholarship in the United States as a student of educational linguistics, where I began to talk about communicative repertoires and communities of practice in place of the Language and its People. Experiences working in non-governmental organizations (Save the Children and the Center for Applied Linguistics), academic outreach projects (the Breath of Life Archival Institute for Indigenous Languages), and participating in a study of the reclamation of a sleeping language (Hornberger, De Korne, and Weinberg 2016; Weinberg and De Korne 2016) have further influenced my perspective. As a result of my participation in a variety of scholarly and activist domains, my own orientation is towards minoritized languages and speakers. I often focus on the scale of a language, but also aim to incorporate the social, historical, and contemporary context responsible for giving speakers of the language the status that they have.

Having myself participated in different research and education traditions, I see them all as part of the wider social project of language activism and linguistic equality. Each community of practice projects a slightly different imaginary of what the problems are and how to address them in relation to socio-historical positionings and disciplinary norms, yet there is a common concern for the inequalities that have been and continue to be created along linguistic lines. Over time I have come to reconcile these different paradigms by viewing them as part of the same compelling, albeit elusive social imaginary of eradicating the inequalities produced through language. Taking these diverse viewpoints into account, I view Diidxazá, like other named languages, as a deictic or indexical which acquires its meaning in relation to its social positioning within a community of practice (Silverstein 1976). For some people it is part of their identity and spirituality; for some it is an under-valued educational resource; for some it is the VSO tonal language defined by the ISO 639–3 code 'zai'; for some it is a legal right; for some it is a uniquely appropriate form of self-expression; for some it is a problem and mark of shame. Working as a language activist, it is helpful to acknowledge the deictic nature of language, and the myriad significance it has both within the speech community and within scholarly communities. I return to this point in the concluding discussion in chapter 8.

As Makoni and Pennycook (2007) have noted, sometimes the answers to linguistic problems require a deconstructivist, interpretive approach, while sometimes they may require essentialist categorization and definition – among other approaches. The notion of 'strategic essentialism', or use of essentialist rhetoric for strategic social purposes in favor of marginalized groups (coined, and later critiqued, by decolonial theorist Gayatri Spivak (Spivak 1996)) has been taken up by multiple scholar-activists as an apt term for one of the key strategies employed in language activism (Leonard 2012; Zavala 2014). Digging in and holding fast to a specific point of view can be considered essentialist (and endangered language advocates have been critiqued for this (eg. Cameron 2007)), however this kind of persistence and focus is also a tool which activists often use in efforts to change unequal social structures and norms. As an activist scholar, I aim to take up the challenge of deconstructing *and* reconstituting language, of critically questioning *and* joining in decisive, goal-driven actions. The following section examines some of the ways that researchers can aim to be reflexive, constructivist, and attempt to contribute to positive social change in specific ways.

3.1.2 Methodological choices in support of language equality

The relationship of academia as a whole to marginalized communities has come under greater focus in recent decades, with calls to develop academic culture away from its roots in European colonialism, racism, and sexism. The legitimation of Eurocentric, white, male, cis-heterosexual knowledge above other forms of knowledge has led to 'cognitive injustice'; in order to counter this imbalance diverse forms of meaning-making need to be recognized, allowing for what theorist Boaventura de Sousa Santos has called an ecology of knowledge (Santos 2007, 2014). Calls to 'decolonize' academic research include consideration of which research questions are asked, who is participating in research, and how research is conducted, with particular attention to whose knowledge is valued, who has power in the process, and who ultimately benefits (Smith 1999). Work done within linguistics, anthropology, and education, among other academic disciplines, has been part of creating injustices and shaping prejudices towards certain languages and people (Errington 2001; Skutnabb-Kangas 2009; Battiste 2013), meaning that efforts to decolonize these disciplines require rethinking key concepts and paradigms, as well as changing who is participating and making decisions (Brayboy et al. 2012; Leonard 2017). Research and education interventions involving Indigenous groups have historically been fraught with biases, leading to movements for Indigenous-run research (e.g. Smith 2005; Wilson 2008). While still a minority in academia, Indigenous scholars have made significant contributions to broadening academic paradigms and reorienting methodologies and priorities in multiple disciplines. Both Indigenous and non-Indigenous scholars working towards an imaginary of linguistic equality have engaged in reflection and debate on how to shift the paradigms of their respective disciplines in order to conduct research that helps to reverse the colonialist heritage and structures of academia.

In their classic discussion of research on language, Cameron, Frazer, Harvey, Rampton, and Richardson (1992, 1993) described different approaches as research *on*, *for*, or *with* a population. They include anthropology and sociology, as well as linguists, in the argument that language researchers with a social justice agenda should aim for research *with* a community through "the use of interactive methods, the acknowledgement of subjects' own agendas and the sharing of expert knowledge" (Cameron et al. 1993: 87). In relation to her work with First Nations language revitalization in Canada, Ewa Czaykowska-Higgins (2009) extended this typology to include research *by* the speech community as a possible positive outcome of linguistic scholarship. As both a member of a linguistically minoritized community and a linguistic anthropologist, Ana Celia Zentella advocated for an "anthro*political* linguistics that never loses sight of [minoritized children's] reality and struggles to change it" (Zentella 1997: 4, italics original). Her work with bilingual Puerto Rican families within this paradigm was instrumental in both political advocacy and in weakening the dominance of deficit models of bilingualism and code-switching in academia. These are just some of the efforts to build a more direct and meaningful interface between scholarship and positive social change put forward by scholars in a range of disciplines. How to use research in favor of greater equality for marginalized groups, including issues of representation, participation, and intervention, continues to be an area of concern and inquiry (Warriner and Bigelow 2019).

Whether or not the scholar is a member of the minoritized community, reflective research and collaborative models are encouraged as an important step in changing the legacy of exploitation of Indigenous (and other marginalized) communities through research (Stebbins 2012). How to collaborate in meaningful ways has been a topic of discussion, including the establishment of research goals, outcomes, and roles at the outset of research (Leonard and Haynes 2010), and fostering long-term, emergent collaborations (Pérez Báez 2018). From the field of Indigenous education, Anthony-Stevens, Stevens and Nicholas (2017) highlight the importance of efforts by community insiders, and support or alliances by community outsiders in "interrupting power structures that impede and delegitimize Indigenous efforts to enact education sovereignity" (Anthony-Stevens, Stevens, and Nicholas 2017: 21). Balancing disciplinary expectations of objectivity and generalizability with the desires of community members (and potentially one's own desires as a language activist) is a common conundrum, but one which has led to fruitful collaboration in some cases. Pérez Báez (2016) discusses the dilemma of being an outsider researcher-activist working in a context where not all speakers are interested in promoting greater use of a minoritized language. She encourages the use of research activities and results to spark discussion around issues of language use, education, and community rights, rather than adopting a passive stance or imposing the views and assumptions of the researcher. Yamada (2007) discusses a documentation project in which she, as a non-community member, attempted to put community learning goals as a priority alongside linguistic description. Hermes and Engman (2017) illustrate the ways in which a documentation project involving a mixed team of Indigenous and non-Indigenous scholars improved through the involvement of Indigenous language learners in data collection and analysis.

Even where the researcher is a member of the speech community, diverse perspectives and priorities within the community need to be negotiated in any research project. Chickasaw linguistic anthropologist Jenny Davis describes her research as "Native ethnography" due to the fact that she is a member of the community she studies, which has traditionally been a subject of research rather than a producer of research. At the same time, she highlights that "because individuals and the communities of which they are members are multifaceted, varied, and even contradictory in characteristics, the ways in which a researcher may be positioned as an insider are equally complex" (48). In all cases it is likely that research relationships and goals may shift throughout a project, as participants gain new understandings and perhaps new priorities and identities. For example, Rouvier (2017) describes a change in the priorities of a language revitalization project from focusing on Elder speakers working one-on-one with younger learners, to include the facilitation of group events and discussion circles where Elders had the chance to speak among each other and to practice language instead of just teaching it. Ongoing reflexivity as to the goals, roles, and power dynamics within a project, such as this, may help to avoid exploitative, extractive research practices. Whatever collaborative approach is taken, it is crucial that participation be voluntary and genuine, avoiding superficial and tokenized participatory approaches that have been observed in international development research (Cooke and Kothari 2001).

There are many approaches to participatory action research and practitioner inquiry, each of which has advantages depending on the circumstances of research and the identity and affordances of the researcher (Lewin 1946; Burns 2005; McIntyre 2008; Ravitch and Riggan 2012). Action research is better established in some scholarly disciplines than others, and in particular has gained respect in education research where all teachers are often encouraged to become practitioner researchers in their own classroom (Cochran-Smith and Lytle 2009). In seeking an approach that would allow me to combine some form of research and some form of activism, I have chosen to use the flexible methodological umbrella of *ethnographic monitoring*, a combination of ethnography and emergent action research developed for use in minority language education initiatives. Sociolinguist Dell Hymes formulated ethnographic monitoring as a methodological paradigm through which to research educational realities and contribute to their improvement, taking into account that *improvement* or *success* may have different meanings in different settings (Hymes 1980). Ethnographers are frequently in a position to observe effects of hierarchical language norms, but they are less often believed to be in a position to challenge either the norms or their negative effects. Ethnographic monitoring counters this, combining the thick description and cultural relativity achieved by ethnography (Hymes 1968; Blommaert and Jie 2010) with a critical perspective and commitment to supporting educational practice for social change. As Hymes (1980) argues, "Ethnography must be descriptive and objective, yes, but not only that. It must be conscious of values and goals; it must relate description to analysis and objectivity to critical evaluation" (104). Crucially, this critical evaluation is undertaken on the base of initial description and careful interpretation of emic perspectives and values. While Hymes proposed ethnographic monitoring as a way to conduct activist research in and with bilingual schools, it has also been usefully applied in other kinds of social projects (Van der Aa and Blommaert 2011; Hornberger 2013b).

Ethnographic monitoring can be understood as "structured around three fundamental tasks: observation and description, analysis and interpretation, and evaluation oriented towards social change. These tasks build upon each other, may occur in overlapping cycles and/or in collaboration with stakeholders, and may be achieved through a variety of methods" (De Korne and Hornberger 2017: 247). The ethnographic monitoring framework does not establish specific methods, but rather encourages collaborative and critical ways of conducting research, and the use of ethnographic research towards social ends in whatever way may be appropriate in the context. In this way, ethnographic monitoring builds connections between traditional ethnography and the range of established methodologies and methods for engaged, action, or practitioner research, where researchers have some degree of participation and engagement in the context that they are studying.

In my work in the Isthmus I have followed this trajectory from description through analysis and interpretation, to evaluation aimed at social improvements, with constant cycling back through on-going description and (re)interpretations. I aim to provide a thick description of what people are doing with and through Diidxazá activism, based on participant observation, semi-structured and unstructured interviews and focus groups with a wide range of stakeholders, semiotic landscape documentation, and document collection in Diidxazá promotion and education contexts. Thematic analysis of this data informs my interpretation of local meanings, imaginaries, and ideologies in relation to language, inequalities, and social well-being. I have sought out ways to support linguistic equality based on my evaluation of the factors influencing potential for positive social change in this context, and have collaborated in several activism projects in particular (see also 1.6). At times this has resulted in very concrete actions and proposals on my part, while at other times my participation has consisted of providing information, reproducing a discourse, or supporting the actions of other activists, as discussed further below. As a researcher working in speech communities of which I am not an organic member, I have found this methodology to be appropriate to my social position, personal style, and goals as a non-prescriptive scholar-activist.

Aside from seeking out ways that the researcher can contribute positively to the setting they work in, the ethnographic monitoring paradigm also considers the biases that researchers bring with them. Hymes (1980) states that an ethnographer "must come to understand his/her own attitudes [. . .] and the reasons for them. Only explicit concern with values, in short, will allow ethnography to overcome hidden sources of bias" (104). As Hornberger (2013a) discusses, reflective engagement is a crucial component of critical ethnographic work, which

> may take a number of forms – it may be about working with multiple members of a research team; it may also be about relationships between researcher and researched; and may range from consultative to fully participatory relationships. It may be about collecting and analyzing data; it may also be about writing up and reporting findings. It is without doubt about reflecting critically on all of these. (2013: 105)

By recognizing oneself as a social actor with the potential to impact a context of research, a researcher automatically becomes a practitioner, someone with a role and a stake in the context. All researchers are also practitioners in knowledge creation within their disciplinary communities of practice and can benefit from on-going critical reflection on the foundations, processes, and uses of their research.

In summary, recognizing the socio-political role of research and researchers, and seeking to shift academic power balances through collaboration, are important considerations for socially-beneficial research. Despite the legacy of marginalization and exploitation of Indigenous people through academic research, there have also been positive contributions and collaborations; the increasing role of Indigenous researchers defining the agenda and terms of research will hopefully continue to strengthen the capacity of academia to engage in and respond to linguistic and other social inequalities in the future. In the following section I analyze the strategies of scholar-activists I observed in the Isthmus, as well as reflecting on my own strategies.

3.2 Scholar-activist strategies in the Isthmus

Linguists, anthropologists and education researchers were among the language activists who I observed and interviewed, and whose practices I considered in developing the framework of activism strategies presented in chapter 1. While researchers can and do engage in a range of strategies, I observed the *creation* or production of *resources* (including archives, academic texts and didactic materials) to be an especially common strategy among scholars. It was also the strategy I adopted instinctively when I began my work. In addition, scholars also have a significant role in representing the focus of their work through a specific ideological lens. In the case of linguists, there is a tendency to *represent* certain *communication practices* (in particular those of idealized native-speaker monolingual elders) as a treasure of universal value, as discussed in the opening of this chapter (Hill 2002). In contexts like Oaxaca, these representations may be in stark contrast to the low status which Indigenous language speakers often hold in society, and the widespread perception that Indigenous communication practices are *dialectos*, not languages. At the same time, they may be helpful in addressing the social stigma that Indigenous language speakers experience. Researchers may also be in the position to make important *connections* – such as between existing *resources, people*, and *spaces*, and among different people – a strategy which I have come to value more and more highly. In this section, I illustrate some of the common scholarly strategies I observed among colleagues, and through reflection on my own practices.

3.2.1 Creating resources

The production of archival or scientific resources related to a language is viewed by many documentary linguists as their primary goal and potential. Scholarly resources, such as grammars, dictionaries, analyzed recordings, and articles can contribute to language activism in a variety of ways, including bringing increased attention and respect to a communication system which has been viewed as less valuable and interesting. They can potentially assist activists working in education initiatives if they are accessible to non-linguists and produced in a language which local activists know. For example, Isthmus Zapotec linguist-historian-writer Víctor Cata has documented ceremonial marriage discourses which are no longer in use in the present day, based on fieldwork with elderly men who were trained to deliver these addresses in their youth (Cata 2012). He has also collected oral history narratives from elder speakers in the Tehuantepec dialect of Diidxazá, motivated by the fact that they are among the only speakers of this dialect, which has not been transmitted in recent generations (Cata 2003). His scholarship has been published with support from government research funds and made available to readers in the Isthmus. Mexican linguist Gabriela Pérez Báez has produced an ethnobotanical dictionary which is trilingual in Spanish, Diidxazá, and English in order to meet the needs of different audiences locally, nationally, and internationally.[18] She strategically used the popular alphabet for Diidxazá in order to maximize accessibility in the Isthmus, rather than the more phonologically precise system she has used in her documentation work and which would likely be preferred among linguist readers. In these ways, Víctor and Gabriela have produced scholarly resources that may be of interest to Diidxazá teachers or learners in addition to other researchers.

Several of the scholar-activists working in the Isthmus have additionally created resources directed at learning Diidxazá. Noting that community members may not find dictionaries or grammars written primarily with academic audiences in mind to be the kind of resources which meet their immediate needs, linguists have engaged more and more in the creation of learning materials, with various degrees of success (Cope and Penfield 2011). Gabriela has facilitated the creation of a range of didactic resources, from games for all ages, to a literacy workbook (Pérez Báez 2015), and bilingual informational cards on common plants and their uses in the Isthmus. All of these resources draw on data from her extensive documentary research of the Juchitán variety of Isthmus Zapotec and have been created in collaboration with various members of the community as well as botanists and visual artists from elsewhere in Mexico. Gabriela, as an activist linguist, incorporated the production of learning materials throughout the process of her work, engaged in consultations with a variety of community actors about the kinds of materials that might be of interest, and has sought feedback on the materials once they were in circulation (Pérez Báez 2018). A similar strategy has been employed by a team of researchers affiliated with the Faculty of Philosophy at the University of Querétaro, in central Mexico, who produced posters of the Isthmus Zapotec popular alphabet and a translation of the popular *lotería* [bingo] game and distributed them to bilingual schools. A member of the team from San Blas Atempa in the Isthmus, David Eduardo Vicente Jiménez, has gone on to produce Diidxazá translations of popular comic books for public dissemination, aiming at younger speakers and learners.[19]

---

18 https://dictionaria.clld.org/contributions/diidxaza
19 http://conacytprensa.mx/index.php/ciencia/humanidades/25230-superheroes-mexicanos-zapoteco-ninos?fbclid=IwAR02Cq9h1wVMjUSxRhuK-Q2fldmBiM8AGiTzck6vmJH5Ctap8IhLGr3dz1A

Ways of creating resources vary greatly depending on the durability and content of what is created. The production of written or digital materials generally takes a reasonable amount of time but may become highly visible through promotion across social networks. For example, the plant-themed didactic games created under the umbrella of the Smithsonian ethnobotany project took around a year to create. They were subsequently distributed in hard copy to cultural centers, libraries and schools across the Isthmus, reaching a regional level of visibility. Additionally Gabriela distributed copies to libraries in Oaxaca City and took copies to display within the Smithsonian in Washington, DC, and a news piece about the games appeared in a regional newspaper (Cha'ca 2013). Digital learning materials, such as the literacy workbook which Gabriela made available in pdf form on-line,[20] can achieve even greater visibility and mobility. In addition to making materials which are accessible, resource production requires editorial choices about inclusion and exclusion of information and images. For example, when I asked for feedback on the first botanical game produced by the ethnobotany project from some of the teachers and librarians who had received copies of it, although there was much positive feedback, multiple users also commented critically on the fact that the game was almost monolingual in Diidxazá. They expressed a desire to have Spanish included in order to make it more accessible to learners of different levels. One librarian noted that the plants used in the game were from the countryside, while the children who she works with live in the town and are familiar neither with the image of the plant, nor with the Zapotec name of the plant. The editorial choices made by the team in order to privilege Diidxazá and showcase regional plants did not coincide with the view of these actors who preferred fully bilingual materials and content that would be more familiar for younger learners.

While scholars may often be in a position to access financial support and may have expertise that can be channeled into the creation of resources, they must also consider what kind of resources will be useful and aim to fulfill the expectations of as wide a user audience as possible – or choose to focus on a limited user group. Additionally, the timeframe it takes to create something is important to consider, with some projects allowing for a quick production cycle and others requiring a longer process. Finally, the creation of tangible resources often occurs by a restricted group, or even one individual, and is characterized by an unavoidable editorial or authorial control over what will be included and what will be excluded. Scholar-activists often try to produce a perfect, authoritative resource which will endure indefinitely, however in some cases it

---

20 https://neho.si.edu/about-la-ventosa-collection

may be more effective to create resources as drafts and expect multiple revisions and new versions over time (Schreyer 2017). The production of resources – from technical to entertaining – is a concrete way which scholars may use their expertise in collecting and presenting information. Through these resources, and their practices and interactions, scholars are also constantly engaged in representing Isthmus Zapotec, as examined next.

3.2.2 Representing communication practices

The resources created by scholar-activists, and the choices that are made regarding what to include and how to present the information (from orthography options, to aesthetic styles, to material forms) function as social representations that often carry the weight of authoritative knowledge. Scholar-activists must choose what kind of aesthetic symbols to draw on in their representations; some may choose to highlight historical and traditional motifs, others may want to link the language with images viewed as contemporary or global. Both of these socio-historical orientations can be strategic. The use of traditional motifs or historical content can serve to legitimate and show respect for local aesthetics, and to make the materials recognizable to local users. On the other hand, the use of non-historical content and non-local references can also serve to represent materials as cutting edge and attractive to younger users. For example, the ethnobotanical materials produced by Gabriela's ethnobotany team help to represent Diidxazá as a source of technical, botanical knowledge and a medium for scientific communication. The superhero comic books produced by David Eduardo Vicente Jiménez and colleagues help to represent Diidxazá as a modern, fun, and fashionable way of communicating, linked to excitement and action. Both of these representations are strategic ways of resisting the stereotype of Indigenous language speakers as unsophisticated, isolated, relics of the past. They present an imaginary of Indigenous languages as refined sources of knowledge, and a vital part of global, digital culture.

Representations also occur through interactions. In my orientation as an applied or educational linguist, I represented Isthmus Zapotec as part of a multilingual language ecology and as an enjoyable part of daily life in the Isthmus in presentations which I gave on several occasions. From late 2013 I worked with colleagues from the local branch of the Faculty of Languages of the state university (UABJO) (see further discussion in chapter 5) to plan and facilitate a two-day event on Isthmus Zapotec which was held in April 2014. The event was aimed at teachers and activists, as well as members of the public who might want to participate in language workshops. This event received quite a bit of local media attention. One newspaper article where the reporter had asked me for input was titled *"Promueven multilinguismo"* [They promote multilingualism].[21] Other news articles in which I had much less influence where published, including *"Promueve UABJO rescate del zapoteco"* [UABJO promotes saving Zapotec],[22] a representation that I was less pleased with, but which is common in relation to Indigenous languages of Mexico, as elsewhere in the world. In a radio interview about the event shortly before it happened, UABJO teacher Ximena Leon Fernández and I described the event as a meeting of researchers and teachers, with participatory workshops and cultural presentations. I concluded a description of the offerings of the event saying *"Y finalmente, habrá muestras culturales porque un idioma no es solamente una gramática o un objeto de estudio; es algo que . . . que disfrutamos. Que vivimos todos los días"* [And finally, there will be cultural presentations because a language is not only a grammar or an object of study; it's something that . . . that we enjoy. That we live every day] (Audio 140402). Ximena summed up the many activities saying *"Básicamente lo que estamos eh . . . buscando es fomentar el multilingüismo que sabemos que se da aquí en la región"* [Basically what we're um . . . looking to do is to foster the multilingualism that we know is here in the region] (Audio 140402). We represented the event as an inclusive space, where research and resources would be present, as well as interactive learning opportunities. We represented Diidxazá as part of the multilingual reality of the region, and promoted multilingualism as a desirable thing, in contrast to the common perception that use of Zapotec would impede use of Spanish (see chapter 2).

The radio host noted that our representation contrasted with popular representations in several ways:

> Locutor   Lamentablemente . . . a veces . . . hemos dejado de . . . admirar, de amar, de profundizar nuestro conocimiento sobre nuestra propia lengua. Aunque dicen por ahí de que el zapoteco va a morir el día en que muera el sol, a veces, digo: no, creo que primero va a morir nuestra lengua porque . . . en muchas comunidades zapotecas se ha perdido ya el número de hablantes.
>
> Ximena   Por eso es importante no dejar de hacer esfuerzos en ese sentido, ¿no?

---

21 http://www.noticiasnet.mx/portal/istmo/general/educativas/202824-promueven-multilinguismo
22 http://www.imparcialenlinea.com/portal/?mod=nota&id=37003&cat=istmo

80 — Chapter 3 Creating knowledge and resources: Strategies in scholarship

Locutor Claro.

Ximena   Porque si uno piensa: 'ay, no va a morir nunca', pues todos nos sentamos en nuestros laureles y no . . . no hacemos nada por . . . por propiciar que se siga hablando, ¿no?

Locutor   Darle importancia a este encuentro: Compartiendo experiencias, guendaruchaaga, guendanabani. Enseña, aprende, vive el zapoteco. Bisiidi, biziidi ne bibaani . . . diidxazá. ¿No?

Host   Unfortunately . . . sometimes . . . we have stopped . . . admiring, loving, deepening our knowledge of our own language. Although they say around here that Zapotec will die the day that the sun dies, sometimes, I say: no, I believe that our language will die first because . . . in many Zapotec communities the number of speakers has already been lost.

Ximena   That's why it's important not to stop making efforts in that way, right?

Host   Clearly.

Ximena   Because if one thinks: 'Ah, it will never die', well we all rest on our laurels and don't . . . don't do anything to . . . to encourage that it continues to be spoken, right?

Host   Give importance to this event: Sharing experiences, *guendaruchaaga, guendanabani*. Teach, learn, live Zapotec. *Bisiidi, biziidi ne bibaani . . . diidxazá*. Right?

(Audio recording 2 April 2014)

The positive representations of Indigenous languages (or a multilingual repertoire containing Indigenous languages) articulated in public ways by scholars differ from the lack of social prestige or admiration noted by the radio host. The statement that 'Zapotec will die the day that the sun dies' is a reference to a popular poem written in Diidxazá by *Istmeño* poet Gabriel López Chiñas and first published in 1971, which concludes with a positive representation linking the vitality of Diidxazá to the vitality of the sun (see also 6.2). Nonetheless, discourses about the displacement of Zapotec are common, such as the host's assertion that 'the number of speakers has already been lost' and his disagreement with those who say that it will continue. The title of this event and our comments in promoting it contributed to a counter discourse, similar to that of Chiñas' poem. By drawing attention to the fact that for many people in the Isthmus, Zapotec is 'something we live everyday' and that the Isthmus is a multilingual region, we were representing Isthmus Zapotec as a vital part of life in the Isthmus, rather than something that is fading away. While the host aligned with our statements by encouraging his listeners to 'give importance to this event', the effects that such representations may have in the wider social space are all but impossible to trace with confidence. A representation that is produced only once or infrequently is certainly less likely to have an influence on the perspectives and practices of a community than a representation that is repeated over time.

Scholar-activists have an especially powerful position when it comes to representations, in that they usually enjoy expert status and a heightened degree of respect, meaning that their ways of representing may carry greater weight and even be broadcast on the radio. The kinds of language produced in texts or didactic games is likely to be viewed as 'correct', at least by some of the users, simply by dint of being produced in connection with scholarship. Scholars with national and international ties may also enjoy higher degrees of respect. As I was told many times by local language activists, *'nadie es profeta en su tierra'* [no one is a prophet at home/ in their region], meaning that local experts would often receive less attention and respect simply by being from the local area. Researchers from elsewhere in Mexico or from abroad sometimes seemed to receive more respect simply because we were from far away – this was the case not just for me as a foreign researcher, but also for Mexican researchers from outside the Isthmus. An outsider positionality is not generally an advantage in scholar-activism, due to the need to build understanding and trust within a social context, however in this small respect it may have some advantages. At the same time, it necessitates even greater reflexivity over how one is using the (arguably unearned) authority and status that can come with being an outsider or a researcher. Vanessa Anthony-Stevens, a European-American scholar-educator, has reflected on the ways that those who are not members of a minoritized group may work as an ally with minoritized groups (Anthony-Stevens 2017). She outlines that it is necessary to step up and use white (or other forms of) privilege at some points, and to step aside, follow, and give space at other points. It has been a common challenge for me to determine when to step up and when to follow, when to offer my perspective and when to listen silently. These are conerns that all language activists working in collaboration must face to some degree, but they are especially acute for those of us who carry various forms of privilege, and/ or identify primarily as outsiders in the contexts we are engaged in.

3.2.3 Connecting people, spaces and resources

The production of the 'Teach, learn, live Zapotec' event (and others) was a strategic choice which responded to the lack of contact and exchange which my colleagues and I observed among different language advocates in the region. Through the creation of this temporary social space we hoped to support new or improved connections among different actors that might strengthen the needed long-term spaces and structures of learning (discussed further in chapters 4 and 5). As I worked to gain an overview of people and groups who were engaged in language activism, I began to try to connect activists to people with similar interests, and to materials which they were not aware of, locally, nationally, and internationally. On one hand this was simple reciprocity, as people I interviewed often connected me to others I had not met yet, or informed me about resources I was not aware of, and I followed suit and did the same whenever possible. I also attempted to give copies of materials directly to people involved in teaching Diidxazá whenever possible, rather than simply informing them of their existence.

Over time, my position as an informed outsider allowed me to make connections in support of language advocacy networks in the Isthmus and beyond, and this became a conscious strategy. When a group of Diidxazá speakers who were participants in Gabriela Pérez Báez's ethnobotany project were interested in offering workshops for children in their community but were unsure how to go about this pedagogically, I invited a young woman with some experience teaching Diidxazá to visit and talk with them. She shared her trajectory of beginning to teach Diidxazá, a language she had always spoken at home but had never used in a formal domain until she was invited to teach it to adult learners. She described how she had to invent her own materials and approaches in order to do so. The conversation which ensued was animated on all sides. The group seemed much more engaged than when I had discussed learning goals and teaching techniques with them on previous occasions. The group commented afterwards on how bright and talented the young woman was, and that they were encouraged by her confidence and experience. Connecting these would-be teachers to a Diidxazá teacher role model had clear positive effects.

The outcomes of strategic connecting, such as finding a role model or gaining new confidence, are often less tangible than producing a game or a book. However, this strategy may help to build social networks with the potential to amplify advocacy initiatives, and may provide crucial solidarity to language activists. Anthony-Stevens (2017) has referred to this as 'brokering', whereby outside scholar allies "negotiate value exchanges" and "consciously leverage available resources" in support of the interests of a marginalized group (96). This strategy is not unique to scholar-activists, but is one which we may often find ourselves in a good position for, due to access to educational networks and resources.

3.3 Summary: Characteristics of scholar activism

Is scholarship an impactful form of activism? As a community of practice with the social power to produce legitimate knowledge and people who are perceived as experts, it has an undeniable influence and potential in social change projects. Scholars can propose representations, such as categories and definitions, which may come to divide or unify, legitimize or erase. Scholarship that prioritizes questions about social inequalities and well-being can channel resources and attention in directions which have been neglected. Depending on the specific context and positionality of the researcher, various forms of activism are possible, including supporting and amplifying initiatives and networks that are underway (connecting), (re)producing positive perspectives on language and culture (representing), and participating in or proposing active interventions and tangible products where appropriate (creating). The following Table 1 illustrates some of the key language activism strategies described in this chapter.

Table 1: Key language activism strategies among scholars in the Isthmus.

Actions →	Goals →	Examples
– Creating	– Resources – Events	– Production of dictionaries, learning materials, didactic games – Facilitating one-off events such as workshops or lectures
– Representing	– People/ Identities – Communication practices	– Indigenous language speakers represented as valuable – Isthmus Zapotec represented as valuable – Multilingualism represented as normal/ positive
– Connecting	– People/ Identities – Resources	– Supporting and expanding activists' networks – Providing reources to activists – Collecting and archiving resources

The mobility and non-local ties of researchers can be an advantage in assembling and distributing resources, and their technical skills are assets in the production of certain kinds of resources. Researchers who are outsiders may experience their novelty to be an advantage in drawing attention and respect to what they do and the representations that they produce – or it may make them less trustworthy and respected, depending on the context. Researchers who are community insiders may be able to benefit from extensive contextual knowledge and networks, but may also be faced with negotiating diverse perspectives and priorities among fellow community-members. In either case, scholarship often remains fairly removed from homes, parks, markets, and the spaces of interaction and subsistence which form the heartbeat of life day to day. Research projects usually have a start and an end date; while some research products become a lasting part of the linguistic ecology and the collection of resources which activists draw from over time, others inevitably do not. Scholars often aspire to make a lasting impact, however if they are based in a city or a country far away it is less likely that they can contribute to the establishment of long-term structures of language promotion. In other words, there is much that can be done, but there are also many limitations.

The social impact of research is infamously muffled or indirect in many instances, in particular where the primary products of scholarship are destined for academic consumption. The kind of knowledge and resources that are produced may not be immediately usable, or may be usable in limited ways. Additionally, scholarship is deeply intertwined with colonial categories and logics, and in some cases neo-colonial enterprises such as missionary organizations or development projects, running the risks of doing more harm than good. There is still variation and potential for conflict in the different understandings of language (from object to action) and different imaginaries of social change via research (from supposed 'objective neutrality' and correction of errors, to different forms of engagement and alliances) across scholarly communities (see 1.2–1.3). The risk that research initiatives may impose unwanted definitions, categories, and forms of change remains. However, Indigenous scholars and allies have made important impacts in pointing out the need to critically examine the concepts and research paradigms that have served to reproduce Euro-centric understandings and structures of privilege, and the need to recognize other ways of knowing. As Anthony-Stevens (2017) puts it, all scholar-activists – but especially outsider scholar-activists – need to show up with "ongoing attention to complex relationships, uncomfortable acknowledgements of power differentials, and a commitment to antiracist, anticolonial education" (100–101).

Through calls for collaborative and decolonized research, including participatory research with communities and research lead by Indigenous scholars, some disciplines attempt to respond to the weakness of the juncture between scholarship and social change. Engaged research has a long history in education and anthropology scholarship, but linguists have been slower to join the party. In the years that I have been part of scholarly communities of practice around minoritized languages, I feel that it has become more and more common to expect reflexivity on the part of the researcher, whether they are collecting data for a dictionary, examining bilingual practices in a classroom, or studying how identity and gender are indexed in an Indigenous language. It is also more common to see community insiders taking on roles as scholars and knowledge-producers. Additionally, scholars have been taken to task over the discourses and representations that they produce, leading to changes in the discourses about so-called 'dying' or 'extinct' languages, and more acceptance for community-based definitions of language and community priorities in language-related projects (McCarty 2017). With continued collaboration among scholars and other language activists, I am hopeful that scholars can learn from other activists and make further progress in harnessing academic work to meet social needs. The opportunity to observe and collaborate with language activists in the Isthmus has taught me about the benefits as well as limitations of what I have to offer as a scholar-activist – and I still have plenty more to learn in that regard. I hope that the increasing legitimation of various action research paradigms, such as ethnographic monitoring, will lead more scholars of language to contribute to socially-engaged research. Research which supports linguistic equality will require greater attention to who is viewed as a creator of authoritative knowledge, what kinds of representations and discourses are being (re)produced, and a humble, learning approach to making and re-making resources that are aligned with the changing interests and needs of dynamic communities of speakers and learners.

Chapter 4
Connecting community and school spaces: Strategies in primary and secondary education

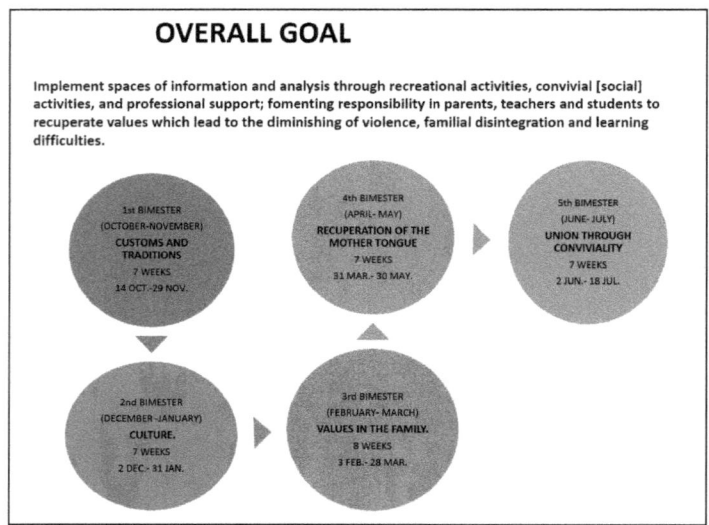

Figure 11: PowerPoint slide from primary school initiative; Original by Delia Ruíz Álvarez; English translation mine.

The above flow chart (Figure 11) represents a pedagogical project planned and implemented by a team of primary school teachers in an officially monolingual primary school in Juchitán between 2013 and 2014. The first image is the original slide from a PowerPoint by one of the teachers and project leaders, Delia Ruíz Álvarez, an experienced teacher from the Isthmus who was pursuing her Master's degree at the time of the project. The second image is a reproduction of the slide with an English translation. The aim of their project as noted in the chart was "*Recuperación de valores en la sociedad, asumiendo responsabilidades tanto padres, maestros y educandos para combatir la violencia, desintegración familiar y las dificultades en aprendizaje*" [Recuperation of values in society, taking responsibility among parents, teachers and learners in order to combat violence, family disintegration and learning difficulties]. In order to achieve this, the 'overall goal' included creating spaces and activities where students, teachers and parents would share information, analyze the challenges facing the community, and ultimately take responsibility for addressing some of these challenges. The flow chart shows the 5 thematic units of the project, each developed in 7–8 week periods and carried out sequentially over the course of a school-year. Each thematic unit had specific goals and activities designed to contribute to the overall goal. The thematic units the teachers chose were 'Customs and traditions', 'Culture', 'Values in the family', 'Recuperation of the mother tongue', and 'Union through conviviality', all topics that went beyond what the normal curriculum would have covered. The teachers in this school framed traditional language and culture as part of the solution to academic and social problems, and they chose to reach out to children's families in order to connect community practices and community knowledge with the school space in tangible ways. Their projects included having the students record their own radio broadcasts, create newspaper posters about local history, paint a mural of local customs on the school wall, participate in Diidxazá literacy classes, and participate in dancing and singing *Istmeño* music. In the teachers' imaginary of social change, all of these activities are relevant to the academic success of their students. For example, in describing the radio activity in a report about the project they stated that they aimed to: "*Impulsar una radio escolar donde los alumnos comenten diversos temas de interés sobre costumbres y tradiciones de la comunidad, participando y dando opiniones para formar alumnos críticos y rescatar valores*" [Foment a school radio where the students comment on various themes that are of interest in relation to community traditions and customs, participating and giving opinions in order to shape critical students and recuperate values]. These teachers viewed the exploration of themes related to local customs and traditions as a way to support quality education and encourage critical thinking.

The perspectives and priorities of this teaching team contrast with the approach to Indigenous languages (and cultures) that has historically been common in public schools in Mexico, and indeed in much of the world. Indigenous languages, traditions and values have not been viewed as resources for academic success in nation-state education systems, rather as problems to be overcome (Battiste 2013; Maldonado Alvarado 2002). As spaces of socialization with high social status, schools have had significant impacts on language ideologies and practices, leading to increased dominance of Spanish in the Isthmus, as discussed in chapter 2. The most common motivation mentioned in interviews and conversations for not speaking Diidxazá to children was the exclusion and punishment that previous generations experienced in schools and in society as speakers of Diidxazá. This was noted as more common in the past, but also something that carries on in some places in the present, and certainly in the recent past. A young woman in her early twenties was one of many people who described the legacy of school-based discrimination in an interview:

> Ahí [en la escuela primaria] tenía varios compañeros que sí hablaban el zapoteco y para eso deben estar callados toda la clase porque no se les permitía hablar el zapoteco. Entonces se quedaban sin recreo si hablaban, una palabra y se quedaban; entonces ahí fue donde ya se fue perdiendo poco a poco y dice mi mamá que desde que ella estaba, cuando ella empezó ir a la primaria le hicieron lo mismo que ya prohibían desde ese entonces que aprendieran, que hablaran el zapoteco dentro del salón, dentro de la escuela más bien. Desde ahí ya como que ya se fue perdiendo.
>
> There [in primary school] I had several classmates that spoke Zapotec and because of that they have to be silent for the whole class because they weren't permitted to speak in Zapotec. So they stayed in without recess if they spoke, one word and they stayed; so that was where it went being lost bit by bit and my mom says that since she was there, when she began to go to primary school they did the same to her, that they already forbid back then that people would learn, would speak Zapotec inside the classroom, inside the school rather. From there already, like that's how it's been getting lost.
> (Interview November 2013)

While a project like that of Delia Ruíz Álvarez and her fellow teachers was in many ways an exception to normal practices, going against the grain of public schooling, it was also supported by rhetorical and political currents within the state and national education systems which characterized the language ecology of Oaxacan schooling at that time. A state-wide initiative developed by the largest teachers union in Oaxaca (Section 22), the *Plan para la transformación de la educación en Oaxaca* [Plan for the transformation of education in Oaxaca, hereafter PTEO] seemed to be having not just rhetorical but also tangible effects. At the time of my study the teachers union was promoting the PTEO, a framework for school-initiated projects to bring local knowledge and traditions into the school and to 'transform' education at the local level. Although not all of the schools I visited were attempting to implement the PTEO, many of the schools were taking up this challenge in different ways. The project of Delia and her fellow teachers was recognized and supported by the PTEO policy. With the initiative of the local teaching team at the core, the project benefited from the opportunities opened through the active state-level support in the form of PTEO and the passive support for (or diminished resistance to) Indigenous languages in schools following their official recognition at the national level.

The social project of formal schooling creates countless communities of practice in individual schools, each an important site of negotiation and reproduction of language ideologies day to day. Formal education plays an undeniably central role in socialization, including the formation of language ideologies, norms and identity (Bourdieu and Passeron 1970; Levinson, Foley, and Holland 1996; Wortham 2005). Education has been a key domain in which linguistic hierarchies are created and reproduced, and correspondingly it is also a key domain for initiatives which seek to establish greater linguistic equality (Heller and Martin-Jones 2001). Additionally, it is a meeting ground of top-down policies and bottom-up politics. In this chapter I discuss the spaces of activism and potential change within formal education, as well as the legacy of exclusionary schooling which these efforts must work against. Like the domain of scholarship, there is a history of marginalization of Indigenous languages in formal education, however there are also numerous actors engaging in different forms of activism to change the way minoritized languages are represented in schools, and to connect community knowledge with schooling.

This chapter discusses education as a social project with special potential to create and/ or dismantle language-related inequalities. I provide an overview of the issue of language (in)equality in education (4.1) and discuss ways that language diversity is supported in education today (4.1.1). The context of schooling in the Isthmus is sketched out (4.2) followed by an analysis of the different approaches to language diversity manifested by teaching teams in several primary schools (4.2.1). I highlight several language activism strategies which I observed in primary and secondary schools (4.3); *connecting* the *spaces* of school and community, as well as *connecting* the *people* in these often separate spaces (4.3.1), and *representing* Isthmus Zapotec *communication practices* as part of formal schooling (4.3.2). I conclude with reflections on the characteristics of language activism in schooling (4.4).

4.1 Language (in)equality and education

Language use in formal education settings has patterns of form and function that are considerably narrower than those which exist across human language behavior in general. The varieties of language (standardized, national languages, often through written modes), the roles that interlocutors take up (expert teacher, novice student), and the kinds of turn taking exchanges that occur (initiation-response-feedback) provide a more or less rigid structure to the linguistic practices of participants (McHoul 1978; Dalton-Puffer 2007). Education typically aims to socialize participants into specific language practices and away from others, with the practices that are chosen generally being those that will privilege people already in positions of power (Bourdieu 1991). As such, formal education has often been a key means through which nation-states have attempted to govern and ultimately assimilate internal diversity, whether through overt means such as obligatory boarding schools for Indigenous children established in the Anglophone colonial countries (Canada, US, Australia; see McCarty 2013 for an overview in the US context) and elsewhere in the world, or more subtle forms of assimilation. In many contexts around the world this has meant that languages in use in a certain place have been excluded from the schools established in that place, because the schools orient towards linguistic practices that are in use in a center of national (or international) power, elsewhere (Heller and Martin-Jones 2001; Tollefson and Tsui 2004). Languages that are excluded from education are pushed down the linguistic hierarchy in their place of origin, becoming minoritized (May 2006) or displaced, and eventually may cease to be used.

Nationalist schooling has not only been detrimental through fostering language hierarchies, but more significantly it can create multiple forms of disadvantage for those who are erased by the school's language regime (Irvine and Gal 2000). Ivan Illich (1970) has argued that obligatory schooling as designed by a dominant social group is a key mechanism for creating and controlling social hierarchy in Latin America and in the world in general, as poorer classes with less access to formal education are "schooled in a sense of inferiority" (7) on the grounds of having restricted membership to the discourses and communities of formal schooling. Illich (1970, 1973) discussed the potential harms of certain forms of institutionalized education, characterized as inherently *manipulative*, in contrast to the potential benefits of "learning webs" characterized as inherently *convivial* (see also chapter 6). Rebolledo (2008), writing about education for Indigenous students in Mexico City, describes the "national monolingual educational model imposed on bilingual students" as characterized by "a series of conventional teaching patterns and the curricular rigidity of basic education: school has been designed for a culturally homogenous population, within which Indian characteristics do not fit" (104). In the Oaxacan context, Maldonado Alvarado (2002) describes how formal education has been used as a site to erase Indigenous practices and perspectives; a colonial endeavor which Indigenous people have long resisted.

The exclusion of local language practices from formal education, and the adherence to a prescriptive, non-local speech norm is detrimental to children's acquisition of literacy and content material, as well as their social and psychological development (Thomas and Collier 1997; Cummins 2009). Conversely, inclusion of these languages can have positive effects on overall academic outcomes and identity development (Hornberger 1998, 2005; García 2009a; Blackledge and Creese 2010). Overt assimilation policies have fallen out of favor since the post-WWII human rights era, and policies that promote language diversity have increased in many parts of the world, as discussed in chapter 1. A variety of what might be called *pro-diversity* education approaches now exist, aiming to include diverse learners in formal education. Implementation and political support for such approaches is far from stable in many contexts however, as discussed in the context of Mexico and Oaxaca (see chapter 2) where so-called bilingual schools serve to transition students to monolingualism. Schools alone can neither eradicate Indigenous languages nor ensure their social acceptance (May and Aikman 2003; Hornberger 2008); however, education initiatives remain central to any project that seeks to create new potentialities for marginalized languages and peoples (Levinson et al. 1996: 19). The following section examines some of the different ways that education initiatives have sought to make space for diverse languages.

4.1.1 Pro-diversity education: From strict immersion to plurilingual repertoires

Pro-diversity education for Indigenous languages draws on a range of ideologies and takes many forms in practice. Immersion is viewed as the gold standard for endangered language education by scholars of language maintenance and revitalization, exemplified by language nests in New Zealand, Hawai'i, and in a growing number of Native communities in North America (Kipp 2000; McIvor 2005). As Grenoble and Whaley (2006) note, "While many would argue that full-immersion programs are the surest route to language revitalization and maintenance, few communities have the resources necessary to see them through" (50). Mother tongue-based multilingual education (MTB-MLE), as developed by PRAESA in South Africa (Alexander 2005; Plüddemann 2010) and additionally promoted by UNESCO (2003) and other transnational development organizations, prescribes sole use of a "mother tongue" (assumed to be the Indigenous language) for acquisition of literacy, eventually transferring to additional (national) languages

(Benson 2004; Skutnabb-Kangas 2009). Immersion and mother tongue education– while both designed to make spaces for minoritized languages and improve the quality of education for populations that have been marginalized by formal schooling– nonetheless draw on fairly essentializing notions of language and identity, such as fusing language with identity and place while overlooking that people may have multiple "mother tongues" or may develop language capacities in non-linear ways. In practice however, these classrooms may make space for multilingual practices such as translanguaging and recognition of multiple mother tongues despite their rhetoric of positive discrimination in favor of *one* minoritized language. For example, Hawai'ian immersion schools instruct students in Japanese and English as additional languages, and incorporate various forms of visual and spatial expression and different learning styles[23]; Hawai'ian language and culture is thus a base for a wide-ranging and diverse curriculum, rather than being a rigid or limiting frame.

Dual immersion, content-based learning (CBL; or content and language integrated learning, CLIL), task-based learning (TBL) and other program models orienting to a multilingual norm, attempt to incorporate multiple languages into one classroom in a meaningful way (Riestenberg and Sherris 2018). To the extent that they do not prescribe a linear or hierarchical development trajectory (one language mastered before another can be introduced), they may be seen as adopting a more constructivist or flexible approach to language learning than immersion or MTB-MLE models. On the other hand they may also create forms of "separate bilingualism" (Blackledge and Creese 2010) through the common practice of keeping languages apart and upholding a nativist ideal of "parallel monolingualism" (Heller 1999) where learners strive to appear monolingual in each language of their repertoire (Flores and Baetens Beardsmore 2015). Transitional or "subtractive" bilingualism (Lambert 1975) that incorporates a minority language into schooling for the purpose of transitioning students towards improved competence in a dominant language is unlikely to change language practices or power structures, maintaining a monolingual hierarchy. This is the norm in the "bilingual" schools for Indigenous students in Mexico (Coronado Suzán 1992; Hamel 2008a; García and Velasco 2012). The incorporation of Indigenous languages as subjects without using them as a medium of instruction at any time, which also occurs in some "bilingual Indigenous" schools in Mexico, is also unlikely to result in significant changes in language use. Teaching Indigenous

---

[23] As I observed in visits to several schools in 2011, see also http://www.hawaiipublicschools.org/TeachingAndLearning/StudentLearning/HawaiianEducation/Pages/Hawaiian-language-immersion-schools.aspx.

languages as subjects may create new communities of practice and increased awareness around issues of language prejudice and endangerment, however (Hornberger, De Korne, and Weinberg 2016).

Actual practices at the classroom level are not necessarily controlled by program types, and thus it is important to also consider the educational goals and ideologies of each program, and how they put them in practice (Hornberger 1991). Often teachers and/or directors have the ability to negotiate the program model or policies that they are asked to implement, developing their own norms and practices (Ricento and Hornberger 1996; Menken and García 2010). Promising practices in education for linguistically diverse students (and arguably all students, within a pluralist education paradigm) include providing culturally and linguistically relevant and sustaining education (Ladson-Billings 1995; Paris 2012) by recognizing the communicative resources that students bring with them. This requires acknowledging students' multimodal communicative repertoires (Cazden et al. 1996; Kress 2000; Rymes 2010, 2014), including non-alphabetic literacies (López Gopar 2007) and translanguaging practices (García 2009b). Rather than separating languages and communicative practices into categories, multilingual students benefit from incorporating receptive and productive, oral and written abilities, through flexible modalities ranging from simultaneous to successive use of different languages as they develop biliteracy (Hornberger 1989).

Educational communities of practice may foster pluralist language practices through locally-informed, flexible approaches to communication, or they may ultimately pressure students to use only certain standard varieties of socially privileged languages through adhering to top-down norms (Blommaert and Verschueren 1998; Weber 2009; Blackledge and Creese 2010). In this respect it is not enough to have a seemingly pro-diversity society or school program, it is also important to interrogate the ideologies that influence language use in the day to day practices of the educational community. Pro-diversity education in practice has been critiqued as resulting in the commodification and essentialization of minoritized languages and cultures within a neo-liberal framework of sanitized multiculturalism (García 2005; Muehlmann 2008; Paris and Alim 2017). The ways that language diversity is approached in schools– often through pre-existing hierarchical, normative frameworks– may ultimately assimilate and render diverse human subjects governable, with impacts similar to those of monolingual norms (Comaroff and Comaroff 2009; Povinelli 2011). Additionally the promotion of language diversity in the form of marketable plurilingual skills may risk supporting "a commodification of language in service of transnational corporations" and a homogenizing neoliberal agenda (Flores 2013: 515). These concerns indicate the need to pay close attention to minoritized language use in education and the social relations that it creates.

In other words, education may be a space that includes diverse language practices, *and/or* a space that restricts them. While there is an underlying argument in this study that the promotion of diverse, minoritized languages is desirable in education and society, I do not assume that *any* form of promotion is necessarily desirable, nor that all potentially homogenizing actions are undesirable.[24] This chapter attempts to deconstruct practices and ideologies in Zapotec education settings but also to reconstitute them, exploring ways that different actors are engaging in the pursuit of educational quality and equity (Makoni and Pennycook 2007). By observing an educational community of practice in action it is possible to understand what potentials they create or remove for their participants in relation to the socio-political context that they are embedded in, and thus look beyond the more transparent aspects of pro-diversity education models. The following sections examine approaches to language diversity in schooling in the Isthmus.

4.2 Language and schooling in the Isthmus of Tehuantepec

Legally, Isthmus Zapotec should no longer be forbidden in schools in today's era of multicultural tolerance. The national legal changes since the 1996 San Andrés accords, including the 2003 linguistic rights law and ratification of the 2007 UN Declaration on the Rights of Indigenous Peoples give Isthmus Zapotec speakers the right to use their language in schools and other public spaces. At the state level, the teacher's union PTEO program also calls for inclusion of local language, culture and history in the mainstream school curriculum. Unfortunately these pluralist policies are far from being universal practices. In some cases I observed, formal schooling continued to perform the function of discouraging use of Zapotec. In other cases, I observed individual teachers and administrators who chose to promote Indigenous language use to some extent. The PTEO was mentioned much more frequently by the schools that I visited than the national and international policies, and did result in some changes in language practices in certain cases, as examined further below.

Schooling in the Isthmus includes preschool (3 years), primary school (6 years), and secondary school (3 years), after which some students choose to go on to study preparatory school or vocational colleges, as represented in the following Table 2.

---

[24] For example, I choose to group a wide array of languages together to talk about "minoritized languages"; in effect I am restricting a diverse reality through this grouping, but doing so allows for solidarity, enhanced visibility, and wider networks of support which all seem to me to be valuable.

Table 2: Formal education institutions available to students in the Isthmus and Indigenous language inclusion.

Level of schooling	Institution	Indigenous language inclusion
Preschool	Bilingual	Yes; flexible
	Monolingual	No
	Private	No
Primary school	Bilingual	Yes; Subject 1 hour per week
	Monolingual	No
	Private	No
Secondary school	Public	No
	Private	No
Preparatory	Public	No
	Alternative Public (BIC)	Yes; Potentially medium and subject of study

As indicated in the table, there are three main types of preschools and primary schools: public with monolingual mandate (often called *normal*, *general*, or *formal*), public with nominally bilingual mandate (called *bilingüe* or *indígena*), and private (some of which are 'bilingual' in Spanish and English, or identify with European methods such as Montessori). The public bilingual and monolingual schools are run by separate supervision offices, but have only slightly different curriculum (bilingual school curricula calls for one hour per week of Indigenous language teaching) and similar underlying aims. There is a long history of nominally bilingual education in Mexico, yet today's bilingual schools are universally judged to result in transition towards Spanish, rather than development of bilingualism or biliteracy (Hamel 2008b; Rebolledo 2010; García and Velasco 2012). My observations in the Isthmus are generally in line with what these scholars have described in other parts of the country, as discussed below in relation to formal education practices.

There is no bilingual secondary or preparatory school system, however state-level politics have created opportunities, and some actors have seized them, to teach Indigenous languages at these levels. The teacher's union, through the PTEO, created an *asignatura estatal* [state subject] in secondary schools, and gave teachers license to determine the content of this course. Some schools chose to teach local languages within this subject, as well as traditional arts, skills, and Oaxacan history. While most preparatory schools do not include

Indigenous languages in any way, a new form of preparatory designed for Indigenous communities in Oaxaca is expanding throughout the state, and has been established in two communities in the Isthmus. The program for the *Bachillerato Integral Comunitario* [Integral/ holistic community baccalaureate, BIC] was created in 2002, building on numerous alternative secondary school projects at the state level (Pérez Díaz 2008), and includes instruction of Indigenous languages 4 hours per week as well as encouragement to integrate Indigenous language into the broader program of studies. A BIC was founded in Álvaro Obregon around 2011, and another was founded in La Ventosa in the autumn of 2014.[25]

The majority of students in the Isthmus attend schools where Indigenous languages are not part of the curriculum, as the 'general' monolingual schools are more than twice as numerous as the 'Indigenous' bilingual schools. The ratio of schools does not equate perfectly with the ratio of students either, as all of the 'Indigenous bilingual' primary schools I visited were small and had fewer class groups than the 'general' schools. Parents can choose where they will try to enroll their children, and the bilingual schools are generally considered to be less prestigious than the 'general' schools. It is not uncommon for students to travel to another (usually wealthier) neighborhood for primary school, or neighboring towns for secondary or preparatory school. Students from La Ventosa often travel into Juchitán, while students from Juchitán often travel to the neighboring municipality of Espinal, and still others attend preparatory schools in the state capitol of Oaxaca. While not everyone attends preschool or preparatory school and beyond, 95.27% of children between the ages of 6 and 14 attend primary school in the Isthmus (Carpeta Regional Istmo: Información Estadística y Geográfica Básica 2012), which in the vast majority of cases means Spanish-only instruction.

The mandate of a school (bilingual or monolingual) does not always align with the characteristics of the participants in the school; the characteristics of the teachers, administrators and students vary considerably across the Isthmus Zapotec region. There are bilingual schools in areas where most children prefer to use Spanish; there are monolingual schools in areas where most children prefer to use Diidxazá; and a concern which emerged often was that not all teachers in bilingual schools speak the Indigenous language (or the variety of the Indigenous language) of the locality. Among the schools that I visited and the teachers that I interviewed, in the cases where Diidxazá-speaking teachers were working

---

25 Additional education services that were not considered in this study are the *Consejo Nacional de Fomento Educativo* (National Council on Educational Support/ encouragement, CONAFE) that runs programs for students who have dropped out of public schools, and/ or live in remote regions, and the *Instituto Nacional para la Educación de Adultos* (National Institute for Adult Education, INEA) that conducts training for adults.

with Diidxazá-speaking students, and were motivated to develop Diidxazá abilities, teachers often expressed uncertainty with writing the language and with language pedagogy in general. Other teachers commented that they would be willing to teach Diidxazá, but that parents do not want their children to spend school time on this subject. While some teachers and directors expressed appreciation for local language and culture, others viewed Diidxazá as a problem which could hold their students back. The lingering influence of coloniality and prejudice towards Indigenous languages is evident in many schools in the Isthmus, both in discourse and in practice. One common thread among bilingual and monolingual schools was that all teachers agreed that fewer and fewer students arrive at school speaking Indigenous languages.

Schools are part of wider trends, as many of the teachers and directors I met and interviewed impressed upon me. The preferences of parents, the curricula sent from the national level, and programs promoted by the state-level teacher's union influence what they are able and choose to do. For example, in autumn of 2013 public schools in Oaxaca opened almost two months late on October 14th due to teachers' protests against the federal Education Reform of 2013. One of the points of contention with the reform was the system of standardized testing being promoted by the federal government, both for students, and most controversially, for teachers. A national standardized test of students, ENLACE, was in place from 2006–2009 in a sample of schools, but the Section 22 teacher's union succeeded in getting Oaxaca exempt from this testing system on the argument that it was not appropriate to their diverse student population.[26] Despite critiques, the test continued in the rest of the country, having been redesigned and renamed PLANEA (Anzures Tapia 2015). With the weakening of the teacher's union through the restructuring of the *Instituto Estatal de Educación Pública de Oaxaca* (Oaxacan State Education Institute, IEEPO[27]) in August 2015, the revised PLANEA exams have been applied in Oaxaca. In the 2017 and 2018 rounds of testing the results of Oaxaca were not included in the final report because the participation of Oaxacan schools was not sufficient, although it had gone up considerably from the 2015 tests (INEE 2018). Teachers I spoke with in the Isthmus generally did not seem concerned about their students' performance on standardized tests when asked directly, and rarely brought the subject up as a topic of concern spontaneously. This stood out to me because they were much less pressured by testing of their students than teachers I have met in other multilingual contexts; this may change if standardized exams begin to loom larger in schools in the Isthmus, however.

---

26 http://www.enlace.sep.gob.mx/ba/
27 http://www.ieepo.oaxaca.gob.mx

Another recent reform in the Mexican curriculum was the inclusion of an "additional language" to be studied in the monolingual primary school curriculum. I met one teacher who interpreted this as an opportunity to teach a local language to her students, but in general it was viewed as a policy in favor of increased English teaching, a subject which many teachers in the Isthmus were not equipped to teach.

At the local level, each municipality appoints a *Regidor(a) de educación* (Education councilperson) as a liaison between the local government and the schools. Unlike the teachers and directors of schools, the local government liaison is appointed for three years only, limiting the degree of influence that they might have. During the first years of my research (2013–2015), the *regidor* in Juchitán was not active in promoting Isthmus Zapotec in education, although the municipal government provided support for a public campaign and some outreach activities which promoted intergenerational use of Diidxazá (the *Gusisácanu Diidxazá do' stiinu* [Let's strengthen our pure/ good Zapotec campaign]). In the following three-year period (2016–2018) the municipal government supported a project to test primary school children and subsequently provide literacy workshops and a small scholarship to those who were evaluated as speaking Diidxazá, collaborating with the public schools in doing so (*Diidxazá xtinu* [Our Zapotec] project). Whether or not resources were directed to Indigenous language promotion, and what kind of promotion activities were undertaken thus changed from one political term to another.

The earthquakes of September 2017 had significant impacts on the schools in the Isthmus, as many were damaged and others delayed re-opening in order to increase pressure on the government to rebuild damaged buildings. Schools cut the number of teaching hours dramatically, often rotating classes through one or two undamaged rooms while waiting for the rest of the building to be reconstructed. Prior to the earthquakes which also brought the local economy to a halt, poverty and related concerns about students' home environments were mentioned by several teachers as an important factor impacting negatively on school life. Following the earthquakes, many acknowledged the trauma caused by these events in all sectors of the population, making it difficult to return to normal activities and studies. Although schools were less active in the post-earthquake period, numerous civil society organizations attempted to fill some of the gap, offering workshops for children (as mentioned in chapter 2, see also chapter 6 and 7).

Despite the contextual instabilities which have characterized formal schooling in the Isthmus, schools remain an important site for socializing children into representations of their community languages, and of what it means to be an educated person more generally. Within the 'bilingual' school system, students do have the right to one hour per week of instruction in the local language, however the fact that many teachers were not pedagogically prepared to teach this area and some parents resist its inclusion in the curricula meant that Indigenous languages were generally not viewed as a resource which could benefit learners in the future. In all of the formal education sites that I observed or learned about through interviews, Spanish was the primary language of oral and written communication, and efforts to use Isthmus Zapotec, where present, were a relatively small part of academic activities. The trend to devalue the local language was common, but there were also some notable exceptions. I now turn to several of the positive ways which educator-activists have promoted Diidxazá in schools.

4.3 Language activism in education in the Isthmus

Although initially I was told, and later observed, that Isthmus Zapotec was largely excluded from schools, throughout my study I continued to hear about individual teachers and schools who were using Indigenous languages in some way, in many cases due to their motivation, rather than the mandate or established curriculum of their school. The practices may have been limited and somewhat isolated, but there were numerous attempts to promote Indigenous language use in formal education spaces underway in the Isthmus which were not necessarily recognized nor lauded beyond the limited space of the classroom or the school. A common strategy among the teacher-activists I met was that of *connecting* their *classroom space* with the *home and community spaces* of their students. Teacher-activists were also engaged in changing the common deficit representations of Zapotec in schools and were providing an alternative representation of Indigenous languages as resources and rights, to varying degrees. By *representing* Isthmus Zapotec *communication practices* as a legitimate part of the school context, they helped to counter the long-standing exclusion of Indigenous languages from public schools. Here I discuss several initiatives which exemplify these strategies that I observed more broadly.

4.3.1 Connecting school and community

In the opening of this chapter I introduced the teaching team of a monolingual primary school who worked throughout a school year to incorporate local and traditional practices into their regular school activities, including spoken and written use of Isthmus Zapotec. A delayed school schedule due to a labor strike that other schools had told me was preventing them from attempting any extra activities was not viewed as a barrier by this team. The school was located in an urban section of Juchitán, and the director informed me that 80% of the students spoke Isthmus

Zapotec, while the other 20% understood. The school's project received extra support from the teacher's union, as they framed it as an attempt to put the PTEO into practice by involving parents and undertaking school-run projects to meet local needs. I met them when they requested the *Camino de la Iguana* literacy workshop (described in detail in chapter 6) to come and work with their students; they heard about the workshop because one of their students was the niece of Natalia Toledo, the co-instructor of *Camino de la Iguana*. When I visited the school in May 2014 in the company of the *Camino de la Iguana* instructors, I observed a student-made poster with drawings and writing in both Zapotec and Spanish in one of the classrooms, which had been created prior to the beginning of the literacy workshop. Teachers informed me that they had hosted a Diidxazá book fair and invited students to bring in books they had at home, as well as bringing books from the libraries in Juchitán. During the workshop students engaged in writing poems, autobiographies, and other texts, as well as learning the basics of the popular alphabet and being further exposed to Isthmus Zapotec literature in several genres.

Delia, one of the lead teachers, told me that the project began as a way to improve the overall school environment, including students' motivation and parents' participation– not in pursuit of a language-related goal. With a gentle, graceful demeanor, Delia approaches difficult topics directly, pointing towards domestic violence and a toxic school environment as causes for poor learning in school. As a native of Comitancillo, a smaller town in the Isthmus, Delia had been surprised by the challenges she faced when teaching in semi-urban Juchitán. Although she had not focused on Diidxazá as an asset for teaching before, she found that it was important in reaching out to her students' families and attemting to change the atmosphere in the school. This is also clear in the project overview represented in Figure 11, with the ultimate goal to "lead to the diminishing of violence, familial disintegration and learning difficulties." The school director, who had worked in the school for 23 years, reinforced this in an interview, noting that their main motivation was to respond to the violence and lack of participation that they felt were increasing in the school. The pro-active inclusion of the local language emerged as part of their response to these concerns.

In an interview the director and I were talking about the amount of students who spoke Isthmus Zapotec, but when I then asked about changes in the school over time the most salient changes for the director were not linguistic:

HDK   Y . . . ¿en esos años ha visto cambios en la escuela o en el alumnado?

Director   Pues mire, realmente usted sabe cómo está la situación en el país, ¿no? En cuanto a la violencia y las drogas y todo eso. Y sí se ha notado porque . . . hay niños que acá vienen y pues ya platican--- el año pasado egresó de aquí un niño que dice: yo me gano cien pesos si vendo tres bolsitas. [. . .] ¿Qué esperanza

	tenemos en esos niñitos que ahorita ven a sus papás que están haciendo eso? El alcoholismo sobre todo, nos afecta bastante acá.
HDK	*¿Y eso no era tanto así antes?*
Director	*No, antes no estaba así, no. Antes había una bandita pero hasta allá al fondo. No, ahorita, ahorita como a dos cuadras hay bandas. [. . .] Ese es el detalle de esta sociedad. Pero pues aquí vamos construyendo y tratando de reforzar los valores de la familia. De hecho, nuestro proyecto tiene--- está fundamentado en el rescate de los valores de la familia para, para tener un poco más, ir rescatando--- en base a los valores, rescatar todo lo bueno que tenía nuestra sociedad antes, ¿no? Aquel "buenos días". Aquí en México en la cultura zapoteca eso era. [Saludas] "Buenos días", sea tu tío, no sea tu tío, sea tu abuelo, "buenos días".*
HDK	And . . . in those years have you seen changes in the school or the student body?
Director	Well look, really you know how the situation in the country is, right? In terms of the violence, and the drugs, and all that. And yes it's been noticed because . . . there are children who come here and well already talk--- Last year a boy left here who said: I earn one hundred pesos if I sell three little bags. [. . .] What hope do we have for these little children that now see their parents that are doing that? Alcoholism especially affects us a lot here.
HDK	And that wasn't so much like that before?
Director	No, before it wasn't like that, no. Before there was a little gang but over there at the bottom/ end. No, now, now like within two blocks there are gangs. [. . .] That is the detail of this society. But here we're building and trying to reinforce family values. Actually our project has– it's based in saving family values in order, in order to have a bit more, go saving– based on values, save all the good that our society had before, right? That "Good day". Here in Mexico in the Zapotec culture that's how it was. [You greet] "Good day" be it your uncle or not your uncle, be it your grandfather, "good day". (Interview July 2014)

This director was one of many educators who commented on their concerns for the economic and social well-being of their students. For some educators this observation was linked to the need to focus on Spanish and core subjects so that students would advance within the education system, leaving no time for local language within school hours. This orientation in many ways served to create a barrier (perhaps viewed as a protective buffer) between the school space and the community space. This director and teaching team, however, took a contrasting approach by seeking to break down barriers with the community and invite parents into the school on a more active basis in order to foster "family values". Referring to the practice of greeting people in the street with *"Buenos días"* or another appropriate greeting, the director expressed a view of traditional behaviors as more respectful, with tight-knit family interactions. In line with this goal, parents were involved in numerous aspects of the project, including helping students produce texts and radio programs, and painting a mural.

The director commented that the goal of recuperating values was intertwined with that of recuperating language. Their activities were designed *"para rescatar un poquito más. Porque sí, sí se, se ha ido perdiendo bastante la lengua. Y los valores, le digo. Que fue el punto central, ¿no? Pero [recuperar valores] a través de, a través del rescate de las costumbres, las tradiciones, la cultura y la lengua"* [in order to recuperate a bit more. Because yes, yes the language has been getting lost considerably. And the values, I tell you. Which was the central point, right. But [recuperate values] through the, through the recuperation of customs, traditions, culture and language] (Interview July 2014). Isthmus Zapotec education was included in their project as part of a broader program seeking to achieve positive social interactions. In the project goals (shown in Figure 11) educational units on family values, local language, and *convivencia* (conviviality or positive coexistence/ social activities) all make up part of the strategic actions towards their social goals. In this case an extensive amount of Isthmus Zapotec teaching and use as a resource resulted from a project aimed at better serving the population of an urbanizing neighborhood. The teachers developed strategic connections between families and the school space through a convivial or participatory dynamic which they, and the parents and students I interacted with, experienced to be rewarding and to improve the environment in the school. As Delia observed, *"vimos ese resultado de integración, de comunicación . . . porque . . . padres que no conocíamos pues ya los fuimos conociendo, ¿no? . . . Vimos resultados en el hecho de que padres que no se interesaban se fueron interesando"* [we saw that result of integration, of communication . . . because . . . parents that we didn't know, well we started to get to know them, right? . . . We saw results in the fact that parents that weren't interested became interested] (Interview September 2014).

Their initiative was further enabled by the support of the PTEO at the state level, and by other local activists such as the facilitators of the *Camino de la Iguana*. They were able to draw on local and regional resources in resisting the deficit representations of local language and culture. The achievement of this teaching team was crucially dependent on the support of the school's director and the members of the team, however, and was not common among the schools that I visited. This was made especially apparent by the experience of Delia, who moved and started working at a larger (and more prestigious) primary school in 2016. When we met in 2018 on one of my shorter visits to the Isthmus, she told me that she was not able to enlist support for the kinds of extra pedagogical efforts that she had helped to spearhead in her previous school. The disruption and reconstruction process of the

2017 earthquake played a role, but the crucial factor was lack of support from the school team. In the face of this disappointment, she had begun volunteering with a community-based organization that promoted literacy and reading in the towns around the Isthmus. She reflected with resigned regret on the many barriers to implementing innovative projects in the public schools, and for the time being was happier to work with other like-minded volunteers outside of the school.

The need for a flexible repertoire of activism strategies is clear in such a context. The strategy of connecting school and community spaces was supported and made possible by the constellation of people and resources in one school, but was prohibited by the conditions of another school nearby. Delia adapted to these conditions, and took up a new strategy of sharing resources and representing literacy as a positive thing outside of school. Community-based education initiatives are common strategies among activists in the Isthmus, as examined further in chapters 6 and 7.

4.3.2 Representing Diidxazá as a part of formal education

Another strategy that I observed in several schools was the representation of Indigenous languages as legitimate to be used and/ or studied in formal education. Like the teaching team discussed above, another teacher in a monolingual primary school in a northern, Spanish-dominant neighborhood of Juchitán also used the state-level PTEO policy as a justification for Isthmus Zapotec use in her classroom. I met María Isabel García Rasgado when she attended the *Camino de la Iguana* in November of 2013 in Union Hidalgo, where she lives. Nearing 30 years of teaching, she remained enthusiastic and emotional when talking about her students, and her efforts to provide them with a high-quality education and pride in their identity as *Istmeños*. She often wore traditional embroidered blouses when teaching, and had engaged in a range of pedagogical projects and excursions with her students over the years. She invited me to visit her class in Juchitán, saying that she wanted her students to see that someone from far away was interested in their language, so that they might become more interested. None of her 5th grade students were conversant in Isthmus Zapotec, although several understood and spoke some. In her classroom there were several posters relating to the pre-colonial history of Mexico and one sign in Spanish and Zapotec "*Rincon Baduhuiini*" [Children's corner]. Her class was conducted in Spanish, but with more discussion of local culture, history and language than what would typically appear in the curriculum. Her students seemed to react positively to this. On my first visit to her class several students had written or drawn cards welcoming me. One student wrote "*Se un poco zapoteco y un poco de ingles pero mis tatarabuelos, mis bisabuelos, mis abuelos mis tíos y primos como mis padres hablan la lengua materna que es el zapoteco"* [I know a little Zapotec and a little English but my great-great-grandparents, my great-grandparents, my grandparents my aunts and uncles and cousins and also my parents speak the mother language which is Zapotec]. María Isabel and her students did not see Isthmus Zapotec as something to be avoided, nor did they seem to worry that it might cause them to speak poor Spanish– although they all spoke comfortable Spanish already.

María Isabel had taught her class Zapotec songs, which she had them sing for me, and again in front of the whole school when it was their class's turn to present in the weekly *"homenaje"* flag ceremony in January 2014. I attended the flag ceremony, where she made some comments about the PTEO policy to valorize local culture and language, followed by readings by the students in Spanish, and a song in Spanish and Zapotec. Then one student read part of a story in Isthmus Zapotec about a lively iguana, while another read the corresponding Spanish translation, and other students distributed copies of this story to all of the teachers in the school, so that they could look at it with their classes. When I spoke with María Isabel afterwards, she explained that the boy who read in Isthmus Zapotec spoke the most Isthmus Zapotec, although he struggled with some other academic areas, and so she was pleased to have him show off his strengths in this way. I agreed that he had seemed confident on stage. She also commented that her fellow teachers were supportive of her efforts, although what she did was limited to her classroom rather than being a school-wide project. In this case, use of Isthmus Zapotec– largely, but not entirely in symbolic ways– was pursued by a motivated individual who viewed it as an enriching but under-appreciated part of her students' backgrounds, and this use received a degree of support from her colleagues.

A group of teachers from a secondary school in southern Juchitán also worked to incorporate local language into their regular curriculum. I met them in April of 2014 when they attended the event that I co-organized with colleagues at the UABJO (see also 3.2.2, 3.2.3, chapter 5), where they told me that they were taking advantage of the *asignatura estatal* [State subject] slot in the curriculum to develop a plan to teach Isthmus Zapotec literacy with their students. This subject was a required topic for secondary school students, but teachers had free reign to decide what to teach in it. I had heard several other secondary school representatives say they wanted to use this subjet to include Zapotec language, but were unsure how to go about this. The April 2014 event included workshops and talks on teaching Indigenous languages, and thus they had requested time off to attend it, and I was delighted to hear that they appreciated the event. I visited them in their school the following November, and they described their efforts to teach traditional handicrafts, as well as Zapotec reading and writing. They were motivated by the need to create lessons to fill the new class slot in the curriculum, and the fact that most of their students spoke Isthmus Zapotec and responded positively to the classes. They were also motivated by personal interests in promoting Zapotec bilingualism and literacy. They showed me various learning materials that their students had made, including a memory game with images and labels for common objects in the Isthmus, including *xigagueta* [painted gourd container]; *yuze'* [cattle]; and *guchachi'* [iguana], as shown in Figure 12. They were pleased when I offered to give them some Isthmus Zapotec texts for students to read. They were also interested in bringing the *Camino de la Iguana* to work with their students and expand their literacy abilities. School communities like this one are clearly representing Zapotec as a resource, part of local heritage, and something that is worth learning about.

Figure 12: Pedagogical materials created by secondary school students (photo November 2014).

4.4 Summary: Characteristics of language activism in education

The presence and status of Indigenous languages in education has shifted over time, with an increasing number of policies at national and regional levels in favor of multilingual education around the world at the end of the 20th and beginning of the 21st centuries. Over twenty years ago language education scholar Teresa McCarty wrote in the US context that "the legal right for Indigenous language and culture maintenance appears to be won, yet the struggle continues [. . .] A stable but locally flexible system of educational delivery [. . .] still is urgently needed" (1997: 52–53). Nearly two decades after the official recognition of Indigenous languages in Mexico in 2003, the same might be said of the Mexican context. And yet as days and years pass by, and new generations grow up under the same discriminatory regimes, we continue to ask what exactly *is* needed to implement minority language rights or to achieve linguistic equality? The domain of schooling illustrates clearly that linguistic equality does not materialize through declarations and policies alone. In the Isthmus of Tehuantepec, as in many other places, educator-activists are engaging in a variety of creative strategies within the constraints of the institutional, political, economic, and socio-demographic realities in which they work. Certain actors in the chain of education politics may have special significance in efforts to expand "ideological and implementational spaces" for Indigenous language education (Hornberger 2002). Johnson (Johnson 2012; Johnson and Johnson 2015) refers to these key individuals as language policy arbiters, illustrating cases where an administrator or official was able to open up or close down space for bilingual education. This chapter has illustrated the importance of teachers as arbiters in educational language policy in the Isthmus.

Teachers like Maria Isabel García Rasgado and Delia Ruíz Álvarez make important contributions towards changing the negative representations of Diidxazá that have been inherited from decades of monolingual Spanish schooling. Activities such as reading Diidxazá literature during the official flag ceremony can have an important symbolic effect, as do similar events for poetry declamation in other schools. These events go beyond a positive representation of the language itself, to a representation of students who speak Diidxazá as people possessing knowledge, rather than as problems or as weak students as they are viewed in some cases. Educator-activists' strategies include the production of both events, such as a one-time presentation or workshop, and more long-lasting structures, such as a regular class in the curriculum. A sustained structure is more likely to support additive bilingualism (bilingualism and biliteracy in Zapotec and Spanish), while events may be helpful in shifting representations, but may have less influence on language competence. Nonetheless, one-time events in schools occur within the enduring structure of the school, such as the presentation occurring in the flag ceremony, itself an event which happens each week. In this way, the framework of the school lends weight and potentially prestige to the activism initiatives that occur within it, in contrast to some of the events organized by language activists in less formal spaces (discussed further in chapters 6 and 7). Like scholar-activists, educator-activists can take advantage of their social role as knowledge-holders and legitimizers of others' (in this case young students') knowledge, which may give their activism initiatives added prestige and social meaning. At the same time, the structure of the school is far less flexible than some social spaces, and may only allow for limited or short initiatives as teachers change schools and new curricula appear, as illustrated by Delia's experience. The teacher-activists who I observed in the Isthmus were not acting entirely alone, but were often supported by a few key colleagues, and were dependent upon the good will of the director of the school. Weinberg (2021) has pointed out that in some contexts, language policy arbiters are not individuals, but rather a combination of two or more key actors. In this case, a motivated teacher and a director who approved of their efforts both appear to be necessary for greater inclusion of Indigenous langauge in school.

In contrast to scholar-activists, I did not observe educator-activists to focus on the creation of materials and resources. Educator-activists did often engage their students in the creation of different materials– from text to audio recordings and paintings– but the focus was on the students' participation as producers, not the resulting materials themselves. A more common strategy among educator-activists was to connect the space of the school with that of the community. Many teachers commented on the fact that they did not have pedagogical supports or training to include Indigenous languages in the curriculum, but collaborating with families and using children's connections with the community outside of the school was helpful in filling this void. This approach has been widely promoted in education scholarship, with well-known formulations such as the use of "community funds of knowledge" as the basis for learning (Moll et al. 1992), and developing "culturally relevant" (Ladson-Billings 1995) and "culturally sustaining" pedagogies (Paris and Alim 2017). This form of connection creates a convivial relationship, or in Illich's (1970) words a "learning web", among teachers, students, and the wider community. Table 3 illustrates some of the key activism strategies that I observed in primary and secondary schools in the Isthmus, including connecting school and community spaces, and respresenting Zapotec speakers as valuable and legitimate in the school space.

While the teachers who were engaging in activism or advocacy initiatives reported that both parents and students appreciated them (and I was also able to observe this on several occasions), several teachers in schools where advocacy was not occurring commented that the parents of the students do not want Indigenous languages to be taught there and have made this clear to teachers. Additionally, teachers within the same school may have different priorities, with some viewing inclusion of Zapotec as a resource, while some view it as taking time

Table 3: Key language activism strateges in primary and secondary schooling.

Actions →	Goals →	Examples
– Connecting	– People/ Identities – Spaces/ Structures	– Family and community members invited into the school space
– Representing	– People/ Identities – Communication practices – Spaces/ Structures	– Indigenous language speakers represented as knowledgeable – Indigenous languages represented as legitimate in school – School represented as a space where local knowledge is important
– Creating	– Resources	– Participatory creation of games, recordings, murals, etc.

away from subjects of greater importance. In these contexts, Diidxazá education could be experienced as an imposition. Harking back to Mayoli García's argument quoted in the beginning of this book; where Indigenous languages are concerned many education actors seem to agree that "we can't go back to the barbarity of before" and force people to study in or about a language that they do not want to use. At the same time, when it comes to Spanish and, in higher levels of education, English, there seems to be no concern as to whether all students and their families want these languages to be studied; they are simply an undisputable part of the system which youth are required to spend at least 6–12 years of their life participating in.

There are multiple imaginaries of positive social change among educators in the Isthmus – some of which include Isthmus Zapotec, and some of which do not. Educator-activists who pursue the inclusion of local language and a more convivial school environment have noted important benefits from this strategy, despite the contextual constraints that may limit their initiatives. Institutional factors of curricula, testing, and strikes may continue to exert pressure on the limited instruction time, in addition to contextual factors such as poverty, violence, and natural disasters. The education spaces that are created, often temporarily and precariously, through language activism in this context, are nonetheless spaces in which inclusive and convivial Indigenous language education is occurring, and where Diidxazá learners experience more equality and respect than in many other education environments.

Chapter 5
Representing legitimate languages and identities: Strategies in higher education

Kiara Ríos Ríos grew up in La Mata, a small town towards the southeast of the Isthmus. She attended public schools in the region and especially enjoyed learning English, which motivated her to enroll in the bachelor's program in *Enseñanza de Idiomas* (Language Teaching/ Learning) at the Faculty of Languages of the Autonomous Benito Juárez University of Oaxaca (UABJO), first in the Tehuantepec branch campus and then in the main campus in Oaxaca City. In the following extract from an interview conducted when she was nearing the end of her undergraduate studies, she reflects on how her interaction with a supportive teacher and interested peers during her studies led her to reevaluate her own language repertoire, in particular to give more importance to her ability to speak Isthmus Zapotec. She is confident and charismatic while narrating her experiences:

> Kiara *Lo que pasa es que al principio, yo sí, yo, el zapoteco para mí era para como algo para mi casa, así. O para aquí para mi pueblo, y todo eso para mí era el zapoteco. No era, como así pensaba yo, que no era para enseñar. Incluso apenas en la carrera aprendí que es una lengua. Yo pensaba que era un dialecto. Entonces todo, no le daba yo misma, no le daba mucho valor a mi lengua. Entonces fue en la escuela que, más cuando conocí al maestro Mario [López Gopar], que empecé yo a darle valor a mi lengua, porque, para mi antes no era como muy de presumir, así como sentirme bien por saber una lengua, no era algo que presumir.*
>
> *Entonces, pero el maestro, como que, si sabes una lengua, es como para él, 'wuauuu'. Entonces yo misma la fui creyendo también. [. . .] Pues entonces fue así, que más o menos ya, él, él decía, 'no sé'– en mi grupo, así, antes que enseñara zapoteco – 'no sé si ustedes saben pero Kiara sabe hablar zapoteco' . . . [. . .] Y muchos no sabían que yo hablaba, muchos no sabían, solo sabían los– mis círculos de amigos y así nada más, pero muchos no sabían, y '¿Enserio hablas zapoteco?', y era así como, 'Sí enserio'. Este de, y ya te pregunta '¿Y cómo, cómo aprendiste?' y así. Entonces, a ti te va dando menos pena hablar, decir o ya no te da pena decir que hablas zapoteco, al contrario te enorgullece decir que hablas zapoteco. Es cuando, alguien también te ayuda a que le des valor a tu lengua, o que te sientas bien por hablar una lengua indígena.*
>
> The thing is that in the beginning, I yes, I, Zapotec for me was for, like something for my house, like that. Or for here, for my town, and all that was Zapotec for me. It was not, I thought like that, that it was not for teaching. Even just recently in the [university] program I learned that it is a language. I thought that it was a *dialecto*. So all, I didn't give it, myself, I didn't give much value to my language. So it was in school that, especially when I met teacher Mario [López Gopar], that I started to give value

to my language. Because before for me it wasn't really something to brag about, like to feel good for knowing a language, it wasn't something to brag about.

So, but for the teacher, like if you know a language, it's like 'woooow' for him. So I started to believe it myself as well. [. . .] Well so it was like that, that more or less then, he said, 'I don't know'– in my [university cohort] group, like that, before I was going to teach Zapotec – 'I don't know if you all know, but Kiara knows how to speak Zapotec' . . . [. . .] And many didn't know that I spoke, many didn't know– only my circles of friends knew and no more, but many didn't know, and 'Seriously, you speak Zapotec?', and it was like that like, 'Yes, seriously'. And um, and then they ask you 'And how, how did you learn?' and so forth. So it starts to make you less embarrassed to speak, to say, or now it doesn't embarrass you to say that you speak Zapotec, on the contrary it makes you proud to say that you speak Zapotec. That's when someone also helps you to value your language, or so that you feel good for speaking an Indigenous language. (Interview December 2013)

Kiara's experience is echoed in the comments of many other university students at the UABJO Faculty of Languages who note that their time at the Faculty changed the way they view Indigenous languages and Indigenous language speakers – including both students who speak Indigenous languages and those who do not. In her account of going from embarrassment about her language repertoire when she entered university to identifying as an Isthmus Zapotec speaker and taking up an opportunity to teach Isthmus Zapotec to other students in the Faculty as part of her teaching practicum, Kiara highlights the crucial role of her teacher, Mario López Gopar, and the interest of her peers. Despite having come out of primary and secondary education in the Isthmus with the internalized belief that Zapotec was a *dialecto* and "not for teaching", her experiences in higher education were impactful enough to change this perspective. Although primary and secondary education is clearly a period where language attitudes and competences are formed, as discussed in chapter 4, for those who continue into higher education this is also a significant moment where exposure to new and potentially more diverse perspectives can occur. In this case, the perspectives that Mario López Gopar, a Oaxacan scholar-activist-educator working on decoloniality and language education (López Gopar, Morales, and Jiménez 2014; López Gopar et al. 2013; López Gopar 2016), brought into the classroom helped Kiara and other students to question the assumed language hierarchy that they had grown up with. In addition to allowing a wider range of critical perspectives, higher education is also a crucial gate-keeping space where future educational authorities are formed and legitimated, in particular future teachers who will have a say in the language practices and politics of classrooms in years to come.

Chapter 5 Representing legitimate languages and identities

In this chapter, I analyze the inclusion of Indigenous languages, in particular Isthmus Zapotec, within the Tehuantepec branch of the UABJO Faculty of Languages. The UABJO is the largest public university in the state of Oaxaca, and the Faculty of Languages has its main campus in Oaxaca City, with much smaller branch campuses in Tehuantepec (the historical market hub and namesake of the Isthmus) and Puerto Escondido, to the north on the Pacific coast of Oaxaca. The Tehuantepec Faculty of Languages became one of the focal sites that I have spent extended time in, initially observing and eventually collaborating with administrators and teachers, and getting to know several generations of students (see section 1.6 on methodology). I begin with a discussion of the numerous factors influencing how young adults in the Isthmus view their communicative repertoires, illustrating how multilingualism and Zapotec competence are often viewed through a deficit lens (5.1). Against this backdrop, I analyze how administrators and teachers in the Faculty of Languages engaged in language activism to support their students and change the colonialist bias of Mexican higher education (5.2). Their strategies included providing a new legitimacy for Zapotec as an academic language, and legitimacy for younger speakers through positive representations of Indigenous languages and of multilingualism (5.2.1). Furthermore, efforts to prepare young Zapotec teachers and to create new teaching and learning spaces within the structure of the university have been challenging, but hold important long-term promise (5.2.2). In summary, by working to fill a key identity category in the chain of language politics – that of language teachers – the community of the Tehuantepec Faculty of Languages have achieved slow, but structurally-supported forms of language activism (5.3). I consider the imaginaries and strategies of some of the teachers and administrators who were involved in supporting the program and the experiences of young adult learners of Isthmus Zapotec. I highlight the significance of higher education in *representing* local Indigenous languages and multilingual youth (or *communication practices* and *identities*, within the strategies framework) as legitimate. In this way, the gate-keeping and legitimation power of higher education has an important role to play in shaping language ecologies and in some cases in fostering potential language activists. The power to *create* certified language teachers (a special kind of socially-recognized *identity*) places higher education institutions at an especially significant point in the language ecology. A lack of teachers with competence to teach Diidxazá, and a lack of preparation and support among those who were attempting to teach it, was a common complaint within the education institutions I visited at all levels, and is common in Indigenous language education around the world (Whitinui, Rodríguez de France, and McIvor 2018). An institution such as the Tehuantepec Faculty of Languages is uniquely positioned to help supply this lack, and additionally holds the power to define what the qualities and abilities of a recognized Diidxazá teacher should be.

5.1 Multilingualism and identities in the Isthmus

Our identities as speakers and communicators are formed through countless influences in our home and surrounding environments. Our communicative repertoires and what we think and believe about those repertoires are likely to change over time as we encounter new influences or make new choices in our lives (Gumperz 1964; Busch 2012), as Kiara's description of her changing perspective and confidence as a speaker of Zapotec quoted in the opening of this chapter illustrates. The communicative repertoires of Indigenous youth, and their attitudes towards different communication practices, are subject to many, often contradictory, influences. The dominance of Eurocentric ideologies which devalue Indigenous languages, as discussed in chapter 2 in particular, has a clear influence on how *Istmeños* view their communicative repertoires. Ríos Ríos's comment that she viewed Zapotec as a *dialecto* is a common one, as is the view that Spanish and English are inherently superior, leading people to hide their knowledge of Indigenous languages. For many people in the Isthmus and elsewhere in Mexico, the idea of studying languages means studying *European* languages. One student who had migrated to the Isthmus for work and participated in a weekend class at the UABJO commented:

> Student 1 A mis papás les dije . . . les dije 'oye, que crees, mira aquí donde estoy hablan zapoteco, y estoy aprendiendo.' Y se empezaron a reír así burlonamente, 'Oh! Oh! Oh! Zapoteco . . . Hola, aprende mejor el inglés', y se empezaron a reír.
>
> I told my parents . . . I told them 'hey, guess what, look here where I am they speak Zapotec, and I'm learning.' And they started to laugh like this mockingly 'Oh! Oh! Oh! Zapotec . . . Hello, learn English instead', and they started to laugh.
> (Interview October 2013)

This student's parents are not alone in viewing English and other European languages as the only legitimate languages to study. With the long precedent of *castellanización* (Spanish-ization, see chapters 2 and 4) in primary and secondary schooling, higher education has generally served to extend this ideology, eventually carrying it over towards the work place and other prestigious spheres of public life.

In addition to a bias towards European languages, there is also a monolingual ideology which is prevalent in the region as discussed in chapter 2. Warnings that children will become *enredado* [tangled] if they learn both Spanish and Zapotec at the same time are common, as are critiques of what is perceived as mixing, and thus denigrating, languages. Mixed or synthetic communication (incorporating communicative resources perceived as Spanish and resources perceived as Isthmus Zapotec; see Hill and Hill 1986 in the context of Nahuatl and Spanish) is the norm in the Isthmus, yet many people also point to this practice as something negative, a degradation of Zapotec or poor Spanish. This is common in other Indigenous and minoritized communities, resulting in discouraging youth from viewing themselves as speakers (Meek 2010) and devaluing the heteroglossic resources that youth employ, while upholding an idealized, monolingual-like norm (García 2009b). For example, Sheilah Nicholas (2019) discusses how a changing language ecology in the United States impacts the communicative repertoires of Indigenous Hopi youth and results in uncertainties about Hopi identity due to the close link between language and culture. In the Hopi case, she illustrates that identity is bound up in more than language competence, and that competence is not a binary characteristic. Likewise in the Isthmus, young adults' communicative repertoires are often different than those of their parents and grandparents, and some struggle to define for themselves which language(s) they consider to be theirs.

When talking with young adults who had grown up in the region, insecurity with their own communicative abilities was a common theme; many would comment that they speak some Zapotec, but not well, or that they understand but do not speak. Many related how one or more family members (often their father) were particularly opposed to their use of Zapotec. Being mocked or critiqued was also a common experience among young adults. As one university student recounted:

> Student 2 Mi papa era el que siempre me decía que lo hablaba mal o esa no era la pronunciación y en vez de motivarme, no pues yo me sentía muy mal y mejor ya no lo – ya no lo hablaba, dejaba pasarlo y ya. Pero mi mamá sí era la que me decía: 'No, pues háblalo. Es bonito aprender el zapoteco. Le vas a enseñar a tus hijos y pues, para que siga.'
>
> My father was the one that always told me that I spoke it badly or that was not the pronunciation, and instead of motivating me, no, well I felt really bad, and better not to– then I didn't speak it, I let it go, that's all. But my mom, yes, was the one that would say to me: 'No, speak it. It's very good to learn Zapotec. You will teach it to your children and, well, so that it continues.'
>
> (Interview July 2014)

While this student's father may not have been aiming to stop her use of Diidxazá, regular critique undermined her confidence and led her to "let it go". Despite the encouragement of some family members, such as this students' mother, she had experienced long-term discomfort and insecurity as a young speaker of Diidxazá. Situations like this position young speakers at a crossroads of multiple language ideologies or stigmas within and beyond the speech community; they may be critiqued by family members for not speaking the Indigenous language in a certain way and/ or they may be critiqued by family or community members for not speaking the Indigenous language at all. At the same time they may face prejudice in society for speaking an Indigenous language to any degree (Gal 2006). Navigating the various norms and ideologies that surround them is daunting.

A case in point is a university student from Juchitán who explained that although he learned Zapotec from his grandparents, with his parents and younger sister he uses almost all Spanish, partially for fear of making mistakes, partially due to his mother's desire to learn Spanish and avoid discrimination.

Student 3 De hecho, hasta ahorita se siguen dirigiendo en español. Muy pocas veces hablamos en zapoteco, o cuando entablamos una conversación mi mamá me habla en zapoteco y yo le contesto en español. Entonces tal vez no le hablo en zapoteco porque me da pena equivocarme, que no diga bien una palabra.

HDK ¿Estás más cómodo en español?

Student 3 En español, sí. Sí, ella a veces prefiere que le hable en español porque--- como mi mamá vende en el mercado, entonces ahí su vida cotidiana es zapoteco, zapoteco. Jamás habla español, más que cuando está en la casa con nosotros. Entonces cuando ella necesita ir al banco o a otro lado es en español y piensa que su español es malo, pero no. Entonces por eso prefiere hablar español con nosotros, porque así aprende el español. Pero por nuestra parte pues nos perjudica porque no practicamos zapoteco.

Student 3 Actually up until now they [my parents] keep addressing [me] in Spanish. We very rarely speak in Zapotec, or when we start a conversation my mom speaks to me in Zapotec and I answer in Spanish. So maybe I don't speak to her in Zapotec because I'm worried to make a mistake, that I won't say a word well.

HDK You're more comfortable in Spanish?

Student 3 In Spanish, yes. Yes, she [my mother] sometimes prefers that I speak to her in Spanish because– since my mom sells in the market, so there her daily life is Zapotec, Zapotec. She never speaks Spanish, except when she's in the house with us. So when she needs to go to the bank or another place it's in Spanish and she thinks that her Spanish is bad, but no [it's not]. So for that she prefers to speak Spanish with us, because she learns Spanish that way. But for us, well it harms us because we don't practice Zapotec.

(Interview November 2014)

Both the student and his mother experience insecurity with language, whether in relation to Zapotec or to Spanish. While he is worried about making a mistake when using Zapotec, his mother fears how she may be judged when speaking Spanish in the bank or other public spaces. Although he comments that she is wrong to believe her Spanish is bad, that it is not in fact bad, he does not extend the same recognition to himself and his abilities in Zapotec. A 'parallel monolingual' ideology, whereby multilinguals are expected to speak each language in a monolingual mode with no mixing (Heller 1999), is widespread in the Isthmus, among both older and younger generations.

The uncertainty that young speakers navigate is represented in a meme circulated in October 2013 by a popular public Facebook page dedicated to cultural issues in the Isthmus (Figure 13). In this meme, a recycled image of Kermit the frog gazing off into the distance is labelled with a text in Spanish and Isthmus Zapotec, which reads in English as "Sometimes I would like to show off/ put on screen that I know how to speak Zapotec. But then I remember that I only know how to say 'eat shit' [in Zapotec] . . . And I let it go." This quip recycles a frame from other memes of varying topics: "*Aveces quisiera X, pero luego Y y se me pasa.*" [Sometimes I would like X, but then Y and I let it go/ I get over it].

Figure 13: '*Aveces quisiera apantallar que se hablar zapoteco . . .*' meme.

This meme elicited many shares and laughing comments, including comments of other words that might make up a basic Zapotec vocabulary, including *'guchachi'* [iguana] or *'guetabingue'* [a local kind of shrimp and corn dough dumpling]. While the creator of this meme took a humorous approach to the topic, the discourse that a person's communicative repertoire is not adequate to claim that they are a speaker of Zapotec is clearly recognized by many viewers. This is a common challenge in minoritized language communities. Young speakers' insecurity or perceived illegitimacy has been noted and discussed from the artic regions of North America, Europe, and Russia (Johansen 2010; Meek 2010; Wyman 2012; Ferguson 2019), to southern France and the Basque country (Urla 2012; Costa 2015), and many other places in between. Muehlmann (2008) has described a similar dynamic in a Cucapá community in northern Mexico, where younger generations are faced with an essentialized notion of what it means to be an Indigenous language speaker, a category from which they are largely excluded. In the Isthmus, being a 'Zapotec speaker' is not quite as restricted as the situation described by Muehlmann where only a small minority of the community are recognized to speak the Indigenous language, however it is still far from straightforward, and is influenced by the presence of multiple regional dialects as well as intergenerational change.

In a higher education context, monolingual ideologies are typically compounded by the standard language ideology which has characterized Spanish and other European languages in education. Standard ideologies of language promote a supposedly neutral, universal form of language as the norm– even when no such norm is possible (Milroy and Milroy 1999; Gal 2006). Most minoritized languages have not gone through the nation-state sponsored process of standardization, yet standard language ideologies are often pervasive in minority language education and reclamation movements (Costa, De Korne, and Lane 2017). Quechua scholar-activist Serafín Coronel-Molina (2015) critiques how efforts to produce standards and coin new words for Quechua are a central focus of the High Academy of the Quechua Language in Peru, yet are pursued largely in isolation from speakers and everyday language use. He points out that a standardization effort that is disconnected from everyday speakers tends not to be successful "since not only does it not have the support of the speech community, but often the community is not even aware of it" (2015: 212). This can create a double-bind for members of minoritized speech communities, who may be criticized for lacking authority and accuracy in an idealized pure or standard variety, while on the other hand they may be criticized for lacking authenticity if they adhere to a top-down norm or a degree of purism that is not in everyday use in the community (Gal and Woolard 2001; Woolard 2008). Education initiatives, while aiming to promote the use of minoritized languages, may delegitimize or leave out certain communication practices and speakers when shaped by purist, monolingual, or standard language ideologies (Heller and Martin-Jones 2001; Urla et al. 2017).

At the same time, education initiatives can have significant positive impacts on the trajectories and well-being of Indigenous or minority youth, as examined in chapter 4. Scholars have discussed the importance of approaching minority language education through additive bi/multilingualism and multiliteracies (Lambert 1975; Martin-Jones and Jones 2001). When endangered language communities have the authority to define what successful learning and revitalization is for themselves (Leonard 2012, 2017; Davis 2019) and to develop a community of practice which is inclusive of learners (Hermes and Engman 2017; Weinberg and De Korne 2016), endangered language education has been shown to have many positive results.

Students, teachers, and administrators engaging in the teaching and learning of Zapotec in higher education must navigate both the expectations and norms of the local speech community in the Isthmus and those of additional language learning as an academic discipline, neither of which have traditionally been very comfortable with multilingualism. In the following section I examine how the administrators and teachers of the Tehuantepec Faculty of Languages made strategic choices which went against the grain of devaluing Indigenous languages and valuing standard, monolingual communication. Their practices as education authorities and language policy arbiters created a space where multilingual youth could gain a new, more positive perspective on their communicative repertoires and in some cases identify as speakers of Isthmus Zapotec when they previously preferred to erase this part of their repertoire.

5.2 Language activism in the Tehuantepec Faculty of Languages

European languages, and particularly English, have traditionally been the focus of the educational offerings of the UABJO Faculty of Languages, both in the central campus in Oaxaca City, and in the branch campus in Tehuantepec. The Bachelor program offered in Tehuantepec since the branch campus was founded in 2000 was originally called *Idiomas extranjeras con especialización en inglés* [Foreign languages with a specialization in English], and was renamed *Enseñanza de Idiomas* [Language Teaching/ Learning] in 2012 as part of a wider shift in management within the Faculty. Even within the new BA program, English was a required subject for all 4 years of the program, although more space was created for a required additional 'optional' language (depending on availability, usually

French or Italian). In the public courses offered at various levels, including courses directed at children and at adults, English was also the most common course offered, again with French and Italian as possible options if enrollment was high enough. In the words of Ximena Léon Fernández, the coordinator of public courses in 2013–2016 and a former graduate of the Faculty's BA program, for most of the Faculty's existence, "*inglés era el rey*" [English was king] (Interview July 2014). In this way, the language hierarchy in the Faculty reflected the coloniality of the language hierarchy in the region, and in Mexico more generally.

Although influenced by trends in the central campus in Oaxaca City, the Tehuantepec campus exists in a very different language ecology and socio-economic context. Not many of the students in the Tehuantepec campus were fortunate enough to take classes with Mario López Gopar, the professor Kiara describes in the opening citation, who is a prolific scholar and advocate of Indigenous rights and inclusive education, and teaches primarily in the Oaxaca City campus. While the Oaxaca City campus is home to the *Cuerpo académico en Lingüística Aplicada Crítica* [Research group on critical applied linguistics] lead by López Gopar, and benefits from the resources of the state's capital city, the Tehuantepec campus is a 5.5-hour bus ride away from the city. The focus in Tehuantepec has always been on providing basic language and teaching courses in a region with few higher education offerings, with most of the teachers at the Faculty holding Bachelor degrees in English or Education, and often being graduates of the Faculty itself. The Tehuantepec Faculty of Languages offers the BA program in both a full-time and a weekend-based part-time program, as well as individual language courses for the general public on evenings and weekends. There are numerous other higher education institutions in the Isthmus, none of which specialize in languages. There are no programs dedicated to the study of Isthmus Zapotec, although several institutions have engaged in various projects related to Diidxazá from perspectives of tourism, education, and technology development. Within this context, it was significant when the Tehuantepec Faculty of Languages initiated two Diidxazá classes as public weekend classes in February of 2013.

These classes were established through the initiative of Ximena Léon Fernández who became the coordinator of the public courses in late 2012. In the winter semester of 2013 she organized an offering of Diidxazá public courses on Saturdays, opening one group for 'beginners' and one for 'speakers'. The first class in spring 2013 was taught by the director of the cultural center in Juchitán, Vidal Ramirez Pineda. In that first semester many of the students from the BA enrolled, as well as some members of the public. Ximena also ran classes in Ombeayiüts (or Huave, an Indigenous language from the coast of the Isthmus), in 2014 but low enrollment levels meant that the class did not continue. Ximena collaborated with the coordinator of the BA program, Omelino Santos Medina, in order to establish Diidxazá as a possible 'optional' language in the BA program, so that students could have it as one of the languages that they would be certified to teach when they completed the program. In autumn of 2015, the Isthmus Zapotec class offerings expanded to encourage more students in the Bachelor's program to study Diidxazá. Several teachers have taught the classes, including Carlos Celaya Gómez, Didiert Hernández Martinez, Anaxhiely Osorio Sanchez, Leticia Gutierrez Pacheco, Margarito Vicente Santiago, Sergio Acevedo, and other students doing their teaching practicum (as discussed further in section 5.2.2). Zapotec has also been included in the summer programs offered for children and adolescents since 2014, often taught by teaching practicum students enrolled in the BA.

In 2017 the Faculty supported a proposal from an adjunt lecturer, Bania García Sanchez, to host a '*Café Literario*' (Literary Café) focusing on the literature from the Isthmus, using bilingual versions in Spanish and Zapotec, with discussion mainly in Spanish. This was offered first as an extra-credit activity for BA students, and then due to its popularity it became a public course that BA students could enroll in. Bania began collaborating with Faculty employee Mónica Esteva García, who brought in a focus on '*rescate de zapoteco*', [reclamation of Zapotec] into the course as well. Isthmus Zapotec has thus come to be present in the Faculty course offerings in various ways in recent years through initiatives such as these.

Throughout the process of establishing Isthmus Zapotec as part of the curricular offerings at the Faculty, numerous challenges have arisen, which the administrators and teachers have attempted to address. The well-established prejudice against Indigenous languages and the standard language ideologies in society and in Mexican higher education at large remain a reoccurring challenge, and enrollment levels in Indigenous language courses have at times been low. Additionally, the investment in educating Indigenous language teachers– while in many ways simultaneously defining the characteristics of the identity category of 'Isthmus Zapotec teacher'– has been a long-term and complicated undertaking. In the following sections, I highlight several of their most salient strategies, including *representing* Indigenous languages and speakers positively, *creating* space for Zapotec within the high-status space of the university, and *creating* Indigenous language teachers. Many people have participated in initiatives in various ways, and it is unfortunately not possible to provide an exhaustive description of all people and events that have helped to increase the status and presence of Isthmus Zapotec at the Tehuantepec Faculty of Languages. In the following sections, I highlight and analyze some of the initiatives and people working within the Faculty that

I observed and came to know between 2013 and 2018 in order to illustrate the key changes underway.

5.2.1 Representing legitimate languages and multilingual identities

Due to its location in the center of Tehuantepec, a town at the crossroads of multiple Indigenous language communities, the Faculty of Languages has always had students who are speakers of Indigenous languages, especially Zapotec. Ximena Léon Fernández recounted that when she began as a student in the Bachelor's program in 2010 the presence of Zapotec speakers was common, but it was not considered "relevant" for the activities of the Faculty.

> Ximena *Nunca fue algo relevante en la facultad, ¿no? Ya que la licenciatura era una licenciatura en lengua extranjera con especialidad en inglés, nunca fue relevante que tuviéramos, como siempre he habido, alumnos que hablaran zapoteco.*
>
> It was never something relevant in the Faculty, right? Since the Bachelor's was a Bachelor's in foreign languages with specialization in English, it was never relevant that we had, as there has always been, students who speak Zapotec.
>
> (Interview July 2014)

A unitary focus on the target language of English was pursued without interest for the languages that students already had in their repertoires. The notion that the students' existing abilities could serve as resources for them in learning English or any other language was not prevalent at that time.

Ximena is an exuberant, energetic teacher and coordinator, known for her colorful outfits, love of theater and the arts, and ambitious pursuit of growth and quality in the Faculty. She worked as an English teacher in central Mexico for many years before moving to the Isthmus to live with her extended family and pursue her Bachelor's degree. Although she grew up primarily in Mexico City, her family's origin in the Isthmus is meaningful to her, and she is proud to have roots there. She had heard her grandmother using some Zapotec words interspersed in their Spanish conversations throughout her life, and knew that her great-grandparents spoke Zapotec as their primary language. She had always been curious about this heritage, and became increasingly interested when she moved to the Isthmus as an adult and began studying in the Bachelor's program. Remembering that time, she said:

> Ximena *Siendo estudiante solamente de la facultad, era un interrogante, vamos, que había tenido, una pregunta que me había hecho; que ¿por qué no había cursos de zapoteco en la Facultad de Idiomas de Tehuantepec? Pues una vez que estuve en la posición de hacerlo, dije lo primero que tengo que hacer es eso.*

> As just a student in the Faculty, it was a question, well, that I had had, a question that I had asked myself; why weren't there Zapotec classes in the Faculty of Languages of Tehuantepec? Well, once I was in the position to do it, I said the first thing that I have to do is that. (Interview July 2014)

Ximena described the inclusion of Zapotec in the Faculty as more of an instinct than a rational plan; she had a feeling that this should be part of what a higher education institution in the Isthmus would provide. She articulated this stongly, stating that: "*La facultad tiene la responsabilidad de preservar la lengua aquí, ¿no? De preservarlo de la forma que debe ser, lo que es teniendo cursos, de manera constante, de manera permanente*" [The Faculty has the responsibility to preserve the language here, right? To preserve it in the way that it should, which is holding classes, in an constant way, in a permanent way] (Interview July 2014). This conviction that Indigenous languages should be included (and preserved) within the enduring structure of the institution continued to motivate her as she introduced, and later struggled to support, this fledgling initiative. She began with the area of the Faculty under her control, the weekend and evening courses open to the public, and began offering 2 sections of Diidxazá on Saturdays in 2013. These classes were open to both students in the Bachelor program and members of the public. She expanded courses to include an Ombeayiüts (Huave) class when she found that there were students in the Bachelor's program who were speakers of Ombeayiüts and interested in teaching it.

The Diidxazá classes attracted the interest of a sizable group of over a dozen students the first semester they were offered. Some of the participating students had Diidxazá competence and were interested in learning how to write and other formal aspects of the language, while others were new to the language and interested in learning the basics. One of the students from Tehuantepec, whose grandparents had spoken Zapotec but who had not grown up with much exposure to the language, told me that he thought learning a 'mother tongue' would be useful in applying for scholarships. Other students were interested in being able to communicate in Zapotec in the local environment, such as the market, or with their grandparents. One of the members of the public who enrolled in the course was a middle-aged man who worked in a school and described his motivation as rooted in his family heritage:

> Student 4 *Aunque he vivido aquí en la región, yo nací en la región, mi mamá hablaba zapoteco, mis abuelos hablaban zapoteco, pero yo no aprendí el zapoteco. Lo escuché. Porque en el lugar donde yo vivía, no se hablaba el zapoteco [. . .] Siempre había tenido la inquietud de estudiarlo no, en conocerlo. Pienso que por el hecho de venir de familia que habla el zapoteco se me puede facilitar a mí, y entonces fue que me decidí a estudiar el zapoteco.*

> Although I have lived here in the region, I was born here in the region, my mother spoke Zapotec, my grandparents spoke Zapotec, but I didn't learn Zapotec. I heard it. Because in the place where I lived Zapotec wasn't spoken. [. . .] I always had the impulse/ desire to study it, right, to know it. I think that due to coming from a family that speaks Zapotec it can make it easier for me, and so I decided to study Zapotec.
> (Interview October 2013)

This student found it convenient to come to Saturday classes, and to build on the knowledge he already had of Zapotec. Although he had "always had the impulse to study it", this was the first time he was participating in a Zapotec class because he had never found an opportunity before.

While students generally appreciated the classes, there were also frustrations, in particular in relation to the lack of a set curriculum, the different levels mixed together in class, and the issue of dialect diversity. The varying levels of background knowledge and varying expectations of the participating students presented the teachers with a steep challenge. As discussed in chapter 2, there are 4 regionally-recognized varieties of Isthmus Zapotec. Tehuantepec itself is one of the areas of the region where language shift towards Spanish is most advanced, and speakers of Zapotec from Tehuantepec are typically in their 70s or above. However, the adjacent village of San Blas Atempa is characterized by active Zapotec use. For some students, the appropriate dialect to teach in Tehuantepec would be the dialect of San Blas, which is close to that of Tehuantepec. Many Isthmus Zapotec activists and writers have been speakers of the Juchitán dialect, the variety which has the most speakers due to its use in the city of Juchitán and several surrounding villages. This is also the variety that aligns most closely with the *alfabeto popular*, the writing system that is the generally-accepted standard for Isthmus Zapotec (see section 2.5 and chapter 6). The first teacher employed by the Faculty of Languages was from Juchitán; although he made efforts to include dialect diversity into his teaching, this was also an area of dissatisfaction among some students. A student from San Blas commented that she appreciated the efforts to include other varieties, but it was still a source of frustration for her:

> Student 5   Lo que nos enseña más que nada es el zapoteco, la variante de Juchitán. Sí nos dice, no, de repente, 'esta palabra se dice así en Juchitán pero en tal lugar se dice así y en otro tal lugar se dice así' y . . . Quizá es como también una necesidad mía el aprender la variante de mi pueblo y . . . Quizá mí mismo cuerpo se resiste un poquito, no.

What he teaches us mainly is Zapotec, the variety from Juchitán. Yes he tells us, right, suddenly/unpredictably, 'this word is said this way in Juchitán but in such a place it is said this way and in another place it is said this way' and . . . Maybe it is like also a need I have to learn the variety of my village and . . . Maybe even my body is resisting a little bit, right.

(Interview October 2013)

When many students are learning for personal heritage motivations, or to be able to speak with elderly members of their community, the question of which variety is being taught takes on a heightened importance. Although most of the teachers I have observed in the Isthmus attempt to give value to all varieties, this is difficult to put into practice in the classroom.

At the same time, students arrive in class with expectations formed by standard language ideologies, and some would like the teacher to choose one variety to teach. The view that there is one right way to speak or write each word in a language is common in the Spanish and English classes that they have taken, and comes to influence their expectations for learning Zapotec. While some students commented in interviews that they believe the variety of San Blas/ Tehuantepec should be taught for geographical reasons, others commented that they wanted to learn the variety of Juchitán because it has the highest profile in the media, publishing, and is used in more places. This compounded the already-difficult challenge of teaching students with a wide range in prior knowledge. The study whose "body was resisting" learning the Juchitán variety had a high level of comprehension, and could be described as a fluent listener. However, when it came to a written vocabulary test that the teacher gave towards the end of the semester, the student had one of the lower scores in the class and dropped out of the class the following semester. The multi-variety, multi-level nature of the Isthmus Zapotec speech community – and of the students arriving in the class – presented a challenge which teachers at the UABJO continue to work with. The non-standard nature of Diidxazá, and lack of a fixed curriculum, made it harder for this language to be included in the institutional structure of the Faculty in the same way that English, French and Italian were included.

Despite these challenges, the presence of the Diidxazá classes had an effect on students and teachers in the Faculty. As Ximena observed "*El simple hecho de saber en la Facultad había un grupo de zapoteco, empezó a generar un cambio en la gente no, un cambio de actitud ante la lengua*" [The simple fact of knowing that there was a class group in Zapotec in the Faculty started to generate a change in people, a change in attitude towards the language] (Interview July 2014). She argued that this change was significant, even if only a minority of students were choosing to enroll in the classes. Posters advertising courses listed Zapotec (and for a time, Huave) alongside French and English, and Ximena endeavored to promote Zapotec courses prominently in the hopes of increasing enrollment. Figure 14 shows her conducting publicity for the Faculty of Languages by handing out flyers and coupons for 100 pesos off enrollment in Zapotec classes in a public park in the center of Juchitán. The banner advertises the "Autonomous Benito Juárez University of Oaxaca; Faculty of Languages; Campus Tehuantepec; Bachelor's degree in Language Teaching/ Learning; Semester courses; Summer courses; Intensive courses; Zapotec; English; French; Italian; Spanish". Listing Zapotec first in publicity was a strategic choice that Ximena hoped would help to make the classes visible and raise the status of the language, even though in practice there was a much larger demand for English classes.

Figure 14: Ximena Léon Fernández distributing flyers in a public park in Juchitán to promote UABJO courses (photo February 2014).

The Literary Café initiated and run by Bania García Sanchez and Mónica Esteva García, and supported by the coordinators, was another reflection of the wider acceptance and interest in Indigenous languages within the Faculty. Bania and

Mónica are both from parts of the Isthmus where Spanish is dominant, and both grew up using primarily Spanish in families with Zapotec heritage. They completed Bachelor's degrees outside of the Isthmus, and Bania additionally completed a Master's degree where she researched Isthmus Zapotec oral traditions. Mónica conducted research on language shift in Tehuantepec for her Bachelor thesis (García 2020). Both young women have been learning Isthmus Zapotec and have participated in a variety of different classes and workshops; Mónica was among the students in the 2nd semester of the public course in 2013 when she first returned to the Isthmus to conduct research for her Bachelor's thesis and continued to participate in Zapotec classes in the Faculty of Languages and elsewhere. Focused and outgoing, they both aimed to conduct further graduate study (and are both doing so as I write) and to continue working on language issues in the Isthmus. Bania and Mónica were in their 20s when running the class; they fit in with the Bachelor students at the Faculty and spent time socializing with students. Based on their experiences in other Zapotec classes, and their areas of expertise, they developed a unique approach for their own class which aimed to be attractive to a wider range of students than the language classes had been. Their class on bilingual Isthmus literature aimed to challenge the coloniality of literature studies at Mexican universities, which typically hold up European authors and Mexican Spanish authors as those who produce "literature". They wanted to bring attention to the literary heritage of the Isthmus (see also chapter 6) and Isthmus Zapotec by having students read and discuss bilingual texts. They commented that the topic of literature was attractive to some students who were not interested in learning the language, but who might develop an interest through the avenue of poetry and stories. They saw this as complementary with the Zapotec-as-subject classes already offered in the Faculty, as Bania commented:

> Bania El taller está ayudando mucho a entender este otra parte del zapoteco, que no solo es digamos saber aprenderlo, escribirlo, sino que tiene, este, más vertientes, más cosas a fondo. Creo que se esta complementando mucho.
>
> The workshop [Literary Café] is really helping to understand that other part of Zapotec, that isn't just, let's say, knowing how to learn it, how to write it, but rather that has, um, more sides, more things deep down. I believe it is complementing [language classes] a lot. (Interview January 2018)

Their class attracted a respectable amount of interest from students, including some who spoke Diidxazá and many who did not. Bania noted that the focus on literature and giving undergraduate students credit for the course were good strategies, because they also drew in students who were not previously interested in

Indigenous language or literature, some of whom became more engaged through the class. Mónica brought a focus on '*rescate de zapoteco*', reclamation of Zapotec, to the class, and when Bania moved to pursue a PhD in Linguistic Anthropology in autumn 2018, Mónica continued to teach the class for another year in collaboration with other members of the Faculty, and eventually with an expert language teacher from the nearby town of San Blas, Antonio Ortíz.

The successful representation of Indigenous languages as legitimate in the academic space involved explicit changes in the policies and practices of that space, in combination with a shift in perception among members of the Faculty community. Issues such as dialect diversity, lack of formal curricula, and low enrollment due to the prioritization of other languages continued to challenge the initiatives within the faculty, but clear positive results have been achieved. Aside from representing Indigenous languages on a par with European languages, another key strategy within the Tehuantepec Faculty of Languages has been attempts to support the education of potential future Indigenous language teachers. Considering that many people in the Isthmus would share Kiara Ríos Ríos's former view that Zapotec is "not for teaching" (as cited in the opening of this chapter), it is not surprising that there are few people who identify themselves as Zapotec teachers and little discussion of what characteristics a Zapotec teacher should possess. The next section discusses how teachers at the Tehuantepec Faculty have tried to help normalize this particular identity category.

5.2.2 Creating Isthmus Zapotec teachers

The lack of teachers, or lack of well-prepared teachers, is a common lament among minority language activists (Blair, Pelly, and Starr 2018). An expertise in language does not always translate into an expertise in teaching, depending on the interests and needs of the learners. In the case of the Faculty of Languages, the need to employ someone who would be willing to take on a few hours a week of teaching (far from a full-time job), make their own curriculum and exam plans and source all their own learning materials, was understandably challenging at times. Additionally, the students at the Faculty come from across the Isthmus, representing different Isthmus Zapotec dialects, and some with strong opinions about which dialects should be taught at the Faculty, as discussed in the previous section. The issue of recruiting and retaining qualified teachers was on-going throughout the first years of the program. Although the initial strategy was to hire a recognized language expert (even when they lacked a teaching background), the administrators soon saw the importance of investing in the pedagogical quality of the classes, and began to explore other options.

The semester after the first class opened, I attended an event where students in the second year of the BA Bachelor program presented a variety of learning activities and resources as part of a class on *Recursos Didácticos* [Didactic Resources]. The students were asked to make learning materials for one of the main languages studied at the Faculty, and they had divided themselves into groups, focusing on English, Italian, and French, respectively. However, in this cohort for the first time there was a group who had asked – and been granted permission – to make materials in Diidxazá, which at that time was not considered a main language of study at the Faculty. I interviewed the teacher, Manuel David Ramírez Medina, about how the use of Zapotec in his class began. Manuel David is soft spoken and tall, and receives both respect and affection from students as I observed on many occasions. He is not originally from the Isthmus, but has lived there for many years, working in the areas of didactics and English teaching. Personally, and as a teacher, he takes a positive stance towards regional languages, expressing interest in learning Zapotec, although Spanish is the dominant everyday language in the part of the Isthmus where he lives and works.

HDK *Y, ¿cómo, cómo pasó que--- pues yo sé que en tu clase de, de este semestre pasado los alumnos se pusieron a elaborar materiales didácticos en zapoteco. ¿Podrías contarme cómo surgió este proyecto?*

Manuel David *La materia en sí se llama recursos didácticos, estrategias y recursos didácticos y me piden [enseñar] la elaboración de material didáctico. Se supone está orientado a inglés, francés o italiano. Entonces, eh, Carlos, Carlos Gómez levanta la mano y me dice: ¿podríamos hacerlo en zapoteco? y a mí se me ocurre: sí, adelante. Háganlo en zapoteco. No fue algo planeado, fue así de, de improviso. Ya después comentando con [los coordinadores] Omelino y con Ximena decían: es que ahorita ya también estamos tratando de hacer todo el proyecto para [que] el zapoteco tenga el mismo peso que los demás idiomas políticamente fuertes. Entonces fue que ya les empecé a abrir más la puerta en cuanto a elaboración de todo el tipo de material en zapoteco que ellos quisieran . . . en parte para este, que ellos se sientan cómodos con el material que están trabajando, porque para ellos es más cómodo trabajar en zapoteco que trabajar en inglés. Entonces esa fue principalmente la, la causa, la petición de un alumno.*

HDK *¿Ah, sí? Eh, en los años que llevas trabajando aquí, ¿ningún alumno antes había mostrado un interés?*

Manuel David *No. No en la elaboración de material. Sí habíamos tenido algunos que hablan zapoteco, y este--- pero ni uno de ellos se había interesado en enseñarlo o en elaborar algo en zapoteco. Es la primera vez que me encuentro con eso.*

HDK	And how, how did it happen that--- well I know that in your class in, in um this past semester the students started to make didactic materials in Zapotec. Could you tell me how this project emerged?
Manuel David	The subject itself is called didactic resources, strategies and didactic resources, and I'm asked [to teach] the creation of didactic material. Supposedly it's oriented to English, French or Italian. So eh, Carlos, Carlos Gómez raises his hand and says to me: could we do it in Zapotec? And it occurs to me: Yes, go ahead. Do it in Zapotec. It wasn't something planned, it was like that, improvised. Then afterwards talking with [the coordinators] Omelino and with Ximena they said: actually now also we're trying to make a whole project so [that] Zapotec would have the same weight as the other politically strong languages. So that was when I started to open the door to them in terms of creation of all of the kinds of materal in Zapotec that they wanted . . . In part so um, that they feel comfortable with the material that they're working on, because for them it's more comfortable to work in Zapotec than to work in English. So that was primarily the, the cause, the request of a student.
HDK	Oh yes? Ah, in the years that you have been working here, no student before had shown an interest?
Manuel David	No. Not in the creation of didactic material. Yes we've had some students who speak Zapotec, and um--- but not one of them had been interested in teaching it or in making something in Zapotec. It's the first time that I find that. (Interview January 2014)

As a teacher, Manuel David wanted his students to "feel comfortable with the material that they're working on", so as to have a better chance of succeeding in their studies. He acknowledged that having students who speak Indigenous languages was not new, but the interest to include them in certain academic activities of the Faculty alongside European languages was novel. His response to his students' interest, alongside the existing initiative in the Faculty to provide Zapotec classes, helped to raise the visibility and acceptance towards Indigenous languages in the Faculty. Alongside the coordinators, he acted as an arbiter of language policy change through supporting the students' interests.

The coordinators of the public courses, the BA Bachelor program, and motivated teachers such as Manuel David, talked together about how to make the most of the interests and abilities of the Bachelor students as a possible resource for teaching Diixdazá and other languages. The Bachelor program required the students to do dozens of hours of teaching practice, and the coordinators agreed that one way to help make the Indigenous language courses sustainable would be encouraging upper-level Bachelor students to take on teaching and developing curricula for Indigenous language classes. They could then receive credit for these efforts to help meet the requirements of their program and help them towards graduation at the same time.

Four Bachelor students representing 2 different dialects took up the invitation to teach the class as a group in winter 2014. It was their first time in front of a class. None of them had had Zapotec as part of their schooling, rather they used it to varying degrees in their homes and communities. Although they were clearly nervous when they began teaching, over time they acquired both more confidence and more expertise. They applied the pedagogical techniques they had learned through the Bachelor program in order to make the class interactive, with students asked to create their own learning materials, songs, and dialogues. Figure 15 shows students and teachers sharing an end-of-semester potluck meal, after having played some of the games that the students themselves created, and singing songs accompanied by one of the students on his guitar. The student-teachers were pleased with the progress of their students and with their interest in Diidxazá. They worked with a senior language expert to develop some of their lesson plans and to check words that they were not certain of. They also aimed to teach both the variety of Juchitán and the variety of San Blas/ Tehuantepec, benefiting from speakers of these 2 varieties in the teaching team. Although the student-teachers brought in a variety of games, songs and interactive exercises, they also maintained a strong focus on writing, often presenting material on the board for the students to copy.

Figure 15: Students and teachers sharing a meal at the end of the semester (photo July 2014).

The team of teachers had explicitly decided to include both varieties in the class, however this was very challenging in practice. As one of the teachers of the smaller, San Blas variety commented when asked about some of the things that were difficult as a new teacher:

> Student teacher *A veces era difícil enseñar a las personas--- es que se va pronunciar así y se escribe así pero en el momento que . . . .lo pronunciaba ese [un maestro de Juchitán], pues si sonaba bien, con la escritura. Pero en la forma en que yo pronunciaba como que no, no iba. [. . .] Era como algo difícil, a mí, a mí me sigue costando trabajo, trabajar con la escritura que tiene los de Juchitán. Que ellos son los que ya lo establecieron ¿no? Es como que muy difícil.*
>
> Sometimes it was difficult to teach people– you pronounce it like this and it's written like this, but at the moment when . . . [the Juchitán teacher] pronounces it, well yes it sounded good, with the writing. But the way that I pronounced, like it didn't . . . it didn't go. [. . .] It was like something difficult for me, for me it still requires a lot of work, to work with the writing that the people from Juchitán have. That they're the ones that already established it, right? It's like really difficult.
>
> (Interview July 2014)

The prominence of the Juchitán variety in the existing written materials was a challenge as this teacher worked to make their variety of Zapotec understood and legitimate within the class. The writing-focused pedagogy in the class made this additionally difficult for the team of teachers, who struggled with their desire to write "correctly" and to include different varieties, when they had previously used Diidxazá orally and had been schooled only in Spanish through their entire educational trajectories. The student-teachers were given feedback by Ximena and myself, and made significant progress in expanding their pedagogical approaches and becoming comfortable as teachers, although they continued to be challenged by the task of meeting the expectations of a varied student group and making space for multiple dialects in the classroom.

In autumn of 2014 I organized a trip for four of the junior teachers to visit two Indigenous language teachers in Oaxaca City (whose classes I had previously observed and admired), as well as a linguistic library and the *Centro de Estudios y Desarrollo de Lenguas Indígenas de Oaxaca* [Center for the Study and Development of Indigenous Languages of Oaxaca, CEDELIO], strategizing that personal observation, exchange, and a bit of big city glamour might be more helpful and motivating in their development as Zapotec teachers than written and oral feedback from myself and Ximena had been. When visiting the Research Library Juan de Córdova, the librarian had kindly pulled out books relevant to the Isthmus for them to look at, which they dove into eagerly. They commented on how surprised they were to see so many books in Diidxazá, far more than they had ever seen in the Isthmus, and they appeared genuinely excited, taking many photos of pages with their phones. The librarian told them they would be welcome to visit the library anytime. One young man, while paging through a copy of *Mexico South* by Miguel Covarrubias suddenly commented that this was the first book he had ever had a personal desire to read. The visits to other Zapotec classes and the CEDELIO seemed largely successful, as the junior teachers enthusiastically met with other Indigenous language professionals during the trip, and afterwards expressed their inspiration and desire to make their own professional Isthmus Zapotec syllabus.

This, and other positive reactions, made me feel that the strategy of improving the UABJO Zapotec program through fostering competent and motivated teachers (as opposed to writing a curriculum for them) was at least partially effective. The strategy to connect young teachers with potential colleagues and role models seemed helpful in supporting their professional development. Observing and accompanying this program over several years made it clear to me that competent teachers are necessary for a structural change to be sustained and accepted by all members of the institution. In educational efforts for minority language equality, teachers are an invaluable resource. Minoritized language teachers often have extra challenges, including dealing with the language-internal diversity that is the norm in non-standardized, Indigenous language communities, being creative in making or adapting materials, and facilitating an engaging learning environment where students can build communicative competence and confidence, while managing the insecurity and hurt that may have been part of being a minoritized language speaker or learner.

Although a majority of students at the Faculty of Languages continued to choose to focus on European languages, and only a small group of Bachelor students have participated as Zapotec student-teachers, this is an important change in comparison with the European language-only norm that was in place in the Faculty in the past. Ximena argued that these changes were not token gestures in favor of Indigenous languages, but carried an important symbolic and practical weight:

> Ximena No importa si lo chicos estudian 4 años de inglés, 2 de francés y 1 de italiano, y que no llevan zapoteco como materia obligatoria en la carrera, no; importa el hecho de que ellos saben hoy por hoy que aunque así sean sus estudios, ellos pueden dedicarse o hacer su proyecto de titulación o su servicio social exclusivamente en zapoteco se así lo desean. Eso es algo que no sucediera con ninguna circunstancia [antes].
>
> It doesn't matter if the students study 4 years of English, 2 of French and 1 of Italian, and that they don't take Zapotec as a mandatory subject in the program, right; it matters that they know right now that even if their studies are like that,

> they can dedicate or do their graduation project or the social service entirely in Zapotec if that is what they want. That is something that didn't happen under any circumstance [before]. (Interview July 2014)

For students like Kiara Ríos Ríos, quoted in the opening of the chapter, simply being acknowledged as Indigenous language speakers and coming to see this as a positive thing within an educational institution was a significant change. The ability to gain academic credit for work related to Zapotec was an additional important strategy which the Faculty administrators and teachers used in order to change the ideological and practical hierarchy of languages within the Faculty. Although European languages still maintained a high visibility (and were of genuine interest for many *Istmeño* students, keen to learn about other cultures and languages) local languages were no longer made invisible or viewed as irrelevant within higher education.

5.3 Summary: Characteristics of higher education activism

Language activism within higher education has significant potential to dismantle the coloniality and Eurocentrism of the traditional curriculum, and to support new legitimate, high-status identities for Indigenous language speakers as experts and teachers. Additionally, changing the bureaucracy to create new spaces or structures may be more achievable within a higher education institution than within primary and secondary schooling (although it is never straightforward), as discussed in chapter 4. A less-centralized curriculum and relatively fewer layers of bureaucracy can make it easier for teachers and arbiters in higher education to enact changes in what is taught or how teaching occurs. In all formal education contexts, negotiating standard language ideologies in order to teach a language with several accepted variants remains a challenge. The efforts of the coordinators and teachers at the UABJO Faculty of Languages made meaningful changes through normalizing the presence of Indigenous language classes, getting more people involved in teaching them, and providing professional development to Indigenous language teachers. The key language activism strategies in this context are schematized in Table 4. Through representing Indigenous languages and younger speakers as legitimate within the higher education institution, the UABJO has made an impact on the perceptions of future language teachers, whether they speak an Indigenous language or not. The creation of spaces for learning and/ or teaching Indigenous languages within the structure of the university, recognized by university credit, helped to establish a more positive representation, as well as to develop actual language and teaching competence.

Indigenous language teachers have numerous challenges, and connecting them with role models as well as with resources went a small way towards meeting some of these challenges.

Table 4: Key language activism strategies in higher education in the Isthmus.

Actions →	Goals →	Examples
– Representing	– Communication practices – People/ Identities	– Indigenous languages represented as legitimate in higher education – Young speakers represented as legitimate and capable of teaching
– Creating	– Spaces/ Structures	– Indigenous language classes for credit; Teaching practicum in Indigenous language as part of existing BA structure
– Creating	– People/ Identities	– Institutionally certified Indigenous language teachers
– Connecting	– People/ Identities – Resources	– Young teachers introduced to experienced teachers – Young teachers introduced to books and materials

In relation to the characteristics of these strategies, they were carried out primarily at the local level of the Faculty of Languages with little wider visibility, although trends and discourses from national and international sources were also drawn upon discursively in promoting Indigenous language classes. The structural change of including Indigenous languages for credit was also a slow, long-term effort, that required on-going trouble-shooting and adjusting over time. Although the teachers working in this context aimed for a somewhat syncretic approach, by including multiple dialects, the standard language ideology that dominates in education settings exerted a purist influence. As with the activism initiatives in primary and secondary school, the ability for motivated individuals to propose some form of action which was then accepted and supported by the institution was key in this setting. The institutional setting did not allow for fully open participation, but it was flexible enough to allow for new initiatives to emerge and to be integrated into the existing structures.

While there are indications that the changes in perspective and in structures will be sustained at the Tehuantepec Faculty of Languages, there is always a risk that they will not. Returning to the professional-development trip for four student-teachers from Tehuantepec in 2014, described in the section above, it is important to note that the semester after this trip three of the four student-teachers opted to stop teaching Zapotec in order to devote more time to other activities. This does not negate the learning and positive exchanges that occurred, but it does make clear that contextual pressures still go against these language activism efforts. As undergraduate students look to their future employment opportunities, and the score they are required to achieve on the TOEFL test[28] in order to graduate, they may choose to set their work with Zapotec aside no matter how enthusiastic they are about it. Of the numerous students who became involved with Zapotec teaching while studying in the UABJO, many have gone on to work as English teachers or with English in the tourism industry. As a member of the UABJO community of practice they came to value their Zapotec capacities, but when they left the university and entered the job market many of them have oriented towards English as the most immediate source of employment in a difficult economic landscape. The complex links between Indigenous language use, educational success, and professional success put a limitation on the changes that can be achieved within a school, whether primary, secondary, or higher education (Hornberger 2008). Language activism within higher education can extend beyond the walls of the institution, however, as the confident young multilingual professionals who are fostered there become part of the wider language ecology for decades to come.

The coordinators in Tehuantepec have continued to seek and support more new teachers from among the Bachelor students and alumni, viewing this as a crucial area which can make or break the success of the Indigenous language classes in the Faculty. Generating and maintaining enrollment has also been a challenge. In the Oaxaca City campus, Kiara Ríos Ríos, the former Bachelor student quoted in the opening of the chapter, has established a 4-level curriculum of Isthmus Zapotec classes with a healthy enrollment, and other Indigenous languages have been offered on a less-regular basis. Although there have also been challenges in the Oaxaca City campus, the high popularity and effectiveness of Kiara as a teacher is one of the factors which has kept the program running, as well as the strong commitment of the administration (De Korne, López Gopar, and Ríos Ríos 2019). Despite efforts from the coordinators in Tehuantepec, a similar degree of success has been elusive there, where Indigenous

---

28 A standardized test of English as a foreign language which is used extensively in higher education around the world.

languages are in some ways less appealing to students (and student-teachers) because they are so much a part of the everyday. An everyday, which, as discussed in section 5.1, involves denigration of Indigenous language speakers and discouragement of young speakers in particular. This symbolic violence or trauma does not evaporate as soon as young speakers enter a more accepting environment. Even though Bachelor students have become accustomed to the fact that Indigenous languages are valued and part of the curriculum within the Faculty, they continue to face prejudice and ideologies which devalue these languages on their way to and from the Faculty each day.

Language activism that aims to produce a new structure, such as a recognized class or an education system that supports Indigenous language teachers, is slower than the production of some materials or a one-off event, but it has important potential to create more long-term changes. This has also been evidenced in other higher education contexts where groundbreaking choices were made to change educational norms. Just a few examples include the Indigenous teacher education program at PROEIB Andes in Bolivia (Hornberger 2009) and other 'Intercultural Bilingual Education' initiatives in Latin America (Maurial and Suxo 2011), the establishment of the Myaamia Center at Miami University in the United States (Mosley-Howard et al. 2016), and the Indigenous Language Revitalization programs at the University of Victoria, Canada (Czaykowska-Higgins et al. 2017), among others. In order to sustain this process, connections among colleagues across institutional spaces can be helpful in providing role models as well as solidarity and understanding for the challenges that all innovators are likely to face. Here again the importance of arbiters (Johnson 2012), or social actors with a specially-important local position in the chain of language politics, is exemplified in the choices made by key administrators and teachers, and the ways they responded to students' interests. The responsive attitude of the teachers and administrators towards the proposals of students and motivated teachers, such as the Literary Café or the students making Diidxazá materials as a final project, was an important open door in the process of change. If the administrators supported Indigenous languages in a tokenistic way only, these kind of proposals would likely not appear, nor receive tangible support. Ximena recounted that the Tehuantepec Faculty had always had events focused on local culture, and that Zapotec had sometimes been spoken as part of those events, but never outside of them:

> Ximena   *Pero lo hacían [hablaban zapoteco] solo para esos eventos. No recuerdo que mis compañeros, los que hablaban zapoteco dentro del salón, se comunicaran en zapoteco como ahora escucho muchos de los alumnos de la nueva licenciatura que van caminando por los pasillos de la facultad y entre ellos hablan zapoteco, no? No creo que eso succediera tanto en mi época.*

> But they did it [spoke Zapotec] only for those events. I don't remember that my classmates, those that spoke Zapotec in the [cohort], would communicate with each other in Zapotec like now I hear many of the students in the new Bachelor program that go walking through the corridors of the Faculty and between themselves they speak Zapotec, right? I don't believe that that would have happened much in my era [as a student]. (Interview July 2014)

Although Ximena and other higher education language activists have even larger changes as long-term goals – such as establishing Indigenous languages as a curricular requirement, or graduating more Indigenous language teachers – creating a space where young professionals feel confident to use all their languages and where they and their languages are viewed with respect is a laudable achievement.

Chapter 6
Imagining convivial multilingual literacies: Strategies in community-based education

Community-based initiatives outside of government-sponsored education institutions are common in the Isthmus of Tehuantepec, with classes and workshops being held frequently in cultural centers, community libraries, and other civic spaces.[29] A common thread among the community-based or non-formal classes I observed was a focus on literacy and the writing of Isthmus Zapotec, as well as discourses about the value and longevity of Isthmus Zapotec literary traditions. One community-based initiative which exemplifies this is a workshop called *Camino de la Iguana* [Path of the Iguana] created and taught by poet and designer Natalia Toledo and historian, linguist, writer and translator Víctor Cata. Natalia and Víctor are respected and loved writers and cultural figures in their hometown of Juchitán, and have made names for themselves in academic and literary circles throughout Mexico and abroad. On a few occasions I attended events where they gave public readings in Juchitán of books they had written (Natalia) or translated (Víctor) and observed that there was an appreciative local audience, with admiring young people coming up afterwards to ask for a photo or an autograph. The idea for the *Camino de la Iguana* started, as Natalia and Víctor both joked on numerous occasions, because they felt that if they did not teach people to read Diidxazá there would be no one left to read the books that they and others were writing. As Víctor expressed in an interview, the aim of the workshop has been to *"darles a conocer la literatura, darles a conocer el alfabeto, que sepan que se puede escribir el idioma, que se puede crear en el idioma, que hay posibilidades para la lengua"* [getting them to know the literature, getting them to know the alphabet, that they know that you can write the language, that you can create in the language, that there are possibilities for the language] (Interview November 2014). Víctor and Natalia aimed to make the "possibilities" of the language available to all residents of the region through an accessible workshop. The workshop was designed to take place for two to three hours a day over a 2-week period and to be offered in different sites around the

---

[29] A variety of individuals and groups have created courses of varying durations, such as linguist Vicente Marcial Cerqueda in Juchitán and retired teacher Antonio Ortíz in San Blas, who additionally developed his own textbooks, among others. Each initiative merits attention; unfortunately due to space I restrict myself here to a focus on the community education space I observed most extensively.

Figure 16: *Camino de la Iguana* poster 2014 (left); The Juchitán-based publication *Guchachi' Reza* 1982 (right).

region, including schools and cultural centers. They received funding from a nonprofit arts foundation based in Oaxaca City, the *Centro para las Artes San Agustín* (CASA), which allowed them to offer the workshop free of charge and to provide materials and a snack for participants (see also chapter 7 for further discussion of CASA).

A poster promoting the *Camino de la Iguana* workshop (Figure 16, left), produced by the *Comité Melendre*, a Juchitán-based civic organization which hosted the workshop in their independent cultural center in 2014 (see also chapter 7 for more on the *Comité Melendre*), uses an image of an iguana taken from a 1982 publication of the Juchitán-based journal *Guchachi' Reza* (Figure 16, right), in conjunction with a simple modern font and the image of a coffee-stain left from a coffee cup. The iguana image links the workshop to the tradition of Diidxazá literature in the 20th century, while the modern style and coffee mark suggests intimacy and participation, with the poster becoming a page that the writer has just lifted their coffee cup from. In this way, the workshop is presented as both traditional and modern. This captures one of the defining features of the workshop and of how Natalia and Víctor define Diidxazá literacy as both traditional and contemporary, and as both local and international.

As writer-activists, Natalia and Víctor aim to *create* a certain kind of *person or identity*, that of Diidxazá readers and writers. The practices and politics of Indigenous language literacies make this a complicated endeavor, however. What it means to be literate in Diidxazá is not necessarily equivalent to what it means to be literate in Spanish, as these writer-activists are well aware. In this respect, this form of language activism necessitates imagining new ways of being, as much as, or more than resisting the inequalities entrenched in current ways of being (such as the inequalities which scholar-activists and education-activists work to reverse within existing education institutions). While the promotion of alphabetic literacy and the production of Diidxazá readers and writers is the explicit language activism strategy of the workshop, this is characterized by an orientation to both historical and contemporary references (a multi-directional *socio-historical orientation*), by explicit links to both local and international influences (transnational *location* references) and by an inclusive approach to *participation*. Additionally, the teachers engage in a delicate balancing act between promoting maximum use of Diidxazá and adapting to the language practices of students, aiming to avoid hardline purism while still increasing linguistic knowledge and use (a centralist *diversity orientation*).

In this chapter, I analyze the imaginary of Diidxazá literacy that was created by this community-based workshop, drawing on my observations of the workshop and insights gained through formal and informal conversations with the two teachers and a selection of participants. I begin with a discussion of the double-edged nature of literacy education and the potential of community-based education initiatives (6.1), and an overview of the heritage of literacy in the Isthmus in particular (6.2). Then, turning to the *Camino de la Iguana*, I outline the strategic ways in which the teachers pursue their participatory, multi-temporal and trans-local imaginary of literacy (6.3). By bridging history with the current context (6.3.1), and local genres with international genres (6.3.2), and above all through creation of a participatory convivial norm (6.3.3), these writer-activists have achieved many positive results. This community education space encourages participants to engage with a historical and contemporary literary community and to see themselves as authors, in addition to learning the alphabet. The imaginaries of Diidxazá literacy present among participants in the *Camino de la Iguana* illustrate that 'reading' Diidxazá means much more than decoding the phonemes represented in the popular alphabet. An imaginary of convivial multilingualism informs many of the language activism strategies in this workshop. I conclude with a discussion of the key characteristics of the activism strategies employed in this workshop, which may provide a positive example to other community-based education initiatives (6.4).

6.1 Indigenous literacies and community-based education

The potential impacts of writing-focused minority language activism are a topic of debate amongst minority language advocates. Writing is variously viewed as a form of emancipation, a form of repression, and a complex amalgam of the two. I provide a brief overview of these perspectives, with the ultimate aim of considering the potential negative impacts of literacy education, and the role that community-based education projects may play in mitigating them.

Indigenous language educator-activists have cautioned that literacy education must be approached strategically and critically in order to avoid reinforcing language hierarchies which place Indigenous language speakers and non-written literacies at the bottom (Watahomigie and McCarty 1996; Zepeda 1995; Outakoski 2015). European-origin literacy practices remain prominent in formal education, privileging standard forms and limited registers of communication which are endorsed by an official authority (Weth and Juffermans 2018). This can serve to devalue the communication practices of languages without a tradition of writing, and has led to conflicts and debates in the creation of standard writing systems for Indigenous languages in many parts of the world (Hornberger 1993; Costa, De Korne, and Lane 2017; Limerick 2018; Schwartz 2018; De Korne and Weinberg 2021). A paradigm of literacy as 'autonomous' from locally-situated and negotiated meaning-making makes literacy appear neutral, and projects a deficit view of learners who do not produce the designated written standard (Street 1984).

The dominance of alphabetic literacy over other forms of meaning making has been critiqued in the context of Indigenous education in Mexico (López Gopar 2007). López Gopar points out that sophisticated local literacy practices, such as the numeric, aesthetic, and sociocultural literacy which is used in the production of traditional embroidered garments in Oaxaca, are typically overlooked and discounted. Maldonado Alvarado (2002) argues that writing-focused education intensifies colonial dominance in Oaxaca: "*La escritura abre espacios de sometimiento que aprovechan las sociedades dominadoras, y todos los 'analfabetas' dominados, independientemente de su 'ignorancia', conocen y sienten las caracteristicas de la dominación mediante lo escrito*" [Writing opens spaces of subjugation that dominating societies take advantage of, and all of the dominated 'illiterate' people, independently from their 'ignorance', know and feel the characteristics of domination through writing] (41). The predominance of education initiatives that focus on writing as a form of promoting Isthmus Zapotec use may thus be a threat, or at least a double-edged sword. If learners and speakers believe that they need to produce a standard written form to be a competent member of the speech community, yet do not have access to sufficient educational opportunities to acquire this expertise, the promotion of alphabetic literacy as a language activism strategy could contribute to the further marginalization of some members of the community. Gal (2006) has called this a 'double stigma' that minoritized language speakers experience all too often; speakers of Diidxazá may face stigma in relation to their 'non-native' Spanish use, as well as in relation to their 'non-standard' or 'illiterate' Diidxazá use (see also 5.1).

On the other hand, the teaching of alphabetic literacy has also been shown to be a fundamental building block of social change and empowerment (Freire 1969, 1970). Research within the New Literacies paradigm has aimed to change the dominant perspective on literacy from autonomous reading and writing, to contextualized, and ideologically-informed meaning making (Street 1984; Cazden et al. 1996; Martin-Jones and Jones 2001). By focusing on multiliteracies, scholars in this field have argued for the need to recognize multilingualism and multimodal communication, as well as culturally-specific communication practices, as part of the literacies which learners may aim to acquire. In relation to Indigenous literacy practices, Hornberger (1996) discusses a "both/and" approach through which Indigenous educators must negotiate and integrate the many factors influencing language use, literacy and knowledge production, ultimately opening a "door of opportunity for the marginalized" (357). Language activists in Mexico and in Oaxaca have argued the potential benefits of writing and literature in Indigenous languages (Francis and Reyhner 2002; Aguilar Gil 2016; Lillehaugen 2016), and pointed out that Indigenous people have a long history of appropriating writing for their own purposes (Rockwell 2005; Pineda 2014). Jésus Salinas Pedraza, co-founder of the *Centro Editorial de Literatura Indígena* (Indigenous Literature Publishing Center, CELIAC) argues that "Indigenous languages must become written languages. [. . .] Lack of literacy is the most important factor in the deterioration and abandonment of indigenous languages. [. . .] The direct participation of native peoples is essential in development of their writing system and in development of their language in all forms of communication, including film, radio, television, and national newspapers" (Salinas Pedraza 1996: 172–173).

Like minoritized language education in general, as discussed in chapter 4, the promotion of minoritzed language literacy has both potential benefits and potential pitfalls. Even where language activists may aim to side-step this prickly issue, the presence of writing in many aspects of 21st century life makes it difficult to avoid, as Salinas Pedraza points out. Heeding the cautions of literacy education sceptics leads to important questions about how minoritized language literacy education is conceptualized and delivered. If it is shaped by patterns from standard European languages, and conventions from Eurocentric literary genres, it is unlikely to support the 'spaces of otherwise' (Povinelli 2011) or culturally embedded learning (Henne-Ochoa et al. 2020) that minority language activists typically aim to create. Community-based education offers a more flexible space for imagining and implementing new pedagogies and social realities, however, with less influence from the bureaucracy and politics of formal education. In this regard, it may be an especially promising space for the consolidation of new literacy imaginaries.

Scholars and activists in Indigenous language reclamation and education in the Americas have long argued for the importance of community control or influence in education as a way of avoiding the colonial histories and power dynamics which nation-state education usually imposes (National Indian Brotherhood 1972; Cajete 1994; McCarty 2013). Reclaiming education in community contexts is an important contribution towards decolonizing education by shifting what forms of knowledge are valued, and how knowledge is conveyed across generations (Battiste 2013). In his critique of nation-state education, characterized as inherently *manipulative*, Illich (1970) argues that community-based learning is an ideal environment within which to pursue *convivial* learning. Illich's strongly anti-institutional stance on education resonates with social learning theories like the communities of practice (Lave and Wenger 1991) and culturally sustaining pedagogies (Paris and Alim 2017), which also grant community-based education initiatives great potential importance. In the Oaxacan context, forms of education that are rooted in community collaboration are often highlighted as the most successful (e.g. Meyer 2018). Rather than struggling to connect the school space to the community space, as some of the teacher-activists described in chapter 4, community-based educators may create their own contextually appropriate learning spaces embedded in the larger community space. There are numerous options for how they imagine and choose to fill this new space, however, as explored further below.

6.2 Isthmus Zapotec literacies

The Isthmus Zapotec community is known for its writers and musicians, both within and beyond the Isthmus. From the journal *Neza* [Path] produced by students and intellectuals in Mexico City in the 1930s (including scholar Andrés Henestrosa, see also chapter 3), to the journal *Guchachi' Reza* [Sliced Iguana] produced by artists and intellectuals in Juchitán from the 1970s through the 1990s (including scholar Victor de la Cruz), to current writers such as Natalia Toledo, Irma Pineda and Victor Terán, the Isthmus has been home to writers of different genres, many of whom have won praise nationally and internationally. Prior to the 2017 earthquake that caused considerable damage to the *Casa de la Cultura*, numerous pillars in the courtyard of the *Casa de la Cultura* in Juchitán held plaques dedicated to local writers and scholars. One of the initiatives of the "*Gusisácanu Diidxazá do' stinu*" [Let's strengthen our good/ pure/ sacred Zapotec] campaign by the municipal government in 2016 was to compile a book of Diidxazá poetry for use in schools, where poetry declamation is often a yearly event and Diidxazá poems are popular. In this regard, writing and literature is not viewed as something imposed by national authorities or schools, but rather something that has been and continues to be an organic part of the Isthmus Zapotec community.

Isthmus Zapotec writers in the first half of the 20th century used a variety of orthographic norms to write Diidxazá. In 1956, the *alfabeto popular* or popular alphabet was produced by a round table of writers and invited linguists, an initiative spearheaded by Zapotec writer Máximo Valdivieso (Pickett 1993; La Sociedad Pro-Planeación del Istmo 1956). The popular alphabet follows Spanish orthography norms in several ways, while establishing a consistent way to represent the four consonants and two vowel phonations that are present in Diidxazá and not in Spanish (for detailed discussion of this writing norm see Pérez Báez, Cata, and Bueno Holle 2015). Although there was no official authority to recognize or promote this norm, it has been taken up by a majority of Isthmus Zapotec writers. As Víctor Cata recounts, the use of the popular alphabet was required by the journal *Guchachi Reza* while it was published under the leadership of Víctor de la Cruz, director of the *Casa de la Cultura* in Juchitán in the 1980s, an editorial choice which helped to disseminate this norm among readers and writers (Interview November 2014). The missionary organization SIL, through their representative Velma Pickett, participated in the 1956 round table and later published stories, a grammar, and a Spanish-Diidxazá dictionary using the popular alphabet (Pickett, Black, and Cerqueda 2001) (see also chapter 3). The establishment of the INALI in 2003 marked the first time that a nationally recognized authority of this kind existed in relation to Indigenous languages in Mexico. INALI has been active in developing and publishing orthographic norms. In 2007 the 1956 guide to the popular alphabet was reprinted and 20,000 copies were distributed by the INALI. INALI has also sponsored workshops aimed at revising the Isthmus Zapotec popular alphabet, in particular in relation to the representation of lexical tone, with the aim of publishing an officially endorsed orthography in the near future (De Korne 2017b).

The municipal government-sponsored "*Gusisácanu Diidxazá do' stinu*" campaign produced a poster to commemorate the 60th anniversary of the creation of the popular alphabet in 2016, which was distributed through their social media channels. Shown in Figure 17, the poster focuses on a pre-colonial Zapotec stone figure resting on cloud-like shapes, as well as reproducing an image of a Zapotec

Figure 17: Poster commemorating the 60th anniversary of the creation of the popular alphabet (February 2016).

king (Cosihuesa). In the center of the poster several graphemes of the popular alphabet in diverse fonts and bright colors are emerging from (or falling into) a container decorated with the 'Greco' designs used in ancient Zapotec building sites, such as Mitla. This image thus links current Isthmus Zapotec writing to a history which extends far beyond the round table of 1956 to include the precolonial literacies of the Zapotec empire, and represents Zapotec writing as part of a longstanding cultural practice (see also chapter 2). The poster also includes part of the typeface that appeared in the original 1956 alphabet guide, which locates and dates the alphabet to Mexico City, 10 February 1956, and credits the publication to "*La Sociedad Pro-planeación integral del istmo* [The Society for integral planning in the Isthmus], *El Consejo de Lenguas Indígenas* [The Council of Indigenous Languages], *y el Instituto Lingüístico de Verano* [and the Summer Institute of Linguistics]", in acknowledgement of the affiliations of the people who participated.

Perhaps the most often-cited reference in the literary heritage of the Isthmus is poet Gabriel López Chiñas (1911–1983), who wrote a poem called *"Didxazá"* first published in a 1971 collection (López Chiñas 1971) and reproduced countless times in journals and poetry collections. The poem begins *"Nacabe ma ché' didxazá"* [They say Diidxazá is going], and continues for two verses to describe that the language of the *Binnizá* [Zapotecs] is said to be dying, as *Binnizá* now begin to only speak Spanish. López Chiñas concludes with two verses addressed to the language itself, proclaiming that he/ she[30] is loved, has given him life, and that *"naa nanna zanitilu'/ dxí initi gubidxa ca"* [I know you will die/ the day the sun dies]. This last phrase has become a trope in discussions of Isthmus Zapotec; on numerous occasions people would be describing to me how Zapotec is getting lost, how children are not learning it– but– Chiñas said it will die the day that the sun dies, so who knows, maybe everything will turn out well (see examples in chapters 3.2.2 and 7). López Chiñas' grave is prominently marked in one of the main cemeteries of Juchitán, labeling him a *"Juchiteco* poet" and including the name of his famous poem.

Istmeños are generally aware of and proud of the heritage of Isthmus Zapotec writing and publishing, even those who are not involved in literature, teaching or other recognized 'cultural' activities, and who presumably do not follow the municipal government's social media channels. On numerous occasions when chatting with women selling in the market, after mentioning that I was learning Diidaxzá, they would tell me "There are books in Diidxazá", offering this as a resource to help me learn and as a point of pride. I also met people who told me that since you can write Diidxazá, it is a language, not a *dialecto*– although they themselves said that writing is hard, and they can't do it. Many people express respect for the people recognized as knowing how to write Isthmus Zapotec, and living Isthmus Zapotec literary icons frequently appear in public events. In contrast to the traditional framing of writing shown in Figure 21, current writers are often viewed as modern, mobile, and worldly, and are known to have travelled to present their work to audiences nationally and internationally. Natalia Toledo, for example, is the daughter of internationally-acclaimed painter Francisco Toledo (see also chapter 7), was

---

[30] In the poem the Diidxazá language is addressed with the 2nd person human pronoun which does not distinguish male and female gender.

the first woman to win the Nezahualcóyotl prize for Indigenous literature in 2004, and has been invited to poetry festivals around the world. In 2019 she became the *Subsecretaria de Diversidad Cultural y Fomento a la Lectura* [Subsecretary of Cultural Diversity and Promotion of Reading], a high-profile position within the Mexican National Secretary of Culture. Víctor Cata, as introduced in chapter 1, has studied and worked in prestigious institutions in Mexico City, and has travelled and collaborated with international scholars, including Gabriela Pérez Báez at the Smithsonian Institution in the US. Another admired Juchitán poet and activist, Irma Pineda, has achieved wide recognition for her writing and social engagement, and was elected to serve on the United Nations Permanent Forum on Indigenous Issues from 2020–2022. Both the past and the present of Isthmus Zapotec literature is filled with high-achieving, charismatic role models.

Ironically, despite this recent and on-going heritage, writing has never been socialized in the general society. I heard mention of literacy programs that had been run in the past through religious and social development organizations, and unearthed several adult literacy workbooks in the SIL archive, however at present only a small minority of people have had any formal training in writing or reading Diidxazá. It is partially this gap – between a clear source of cultural pride and identity on the one hand, and the majority of the population who do not feel empowered to participate in it on the other – that motivated Natalia and Víctor to put their own writing aside for a while in order to teach. The following sections analyse their imaginaries and strategies of Diidxazá literacy as practiced in their workshop.

6.3 Imaginaries of literacy in the *Camino de la Iguana*

As residents of Juchitán, Natalia and Víctor were well aware of the prestige of the popular alphabet and Diidxazá literature, as well as the lack of learning opportunities. In response, their efforts focused on teaching the alphabet and the literary heritage in a way that would be accessible and attractive to a wider section of the Isthmus Zapotec community. Although the workshop was initially designed to assist speakers of Isthmus Zapotec in becoming comfortable with the popular alphabet, from the very first incarnation of the workshop in the *Casa de la Cultura* in Juchitán in January 2012 there were many people attending who did not identify as speakers, interested in learning how to speak as well as how to write. As a result, the two-week workshop has varied each time, depending on the ages and language abilities of the participants. Participants have varying levels of speaking and listening comprehension. In 3 of the 10 iterations of the workshop that I observed between 2013 and 2015 there were almost no Isthmus Zapotec speakers among the participants; in 4 there were a mix, with non-speakers generally more numerous than speakers; and in 3 locations all or almost all of the participants were speakers. This was due to which geographic area the workshops were held in. The communicative repertoire of the participants impacted the teachers' practices, as they typically switched to Spanish if the participants could not produce Diidxazá.

The basic format of the workshop was the same in all locations, however. Activities in the workshop began with about one hour of *"lectoescritura"* [reading and writing], where Víctor taught and drilled the sounds and symbols of the popular alphabet, often including old vocabulary words as examples, relying on lots of dictation exercises and peer correction. He often taught the Zapotec vigesimal (base-twenty) number system as well, and had participants read texts or poems to practice pronunciation. Víctor's teaching involved lots of copying and dictation, aimed at providing students with the skills to write Diidxazá in Natalia's class, which was structured around students' writing projects. Natalia taught one hour of *"creación literaria"* [literary creation, creative writing], beginning with discussion of the current legal status of Indigenous languages in Mexico and some of the prominent literary icons of Isthmus Zapotec. She then guided participants through a series of exercises in which they produced writing (ideally in Zapotec) in a variety of *"universal"* [universal, international] genres, including surrealism, haiku, and autobiography, as well as genres identified as Zapotec, such as *"adivinanzas"* [riddles], tongue twisters, metaphors, and *"mentiras"* [humorous lies/jokes]. She coached participants in writing these genres, ideally in Diidxazá, although often in Spanish or a combination thereof. She also often taught some Zapotec lullabies and had participants sing. Sometimes a special guest was invited to attend for a day, often one of the young bilingual rappers from Juchitán (see chapter 7) or another Zapotec poet, who presented their poems or songs to the group. Each workshop concluded with a ceremony in which each participant was supposed to read something that they had written and receive a certificate, and in which there was usually some form of food and music. These ceremonies ranged from very formal to very casual, depending on the location of the workshop. Both teachers acknowledged that the two-week time span of the workshop is not sufficient for participants to become comfortable with the alphabet, but they hoped to spark enough interest so that some students will continue learning and writing in the future.

6.3.1 Our alphabet: Sharing sounds and symbols

Víctor's approach to teaching Zapotec literacy has transformed throughout the process of developing the *Camino de la Iguana*. He described how the first class he taught was like a linguistics lecture, which bored the children, adults and elders of Juchitán who were in attendance. He realized that he needed to present content in a more accessible way, and with different activities for different populations, in order to meet the goals of the workshop. These changes were driven by the desire to better achieve the underlying goals of the workshop, as referenced in the opening of this chapter, and stated here in his words in full:

> El taller ha sufrido cambios, se ha ido adecuando a las condiciones, a las necesidades. Pero el objetivo primordial sigue, eso sí no se ha alterado, el de darles a conocer la literatura, darles a conocer el alfabeto, que sepan que se puede escribir el idioma, que se puede crear en el idioma, que hay posibilidades para la lengua. Eso sí mira. La forma es que ya cambió.
>
> The workshop has gone through changes, it's been adapting itself to the conditions, to the needs. But the primordial objective continues, that yes, has not altered, that of getting them to know the literature, getting them to know the alphabet, that they know that you can write the language, that you can create in the language, that there are possibilities for the language. That yes, look. The form is what has changed.   (Interview October 2014)

The teaching of the alphabet (and corresponding phonemes) was still pursued in a linguistically-informed way, but Víctor incorporated a lot of practice exercises and some peer work to help Spanish-literate students acquire the information with greater ease. Víctor teaches in a calm and unhurried way, taking time to explain the issues that his students find confusing or to tell a story that helps to explain the topic at hand. The following field notes describe a typical lesson:

> Víctor begins the first day of the workshop with an entirely adult audience in Tehuantepec by showing the Spanish alphabet, pointing out which letters are not used in Isthmus Zapotec. Then he turns to what I already know will be the main focus throughout the workshop: the 4 consonants and 10 vowels that are in Diidxazá but not in Spanish. He gives examples of words starting with each sound in the popular alphabet. It doesn't take long to come across an example of a word that the participants say in multiple ways: *guelaguidi* versus the more common *laguidi* (sandal), produced through a pattern of dropping [g] at the beginnings of some words, which many interpret as a kind of language decline. Víctor tells the students that 'language always changes, don't fall into thinking about the "correct" and "incorrect"'.
>
> Then he dictates words in Diidxazá and has students write them in silence. Later he calls students to the board to write their answers, asking the group what they think of each answer, and if anyone has anything different. The group compares the different versions, with Víctor asking them how they would pronounce each version. When reading them

back the students start to notice where the writing doesn't line up with the pronunciation of the word. Finally Víctor gives a correct version of each word, signaling correct words with a check and incorrect with a cross.

Víctor then writes some minimal pairs on the board, asking if students know the definitions, and filling them in. One pair is *nisa* (water) and *niza* (ear of corn). Víctor tells a story about a carwash in Juchitán that has painted their name "*Niza yaa*" intending to mean "clean water", but actually meaning "clean ear of corn". Everyone laughs.

(Field notes February 2014)

Much focus is given to the 4 consonants and 3 vowel phonations that are not found in Spanish,[31] learning to recognize them through presentation of minimal pairs and practicing them through dictation exercises. Since Spanish uses the graphemes <s> and <z> to refer to the same phoneme, /s/, this can be a particularly challenging for students, and they find examples like the story of "*Niza yaa*" to be amusing and instructive. As noticeable in the vignette of a typical lesson above, Víctor explicitly espouses a paradigm in which different versions of a word can be correct, however his classes simultaneously emphasize the importance of "correct" spelling, judged at the level of sound-symbol transparency. This approach– accepting the written representation of diverse pronunciations and regional dialects, while adhering to a normative phonemic inventory– can be called a "polynomic" (Marcellesi 1983) approach to literacy, which has been popular in the teaching of Corsican and Occitan in France, as well as other lesser-taught languages (Sallabank 2010). This non-standard approach to dialect is conscious and strategic on Víctor's part, as he encourages students from different parts of the region to adapt the popular alphabet to their dialect variant.

At the same time, as a historian and linguist, he tries to promote the use of Zapotec words that have been or are in the process of being replaced by Spanish, without imposing them in a purist way. He often teaches the traditional vigesimal number system, with the symbols that were previously used to represent different amounts in the pre-colonial Zapotec writing system. In explaining this base twenty number system and the symbols that were used to represent certain quantities in ancient carvings and texts, Víctor asks the students to convert and translate different sums and impresses upon them the sophistication of the system. While his classes aim to take into consideration the language abilities of the

---

[31] Consonants are: dx /dʒ/, x /ʒ/, xh /ʃ/, z /z/. The vowels are the same 5 vowels used in Spanish (a, e, i, o, u), but are produced in three possible phonations: simple (produced as modal vowels and represented as in Spanish or English); "*cortadas*", non-continuous/ final glottal stop (represented with an apostrophe following the letter); and "*quebradas*", laryngealized (represented with a double letter).

students, they also attempt to transmit vocabulary that is often new for students, even those who regularly use Zapotec in daily communication. When discussing his stance on the use of Spanish terms he commented:

> *Cuando está el nombre en zapoteco, no. Entonces sí. . .digo ¿por qué? si tenemos el nombre ¿por qué estás usando el préstamo? Cuando no lo tenemos pues ni modos no lo tenemos: manzana: manzana, pera: pera. Pero sí tenemos "aguacate". . ."yaxhu"*
>
> When the name in Zapotec is there, no. So yes. . . I say why if we have the name, why are you using the loan word? When we don't have it well, oh well, we don't have it: apple: apple, pear: pear. But we do have avocado. . ."yaxhu"
>
> (Interview October 2014)

Víctor explicitly aims to be inclusionary in his teaching of Diidxazá reading and writing and to avoid discouraging students, but he does not adopt an all-inclusive approach and continues to promote the kind of vocabulary and phonemic knowledge that he thinks is most important for students to have. He views an overly normative or pursit approach as a problem, as he discussed:

> Víctor *No me gusta ser como muy normativo porque van a decir "es muy purista" o que me tomen como muy estricto. Hay veces escucho y no digo nada pero si puedo les digo pero----para no hacerlos sentir mal, namás para hablarles de la riqueza del idioma. Pero por lo regular me quedo callado.*
>
> HDK *Sí . . . no creo que te he visto haciendo correcciones [dialectales o léxicos].*
> *[. . .]*
>
> Víctor *No lo hago, no . . . no me gusta porque si de por sí no habla y aparte les digo que no hablan bien . . . Pero van a hablar, mejor que hable, ya sobre la marcha ya aprende. Ahora sí, sobre la marcha aprende.*
>
> Víctor I don't like to be like very normative because they will say "he's very purist" or they take me as really strict. There are times I listen and I don't say anything but if I can I say to them but--- not so as to make them feel bad, just to talk to them about the richness of the language. But for the most part I stay quiet.
>
> HDK Yes . . . I don't think I've seen you making corrections [of dialect or word choice].
> [. . .]
>
> Víctor I don't do it, no I don't like it because if in fact someone doesn't speak and besides I tell them that they don't speak well . . . But they're going to speak, it's better that they speak, then learn along the way. Now yes, learn along the way.
>
> (Interview October 2014)

Víctor was aware that many students have only limited motivation to learn, and that his actions may have repercussions on their future levels of interest.

Although Víctor recognized the risk of making his lessons overly technical and with an intimidating focus on accuracy, he also noted the importance of the linguistic analysis that he brings to his work, commenting:

> Es distinto que tú hables un idioma, que tú analices tu propio idioma. [. . .] Y ahí es cuando te enfrentas realmente a tu idioma y tienes que explicarlo, no puedes decir de que "ah, pos nada más porque así lo ponemos." "No, explícamelo, explícame por qué primero." Eh comienzas con el verbo, luego el sujeto y luego el objeto. . . Entonces por supuesto que me sirvió mucho [mi formación lingüística]. [. . .] Cuando explico una palabra, ya sé cómo explicarlo sin que ellos se enreden, sin que ellos se aburran [. . .] Sí sé hacer un análisis, sé por qué la palabra está ahí, sé por qué cambia, y como siempre me gustó la semántica puedo hacer el análisis del camino de la palabra.

> It's different that you speak a language, than that you analyze your own language. [. . .] And that is where you really face your language and you have to explain it, you can't say that "Ah well just because we put it like that." "No, explain it to me, explain to me why first." Eh you start with the verb, later the subject and later the object. . . So definitely [linguistic training] has been really useful to me. [. . .] When I explain a word, I know how to explain it without them getting tangled up, without them getting bored. [. . .] Yes I know how to do an analysis, I know why the word is there, I know why it changes and since I always liked semantics I can do the analysis of the path of the word.
>
> (Interview October 2014)

Students appreciate Víctor's ability to offer more insight into their questions and a structured approach to learning the writing system. Two young women who took classes with a speaker who did not have linguistic or pedagogical training and subsequently attended the *Camino de la Iguana*, told me in conversation that they were not willing to take more classes with the previous teacher but would love to study more with Víctor because he was able to explain complicated things in a simple way. Figure 18 below shows Víctor teaching independent pronouns and corresponding verb conjugations to a group of adult learners, following a framework that is familiar to those who have studied additional languages or linguistics in a formal way.

Students generally participate well in all of his activities, from dictation and reading aloud, to grading a neighbor's work and translating vocabulary. These pedagogic routines, while relying on the memorization and drills that are generally criticized by more holistic or constructivist approaches to literacy teaching, are very familiar to students who have come through the Mexican education system. When working in a context where all the participants are schooled in Spanish, these norms are hard, if not impossible, to resist. The literacy component of the *Camino de la Iguana* thus has echoes of formal education and linguistics-based teaching, while avoiding the exclusion and

Figure 18: Víctor teaching in the *Camino de la Iguana* (photo February 2014).

shaming that these kinds of standards-focused education can produce, and additionally promoting dialect diversity.

6.3.2 We have a unique way to name the world: Diidxazá in the canon of universal literature

Natalia's goals for her students include familiarity with some of the Diidxazá literature that exists, although more of her time is spent coaxing them to produce and share their own writing, focusing on projects that bring to light their dreams, personal stories, and observations. Her passion for literature as a form of personal and cultural expression is apparent through her teaching. Natalia lectures charismatically and intensely, punctuated by sudden, deep laughter and moments of warm connection with her students. Throughout the workshop she combines projects that relate to a kind of literary production identified as "Zapotec", and projects related to literature identified as "universal" or international– although there is not a clear line drawn between the two in discourse nor in practice. In all their writing, participants are encouraged to use at least some Zapotec, or to translate into Zapotec. The first project she assigns them is to write something (usually a poem) about a dream that they have had and bring it to class the next day. "If you don't remember your dream, ask your grandmother for one of hers, she probably has great ones" she joked on several occasions.

The projects vary from one location to another due to the age of the students, and various scheduling issues that slow down or speed up the workshop. In the workshops that I observed, the main projects following the dream assignment were a surrealist poem, an autobiographical piece (with an example of a poem by Venezuelan poet Luis Brito for inspiration), writing based on a childhood photo, "*guendarusiguii*" (the art of lying, with examples collected and published by Juchitán writer Macario Matus for inspiration), and writing or translating a haiku (often with Zapotec onomatopoeias and/or metaphors, using examples of haikus by Japanese poet Matsuo Basho and Juchitán writer Victor Terán for inspiration). Sometimes Natalia also asks participants to do an interview with someone from their town, and frequently incorporates tongue twisters, old-fashioned games and Zapotec songs, in particular lullabies. In one workshop where all the participants were children, she brought in black and white images by her father, Isthmus painter Francisco Toledo, and had the children color them in and write a story about the image. In another workshop where many of the participants did not speak Isthmus Zapotec she assigned lists of words to be learned.

Participants were always encouraged to write their assignments in Diidxazá– with help if needed– although they were not prevented from writing in Spanish or translanguaging, and both were very frequent practices. Most important was for them to write and be willing to read what they wrote out loud to the rest of the group. A typical lesson is described in the following vignette.

> Natalia is teaching the workshop with adult learners. On the white board at the front she has written "*Bigú- polvo, pedaceria, añicos*" [Turtle [in Zapotec]- powder/ dust, pieces, fragments [in Spanish]], after telling an Isthmus Zapotec legend recorded by *Istmeño* scholar Andrés Henestrosa about how the turtle got a broken shell, resulting in its mosaic shell today (Henestrosa 2009 [1929]). She launches from this story into an explanation of a writing exercise called the "*cadáver exquisito*" [exquisite corpse] where each person will contribute a random phrase and these fragments are then assembled together to make a surrealist poem. She gives a brief description of the era of French surrealism in the 1920s and mentions several French poets associated with this movement, including forerunner Lautréamont. She aligns with their philosophy that "*La poesía debe estar hecha por todos*" [Poetry should be made by all], which she writes on the board.
>
> (Field notes February 2014)

By combining Isthmus Zapotec literature with French surrealism, Natalia draws a clear bridge between local and global literary traditions. Additionally, she prioritizes the students' participation through accessible exercises like the exquisite corpse, and welcoming writing in any combination of languages.

One of the resources Natalia often brought to the workshop was a recent reprint of the 1578 dictionary of Zapotec compiled by Fray Juán de Córdova. Natalia told students that the 1578 dictionary holds many archaic words, but that they can find subtle and beautiful things there, and it is still the largest dictionary of Zapotec to date. Natalia attempts to inspire interest in the intricacies of the language among her students with examples like the onomatopoeia in the 1578 dictionary, most of which are no longer in use (such as the sound pain makes when it walks through the body). She reiterates again and again that being bilingual or multilingual is a source of pride, that Diidxazá lends itself well to creative expression, and that Zapotecs have their own forms of expression that are just as valid as those of other people and places. In an interview she commented:

Natalia Es complejo porque es una manera de pensar. No, no puedes enseñar palabritas--- claro, ese es el inicio, ¿no? Pero por ejemplo, cuando yo pongo este . . . esto, ¿no? de las metáforas. Estábamos viendo el otro día, entonces yo les dije que algunas metáforas que existen naturalmente en el zapoteco. Cómo cuando dices que: ay, fui a la marcha de ayer y te--- y alguien te dice: ¿y hubo mucha gente? Dices: "binni biri", gente hormiga. O sea, había mucha gente como hormiga, ¿no? Eso es un pensamiento, si yo lo digo en D.F. nadie va a saber qué estoy diciendo. Si yo lo digo aquí [. . .] a estos niños de esta escuela no tienen la menor idea. Entonces esas expresiones se mueren, como se murieron las onomatopeyas de cómo camina el dolor en el cuerpo. Imagínate que un antepasado mío tuvo--- o esa cabeza que representa a una cultura, tuvo la posibilidad y la maravilla de escuchar su cuerpo.

HDK Ujum.

Natalia Esas sutilezas del idioma se han perdido y . . . sigue habiendo y existiendo onomatopeyas, pero lo que nosotros hacemos mucho en el taller es también preguntarnos y preguntarles: ¿qué les parecen estas cosas?, ¿cómo lo ven?, ¿no? Porque la literatura es eso, es ese . . . tú sabes que detrás de un libro hay una persona, y esa persona se hizo preguntas y registró muchas cosas de su tiempo. Entonces el lenguaje somos nosotros, el lenguaje somos las personas. Yo me hice persona en zapoteco, el zapoteco a mí me hizo una persona.

Natalia It's complicated because it's a way of thinking. You can't teach just little words--- clearly, that is the start, right. But for example when I put um . . . this, right, the metaphors. We were looking [at that] the other day, so I told them some metaphors that exist naturally in Zapotec. Like when you say that "oh, I went to the march yesterday" and you– and someone says to you "and were there a lot of people?" You say *binni biri* people ant. Like, there were a lot of people like ants, right. That is a thought, if I say it in Mexico City no one will know what I'm saying.

6.3 Imaginaries of literacy in the *Camino de la Iguana* — 155

If I say it here [. . .] to these kids in this school they don't have the least idea. So those expressions die, like the onomatopoeias about how pain walks through the body died. Imagine that one of my ancestors had– or that head that represents a culture, had the possibility and the wonder to listen to their body.

HDK   Uhum.

Natalia   Those subtleties of the language have been getting lost and . . . there still are and exist onomatopoeias, but what we do a lot in the workshop is also ask ourselves and ask them: What do you think of these things? How do you see them, right? Because literature is that, it's that . . . you know that behind a book there is a person, and that person asked themselves questions and documented many things of their time. So the language is us, we people are the language. I made myself a person in Zapotec, Zapotec made me a person.

(Interview November 2014)

Her goal is not to teach skills, but to foster an attitude of pride and a "way of thinking" that is critical and engaged. She has drawn great inspiration, identity and opportunity from Diidxazá and encourages others to do likewise. Natalia often comments that it is because of Diidxazá that she and Víctor have left the Isthmus, received grants and prizes, and travelled around the world. She tells participants to keep writing, to follow whatever dreams and aspirations they have. For example, when teaching in a secondary school in a rural community outside of Juchitán where many students do not continue to study beyond secondary level, she hung up a poster on the otherwise bare wall for an annual writing competition for Zapotec writers (of all varieties), supported by the *Centro para las Artes San Augustín* (CASA), the same foundation that supports the *Camino de la Iguana* workshops (see also chapter 7). Using the poster, she talked about opportunities like this to encourage students to keep writing, and to submit the work that they do to try for prizes.

Figure 19 shows Natalia teaching to a captive young adult audience in Tehuantepec. On the whiteboard she has written two possible ways to discuss poetry in Isthmus Zapotec; *diidxa guie'* glossed as *palabra flor* [word flower] and *diidxa do'* glossed as *palabra sagrada* [sacred word]. With characteristic passion, she discusses poetry as an entrance into a unique way of naming and talking about the world. She is a vocal supporter of other forms of artistic expression, including traditional music, cuisine, hip-hop and graffiti, and often teaches wearing *huipils* or *bidaani* (blouses) that use traditional embroidery styles (also shown in Figure 19).

While Víctor may talk non-confrontationally about "the richness of the language" in order to motivate people, Natalia is more direct about her concerns and frustration with the current state of Zapotec use (or lack thereof).

Figure 19: Natalia teaching in the *Camino de la Iguana* (photo February 2014).

She described some of her interactions with students from a well-respected monolingual primary school in a wealthy section of Juchitán:

> Natalia Les dije: ¿por qué dicen que son la mejor escuela de Juchitán si no hablan zapoteco? Estaban así [expresión de sorpresa]. Les digo: "sí, ustedes saben que---" ay, empecé . . . les dije cosas, ¿no? Este, les dije: "de ustedes depende que este idioma se siga hablando. Qué responsabilidad tan grande, yo no la voy a tener porque yo sí lo hablo. Pero ustedes no lo hablan, se va a morir." Y así.
>
> HDK ¿Cómo respondieron?
>
> Natalia "¡No, no se va a morir porque dice An--- este, Gabriel López Chiñas que no se va a morir!" [risas]. Les digo: "sí, pero ese es un poema muy bello. Pero el sol es más fuerte que nosotros, entonces sí tenemos que hacer algo. Imagínense, hace unos años se hablaba tantos, ¿no? tantos hablantes. Ahorita ya hay poquitos, treinta y cinco mil de este pueblo tan grande . . . y ya--- entonces, ¿qué vamos a hacer?, ¿le van a echar ganas o, o nos vamos todos y cerramos la puerta?" "No, no, no." Y así pero ya--- pero les tiene que meter la cosa esta, ¿no? el gusto [. . .]
>
> [risas] "A ver pinches chamacos, piensen que tienen una manera de nombrar única el mundo, y ustedes le están dando la espalda."

Natalia   I said to them "Why do you say that you're the best school in Juchitán if you don't speak Zapotec?" They were like this [shocked expression]. I said to them "Yes, you know that–" oh I started . . . I said things to them, right? Um I said to them "It depends on you whether this language continues to be spoken. What a big responsibility, I won't have it because I do speak it. But you don't speak it, it will die." Like that.

HDK   How did they respond?

Natalia   "No, it won't die because--- um, Gabriel López Chiñas says that it won't die!" [laughs]. I say to them "Yes, but that is a really beautiful poem. But the sun is stronger than us, so yes we have to do something. Imagine, a few years ago lots spoke, right, lots of speakers. Now there are already few, 35 thousand of this really big city . . . and now---so, what are we going to do? Are we going to make an effort or, or we're all going to go and close the door?" "No, no, no." And like that but---but you have to give them something that, right, the appreciation/ enjoyment. [. . .]

[laughs] "Let's see you darn kids, just to think that you have a unique way to name the world, and you're turning your back on it!"

(Interview November 2014)

Talking about the "death" of the language was not a dominant theme in the workshops, but was occasionally introduced in particular by Natalia to motivate participants. Natalia makes her interaction with these young students sound harsh as she retells it, although her personal interactions with participants, especially children, were always warm and playful, even when teasing or discipline was involved. The passion that Natalia and Víctor have for Diidxazá– as a way of being and communicating, and as a linguistic artifact– is clear, and they attempt to pass it on to the participants in whatever way they can.

Although Natalia loosely structures her teaching around recognized literary genres, she in no way views "*creación literaria*" as a series of skills that she can transmit, nor as something autonomous from the dynamics of life in the Isthmus. Speaking about her own experiences and desires as a writer, she said:

Natalia   *Pero por supuesto, que como tú eres un poeta indígena, todo se vuelve político.*

HDK   *¿Ah, sí?*

Natalia   *Porque eres una minoría yo creo. [. . .] No es que tú escribas sobre la política, sino que también pienso yo que ser poeta es una postura ante la vida, porque tú celebras la palabra. Otros están haciendo las grandes cosas, los poetas no. Los poetas están escribiendo palabras, son como esos loquitos que están haciendo versos, están en otro mundo. Y haciendo un mundo más habitable tal vez . . . porque el horror que acompaña a la vida a veces no--- es como dice Raúl Zurita, ¿no? Si . . . si fuéramos felices no existiría la música, no existiría la literatura. Pero como no hemos sido felices tenemos que agarrar de aquí para cantar, para decir, para este--- mirar una belleza. Algo así que te provoque humanidad, que es lo que nos falta ahorita.*

Natalia   But definitely, since you're an Indigenous poet, everything becomes political.

HDK   Oh yes?

Natalia   Because you're a minority I think. [. . .] It's not that you write about politics, rather that also I think that being a poet is an orientation towards life, because you celebrate the word. Others are making big things, not the poets. The poets are writing words, are like those crazies that are making verses, they are in another world. And making a world that is more habitable maybe . . . because the horror that accompanies life sometimes doesn't– It's like Raúl Zurita says, right. If . . . if we were happy there wouldn't be music, there wouldn't be literature. But since we haven't been happy we have to grab from here to sing, to say, to um--- look at something beautiful. Something like that that provokes humanity in you, which is what we're missing now.   (Interview November 2014)

Referring indirectly to the disadvantaged condition of Indigenous people under the Mexican government, and the social-political turmoil of life in the Isthmus, Natalia sees writing– especially writing as an Indigenous Zapotec person– as a needed response and a way to imagine a more humane world.

6.3.3 *Convivencia* in the *Camino de la Iguana*

A significant way in which the *Camino de la Iguana* broke from typical formal education practices was in the social and playful atmosphere of the workshop. For most workshops Natalia and Víctor provided a snack and drink to the participants each day, taking time to eat and drink together in between the lessons or at the end. The food was usually a local snack and "*agua fresca*" (fresh beverage of fruit or rice and water), prepared by Natalia's sister-in-law and served on the leaves of almond trees, a traditional practice that has now largely given way to styrofoam, but which Natalia and Víctor intentionally promoted. Discussion before and after the workshops often turned to local politics, or what festival was coming up next. On one occasion Natalia and Víctor delayed the start of the workshop to join in an impromptu game of basketball, which the primary school participants had asked them to play in. Neither of them had arrived prepared for this, but they kicked off their shoes and played barefoot with great gusto, much to the students' delight. As participants got to know Víctor and Natalia they become increasingly friendly, and by the end of the workshop there were always many pictures taken and emotional goodbyes exchanged. Each workshop was concluded with a ceremony and celebration, or *convivio*, usually involving food and reading some of the works the participants had written. Figure 20 shows Natalia and Víctor laughing with participants at the start of the closing *convivio* for the workshop held at the Comité Melendre's Cultural Center in August-September 2014. During this workshop they taught in the courtyard behind the Center, with mainly children and a few older adults participating. For the closing ceremony the participants arrived dressed in traditional formal clothing and with festive spirits.

Figure 20: Natalia and Víctor during a closing *convivio* (photo September 2014).

Despite their position as local celebrities and their expert status in the workshop, Natalia and Víctor fostered a convivial education environment through collaborative activities and their personal humor which was often present. This was not coincidental, but relates to their wider vision of how Zapotec can be promoted. As Natalia commented:

> *Estamos hablando el idioma y yo de verdad que obviamente lo que está en los libros es muy importante, pero lo que está, la gente está hablando ahorita zapoteco, esos son los que están salvando el idioma. No en un aula. O sea, algo estamos haciendo porque estamos enseñando, ¿no? "Miren, hay escritores, hay esto, hay lo otro, vamos a jugar. Estos son los juegos zapotecas, aquí hay recetas de cocina, esta es nuestra comida, esto somos nosotros todo el tiempo." Los números, el cuerpo, todo lo que vemos ahí [en el taller], jugamos. Pero realmente los que pueden hacer algo son la--- es la gente que está en casa sentada con sus nietos, con sus hijos, con sus. . . Esos son los que salvan el idioma.*

> We're speaking the language and I, honestly, obviously what is in books is very important, but the people that are speaking Zapotec now, those are the ones that are saving the language. Not in a classroom. Well, we're doing something because we're teaching, right? "Look, there are writers, there's this, there's that, let's play. These are the Zapotec games, here are cooking recipes, this is our food, this is who we are all the time." The numbers, the body, all that we look at there [in the workshop], we play. But really those that can do something are the--- it's the people that are at home seated with their grandkids, with their kids, with their. . . Those are the ones who save the language.
> (Interview November 2014)

Although they were not reproducing these natural interactions in the workshop, they created an environment somewhere between school and home. During the workshop both Natalia and Víctor regularly gave away books that they have written, and occasionally other books that they were able to get copies of, so that participants would have something to read after the workshop ended. In addition to sharing books and the dictionary, they frequently encouraged participants to consult the "living dictionaries" of their families. In this way they oriented towards the more open and inclusive side on the scale of participation, and created something like the convivial 'learning webs' that Illich (1970) advocated for.

Participants were often very receptive and appreciative of the workshop, and several took it multiple times or expressed desire to do so. At the closing of one workshop in a primary school, a young boy who spoke better Diidxazá than most of his classmates and had been the star student of the workshop presented them with a letter he had painstakingly written to them. They often received handmade gifts, cards and tokens of appreciation from participants. When asked what the most interesting part of the workshop was for her, a reserved woman in her 50s who participated with her adult daughter told me that it was the first time she had ever been asked to write something personal– at first she was certain that she had no stories worth telling and nothing to write, but was deeply impacted when she found that she did have things she wanted to express.

The impact of the *Camino de la Iguana* on participants was thus not limited to learning parts of the alphabet, or motivating use of Diidxazá, but also has empowered the personal expression of some participants.

Following the earthquakes of September 2017, both Natalia and Víctor were more involved in reconstruction efforts than in literacy education for a time. Natalia turned her home into an ad-hoc cultural center for children in her neighborhood, and began to sponsor a variety of workshops involving art, games, video production, and theater, among other topics, and to show films. Her primary goal was to give the children a chance to play and ease the stress and tension that came from the major earthquakes and countless smaller replicas which followed them. Víctor collaborated in coordinating community kitchens to provide meals to families whose homes were damaged. For both Natalia and Víctor, language activism is part of broader social engagement in the well-being of their community. While they are both interested in language as an object and discursive tool, it is the convivial social relations maintained through language that they prioritize as writer-activists.

6.4 Summary: Characteristics of community-based education activism

Community-based initiatives have the potential to imagine and enact different kinds of education spaces, hopefully avoiding the negative legacies of top-down colonial education (see chapter 4). 'Diidxazá literacy' as imagined and practiced by Víctor and Natalia is negotiated and collaborative, fostering appreciation of the literary heritage and opening the door for participants to take whatever they have gained and apply it towards their own goals and desires amidst the realities of their lives. Their initial desire to create readers of Zapotec adapted to the students that were present, many of whom had limited speaking competence. Rather than exclude this population, the teachers created new activities and adapted their teaching from context to context. The teachers hoped to give participants more confidence as bilingual or multilingual people and to encourage them to use their communicative repertoires more fully. In contrast to autonomous models of literacy that can leave learners feeling less powerful, literacy practices which provide learners the power to name their world and express their perspectives can help to reduce "literacy inequalities" (Street 2011). This positive appropriation and redefinition of literacy is apparent in the *Camino de la Iguana*. The central strategies of creating and legitimating readers and writers of a multi-dialectal and multilingual Diidxazá speech community are illustrated in Table 5.

Table 5: Key language activism strategies in a community-based literacy workshop.

Actions →	Goals →	Examples
– Creating	– People/ Identities – Communication practices	– Diidxazá readers and writers – Reading and writing in Diidxazá
– Representing	– People/ Identities – Communication practices	– Speakers and learners of all levels represented as legitimate – Diidxazá represented as a global and literary language – Dialect diversity represented as legitimate – Syntretic language use/ multilingualism accepted
– Connecting	– People/ Identities – Resources	– Participants introduced to books, writers, and literacy resources

Natalia and Víctor knew that most participants will not master the alphabet and beginning learners will not become speakers as a result of the workshop, but they hoped that the experience of the workshop would spark the motivation or confidence necessary for them to speak, write, and work towards their own aspirations. Although Natalia and Víctor would sometimes joke that all Juchitán residents should be required to study Zapotec, they ultimately acknowledged that fostering personal appreciation is the only viable approach, and that requiring people to study the language will not be effective. They did not want to reproduce the kind of forced learning environments found in schooling, but rather to take advantage of the flexibility of community-based education to create their own norms. Whether or not participants acquired full knowledge of the phonemic inventory of Isthmus Zapotec was less significant than the attitude or ideology that they had towards the language. Awareness of the local literary heritage – as well as viewing that heritage as part of universal literature – was a central aim of the workshop. The knowledge that Víctor and Natalia have as experts from the local context gives them insight into local histories and resources, as well as the diversity within the Isthmus Zapotec community, all of which they used to make their workshop as appropriate as possible to each new group of students. Different dialects were specifically included, albeit within a standard writing norm that can echo mainstream education practices. Although this norm results in telling people that some of their writing attempts are "incorrect", it also gives status and respect within a mainstream system dominated by standard language ideologies, and was evaluated positively by students who had been frustrated by less-normative Zapotec programs. Natalia and Víctor also offset the normative education practices that occured in the workshop with an over-arching convivial atmosphere in which participants became friends, talked, joked, sang and sometimes cried with them as they shared meaningful aspects of their lives. Participants evaluated this experience very positively, and many hoped to repeat it or to continue to learn more about Zapotec elsewhere.

Key characteristics of Natalia and Víctor's strategy to create Diidxazá writers and readers included the connection of the literary heritage to the contemporary context and the connection of local genres with international genres, bridging a local-historical orientation with an international-contemporary one. The inclusion of all learners through a convivial multilingual atmosphere and adaptation of the workshop to the needs of each student group illustrates Natalia and Víctor's commitment to encourage all residents of the region to identify as speakers and writers (at varying levels of expertise) of Zapotec. They viewed a purist orientation as a threat to learner participation, orienting mainly towards syncretic language practices, which they also modeled through their teaching. It is difficult to avoid orienting towards linguistic purism when teaching orthography, but through an explicit polynomic approach, and complementary writing activities where no correction was present, the teachers struck a good balance. Achieving a convivial learning environment in a multilingual context, as the *Camino de la Iguana* did, requires the democratic negotiation of communication practices and norms, where diverse voices are equally able to engage in self-definition. Arguments in favor of flexible (Blackledge and Creese 2010; Weber 2014; Heller 2007), heteroglossic, and dynamic (Cazden et al. 1996; García 2009a) multilingualism have been articulated in relation to these same concerns for improved participation and social justice in education in contexts around the world. The emphasis of these concepts often tends towards the resulting language forms (the fluid, flexible, heteroglossic languaging that is produced), however, rather than on the political processes through which communicative norms are negotiated. While there are many factors which supported the success of the *Camino de la Iguana*, I argue that the creation of a convivial multilingual approach to education in general, and literacy education in particular, was key to the positive outcomes of this activist endeavor.

For most participants, taking a workshop on writing Zapotec is a unique experience, standing out from the rest of their schooling; through a convivial atmosphere and the need to contribute their own voice, it became a meaningful experience for many in which they became part of a community of practice which frames Diidxazá use and users in valued and inclusionary ways. By accepting learners of all levels as "legitimate peripheral participants" (Lave and Wenger 1991), the principal actors in this community of practice encouraged them to take up a shared repertoire as decoders, consumers and producers of Zapotec texts. This community of practice is also investing in a joint enterprise to establish a Diidxazá-as-resource ideology and a new social imaginary of what it means to be literate in Diidxazá. They represent literacy in Diidxazá as something that goes beyond decoding to include creating and sharing new meanings, as well as being aware of the histories and social context of contemporary Diidxazá communication practices. By legitimizing the agency of learners as well as speakers in contemporary acts of meaning-making, and reinforcing an awareness of the histories and humanity inherent in Diidxazá use, the *Camino de la Iguana* fostered conviviality at the heart of communication practices.

Chapter 7
Imagining future traditions: Strategies in popular culture spaces

The *Raptivismo* (Rap + *activismo*, activism) radio show is on the air for its weekly 2-hour slot on a Sunday. In the second story of a building near the center of Juchitán I'm in the room which serves as a small local radio studio with 7 young men, sitting around a table which supports 3 microphones on small tripods. The host of the show is Juchitán-native Dalthon Pineda, who is a primary school teacher and a writer in addition to being a proponent of hip-hop music and culture. He interviews several rappers who are in the studio, including Cosijopi Ruiz López and Antonio Sánchez Ruiz of the Juchitán-based group Juchirap, and a rapper visiting from Puerto Escondido, a few hours away up the coast. The show and the side conversations in the studio are in Spanish; the music that is played and discussed is in Spanish and Zapotec. They take calls from listeners and offer a free CD to the first caller.

In a break, the host tells me about the first time a group of them performed rap at a public event and were met with animosity from politicians and members of the public, who associate hip-hop with vandalism and violent urban culture. He says it has been a challenge to show people that they do '*rap consciente*', conscious rap, which takes up important social issues and promotes critical thinking. One of the rappers in the studio agrees, saying that older people think rap is about gangsters, until they hear that you're rapping in Zapotec– then they shake your hand and ask where they can get your music. Two years ago (2012) one of the first people to rap in Isthmus Zapotec, Vicente Ramírez Santiago, or Rosty, won a prestigious state-level award for Indigenous language writing for his rap lyrics, which remains an important mark of legitimacy and pride for the local hip-hop community. The Juchirap group recounts how they've been invited to perform in several schools now and received an enthusiastic response from the students and a warm welcome from the teachers. Tomorrow they'll perform at 7am in a secondary school in the southern neighborhood of Juchitán, where most people speak Zapotec.

On the air, the host asks the group about the bilingual (Spanish-Zapotec) lyrics of one of their songs, which includes a reference to Juchitán poet Gabriel López Chiñas. At several points the young musicians talk about festivals and events that they have participated in elsewhere in Mexico, and the support and mentors that they have from being part of wider hip-hop networks. Towards the end of the show an adolescent boy and girl arrive at the studio, somewhat timid; they're the callers who have come to claim their free CD. The Juchirap members sign the CD for them, and do a fist-bump handshake with the boy before the teenagers leave. (Field notes July 2014)

Popular culture spaces such as this radio show are important domains of language use where norms of communication and identities are negotiated. The forms of music, visual art and literature that are created and shared through mass media, and increasingly through social media, can also have a significant impact on language ideologies. The Isthmus is home to artists of many genres of music and visual art, as well as the literary heritage discussed in chapter 6. While language activism is not the foremost goal of all of these artists, Isthmus Zapotec does feature prominently for some of them. In the case of the young rappers participating in the *Raptivismo* show, the displacement of Zapotec is one of the many social changes that they observe and comment on through rap; increasing insecurity and violence in their communities, and political corruption are also prominent concerns. The fact that the local hip-hop community had secured a space on the air and had an audience for their program was evidence that they were well on the way to being accepted as a legitimate art form and youth movement. They were conscious of participating in a transnational music culture, discussing their wider networks and influences, in addition to wearing an internationally-recognizable style of clothes and performing other indexes of hip-hop-ness, such as the stylized handshake. At the same time, they were also keen to reach the ears and minds of their peers and neighbors in the Isthmus, and an (old-fashioned) handshake with someone who was previously skeptical but came to be interested in their music was viewed as an achievement. The use of Diidxazá was often discussed as part of what attracted listeners and attention locally, in part because it was an unexpected fusion of something viewed as a foreign, urban, modern art form with something viewed as local, largely rural, and traditional. For the rappers and their listeners, this fusion was also a congruent reflection of their everyday lives, where all of these elements were current and relevant. Most of young hip-hop artists had a foot in local traditions as well as global trends; one continued to play in the 'prehispanic' music group[32] he had participated in since he was young; another occasionally worked with his father painting banners for the *Velas*, saints' festivals, but was also an avid graffiti painter. They knew how to shake hands in both old and new ways.

In this chapter I examine several popular culture spaces which have grown to be important domains for language activism in the Isthmus, including groups which organize events and performances, participation in digital spaces, and the wider networks of civil society organizations that sometimes support local initiatives. These popular culture initiatives are important spaces where socialization and learning occur without the oversight or intervention of formal or informal educators (7.1). The amount of locally organized groups, collectives, events, and

---

[32] 'Prehispanic music', as played for some public occasions in the Isthmus, consists of drumming, turtle-shell percussion, and a whistle instrument.

digital resources that are created in the Isthmus is prolific; describing even a fraction of these initiatives would require a book in and of itself. Here, I highlight examples of some of the initiatives I observed, noting that there are many inspiring initiatives which unfortunately remain unmentioned here for lack of space and time. Rather than attempt to inventory popular culture initiatives, I focus on several key activism strategies which are shared among multiple initiatives (7.2). Salient language activism strategies among popular culture initiatives include *creating events*, such as performances and festivals, and *creating* semi-fluid and participatory *spaces or structures*, such as a yearly writing competition, a radio show, and a social media page. Through these spaces and events, activists are *representing* their own *identities* and *communication practices* as both local and global, and both traditional and modern. I conclude with a summary of the language activism strategies in popular culture spaces, which remain fluid, highly creative and diverse as they recontextualize Isthmus Zapotec in a changing language ecology and society (7.3).

7.1 Negotiating social meanings through popular culture activism

Language activism has often been pursued through artistic, popular culture and media channels. These domains lend themselves to an especially flexible and negotiated form of language activism, where the multiple meanings of Diidxazá– of language– are open for (re)interpretation and negotiation (as discussed in chapter 1). While school-based activism may be inextricably linked with notions of linguistic competence and standard language ideologies, and scholar activism is influenced by the tendency to define, categorize and assert authoritative knowledge, popular culture activism draws from a more eclectic array of social and discursive resources. Like activists in community-based education, popular culture activists have a more open space to work with, and can contemplate a wider range of potential participants and imagine alternative connections among them.

The political power of the aesthetic, creative and performative domains of life has been examined in multiple contexts (e.g. Edelman 1995), not least that of Indigenous activism. Sociolinguist Sari Pietikäinen (2018) examines the new meaning-making achieved by Indigenous Sámi activists through visual art, such as posters and re-appropriated digital images which combine elements of global culture with elements of Sámi culture. For example, the US World War II poster of 'Rosie the Riveter' is redesigned to wear iconic Sámi clothing, with Northern Sámi text, as a representation of Indigenous resistance. She labels this strategy "affective multilingualism", and argues that:

> For this kind of affective multilingualism to work – that is, to transform some of the existing ways of perceiving, thinking and talking about Sámi issues and creating affective solidarity, alliances and politics – requires interconnected and intertextual ways of working and the recycling and reworking of traces and signs already used before: they need to be rooted in expressive rhizomes and engage with multilingual and multisemiotic resources.
>
> (2018: 193)

Pietikäinen points towards a two-fold goal for these activists; they aim to transform ways of perceiving and thinking, and to foster "affective solidarity", what in Mexico would be called *convivencia*, conviviality (see also chapters 4 and 6). She also highlights how they are able to achieve these goals through the recirculation and re-purposing of visual and linguistic resources in social space.

Such recirculating of semiotic resources is described by Bauman and Briggs (1990) as acts of entextualization, decontextualization and recontextualization. Like the Sámi activists choosing to recontextualize Sámi clothing onto a global icon of feminine resistance, the Juchirap musicians chose to recontextualize a piece of the Isthmus Zapotec literary canon (López Chiñas' famous poem) in a global musical genre, as described in the opening vignette. Bauman and Briggs note that producing chains of meaning in this way is a performative, political action. Choosing to "decenter" and "recenter" an image, text, or sound "is an act of control", subject to social limitations of access and resources (1990: 76). Activists who engage in these creative productions are part of the "the process of traditionalization, the telling and retelling of a tale, the citing and reciting of a proverb as these recenterings are part of the symbolic construction of discursive continuity with a meaningful past" (1990: 77–78). Pietikäinen calls this "the politics of becoming", noting that aesthetic activism "does not just reflect contemporary values, identities, and relationships but is an active participant in the creation and recreation of the socio-cultural milieu" (2018: 193).

The semiotic tools which popular culture activists make use of – such as images, music, and text – are also available and used by activists in other domains, but often with a more limited range of expression. While activists in higher education are negotiating the nature of the identity of 'Isthmus Zapotec teacher' (see chapter 5), popular culture activists are typically engaged in negotiating broader categories such as 'Isthmus Zapotec speaker', 'Isthmus Zapotec woman', and 'Isthmus Zapotec person'. Popular culture spaces, such as the hip-hop scene, are important sites for many kinds of activism and political engagement. In these spaces, contested identities, resources and rights may be represented and negotiated, often in intertwined ways. Language activism, where present, is often closely intertwined with other concerns, such as shifts in Indigenous identities and lifestyles or critiques of non-local interventions in the local society and economy. Describing the history of Isthmus Zapotec cultural promotion in the 19th and 20th centuries (see also chapter 2) in an article published in *Guchachi' Reza* in 1984 and reproduced in an edited volume in 1993, *Istmeño* scholar and writer Víctor de la Crúz noted that:

> As the cultural and linguistic movement becomes politicized, its objectives broaden. Now it is not enough to recover native language and culture. It is also necessary to recover the communal lands that are being monopolized and privatized. [. . .] In relation to this our history has taught us, [. . .] that we Zapotecs cannot win the battle by ourselves. We must seek new alliances [. . .] and, in this way, widen our project. (1993: 245)

Making linguistic and cultural movements visible to members of the non-Indigenous society and showing how they are linked with wider concerns of identity and well-being is another part of the activist agenda. Elsewhere in Mexico, Indigenous language activist and scholar José Antonio Flores Farfán has discussed the value of pursuing language activism through multimedia and art in order to build wider coalitions (Flores Farfán 2002). Producing bilingual multimedia resources is "useful to a wide audience, namely, people in the indigenous and mainstream populations looking to establish a respectful and productive dialogue between different sectors of Mexican society" (2002: 231) he argues. Whether through a range of semiotic resources, or through widened solidarity and conviviality, popular culture activism has considerable potential and power.

This activism can take many forms. In the following sections I offer a glimpse of the strategies of several popular culture activists in the Isthmus, including the hip-hop movement (7.2.1), a women's collective (7.2.2), digital spaces (7.2.3), and discuss some of the common characteristics and the wider networks which support these grassroots projects (7.3).

7.2 Popular culture activism in the Isthmus

There is a long tradition of locally run artistic production as well as volunteer-organized groups and initiatives in the Isthmus. From the independent publications of *Neza* and *Guchachi' Reza*, to the founding of the Juchitán *Casa de la Cultura* in 1972, there have continued to be a multitude of publications, radio programs, events, and cultural spaces created by *Istmeños*. Cultural activists have created spaces of exchange and creativity in their own homes or in public parks, and are respected and appreciated by residents of all ages. For example, in Union Hidalgo, a village to the southeast of Juchitán, the *Galería Gubidxa* [Sun Gallery] has been established and maintained by Víctor Fuentes, a teacher and writer, who hosts art expositions as well as workshops and events, often facilitated by other members of the local community. Founded in Juchitán in 2004, the *Comité Melendre* [Melendre Committee] has engaged in social, cultural, and educational outreach with the goal of supporting *"la transformación positiva de la sociedad zapoteca"* [the positive transformation of Zapotec society] through a variety of activities. One of their projects has been the *Centro Cultural Herón Ríos*, which has offered workshops and events aimed especially at children (see also chapter 6).[33] The collective *Binni Cubi* [New People] in Union Hidalgo has been active producing didactic games, murals, films and other creative products which promote knowledge of local history and language (Schwab-Cartas 2018).[34] A variety of virtual spaces and resources have also been created, such as a navigator and vocabulary list hosted on the "Familia Toledo" website,[35] and Diidxazá learning apps for mobile phones created by students at the *Instituto de Estudios Superiores del Istmo de Tehuantepec* [Institute for Higher Studies of the Isthmus of Tehuantepec, IESIT].

Among these and many other spaces and groups across the Isthmus, the role that language plays varies. The valorization of Isthmus Zapotec is sometimes explicit, as the focus of instruction or the medium of communication. In some initiatives it is interwoven indirectly in the activities, events, and creations of these popular culture activists. Here I focus on several communities of practice which have been active in creating events and networks in recent years which valorize Diidxazá in both direct and indirect ways. Beginning with the tangible spaces and events created by the hip-hop and feminist communities, I then illustrate the strategies of representation and connection within virtual spaces. A focus on convivial participation is central across most of these initiatives, as taken up further in the concluding section.

7.2.1 Wake up! Hip-hop events and representations

Among Indigenous language activists in many parts of the world, hip-hop has been a popular medium for valorizing Indigenous language and appealing to youth (Swinehart 2012; Cru 2017). Rooted in Black American activism, this art

---

33 https://comitemelendre.blogspot.com/
34 https://sites.google.com/site/lubilunisa/Home
35 www.biyuubi.com

form has lent itself well to other contexts characterized by resistance to racism and oppression (Alim, Ibrahim, and Pennycook 2008; Williams and Stroud 2013; Williams 2017). One of the first occasions where I heard *Istmeño* rappers was at an event in May 2014 that several rappers had organized; their publicity for the event stated that the theme was *"Libertad y Resistencia"* [Freedom and resistance]. The event was held outdoors next to the *Guigu Bicu Nisa*[36] which runs in between the central section of Juchitán and its western neighborhoods. During the dry, windy season, the levels in the river had fallen very low, and the banks were wildly overgrown, covered in most places by dense grasses and brush, a few small trees holding on to the banks here and there, and a substantial amount of plastic and trash. A group of rappers had worked together to cut down the brush and grasses and to clear a space along the bank. They set up low benches with planks and cinder blocks and had built an open thatched roof structure which housed speakers, a pile of cables and some microphones. The event included performances by several rappers, in both Spanish and Zapotec, with an audience of 30–40 people stopping by to listen and a MC hosting in Spanish in between the songs. Most of the young men wore jeans, baseball caps and t-shirts often with an English logo or slogan on them. A few were painting a graffiti mural nearby. Anyone was welcome to get up and take the microphone, some of the rappers tried out new songs, rapping from their handwritten lyrics on pieces of paper. After a boy who looked younger than the rest, perhaps 13 years old, had performed a song with some obvious difficulties, the MC encouraged everyone to give him a big applause, commenting that it takes real courage to do this.

One of the organizers was Rosty (Vicente Ramírez Santiago), the rapper who had won first prize in the 2012 CASA competition (*Premio CASA Creación literaria en lengua Didxazá (zapoteca)*) in the category of music. His winning song was entitled '¡*Gutaná*!' [¡*Despierta!* Wake up!] and focused on social problems and social change in the Isthmus Zapotec community. The prize is awarded each year in several categories (music, poetry, children's literature, narrative, and text based in oral traditions) by the *Centro de la Artes San Augustín* (CASA), a non-profit organization based near Oaxaca City.[37] CASA was founded by Isthmus-born painter Francisco Toledo, the father of poet and *Camino de la Iguana* co-counder Natalia

---

36 Otter River, often called *Rio de los Perros*, literally Dog River in Spanish following a direct, incomplete translation from Diidxazá: *Bicu Nisa* (water dog, or otter).
37 CASA supports numerous artistic endeavors that raise the visibility of Indigenous languages and forms of expression in Oaxaca, including the *Camino de la Iguana* workshops (see chapter 6) and other literacy outreach initiatives.

Toledo. Francisco Toledo had also helped to found the *Lidxi Guendabiaani*, or *Casa de la Cultura* in Juchitán in 1972 and was active in the COCEI movement in Juchitán in the 1980s (see chapter 2). In the following decades, he engaged in extensive arts-based social outreach from his base in Oaxaca City, including the creation of a public graphic arts library, a photography center, and numerous campaigns for socio-political issues. Toledo achieved a unique level of international and national renown, which helped his foundations and initiatives, but he remained hugely popular and was viewed by many *Istmeños* as intrinsically local, a defender of Oaxacan culture, land, and language.[38] The CASA award gave Rosty's music, and hip-hop more generally, the symbolic backing of CASA and of Toledo, a valuable stamp of approval in both the realm of art and of Isthmus society. On the occasion of the outdoor event by the riverside in May 2014, however, Rosty commented to me that this event was organized internally, through the volunteer labor and interest of the local hip-hop community. The symbolic backing from a state-level authority such as CASA was useful, but not as important as the genuine interest and participation of the local community which was easy to observe. The same was true of the *Raptivismo* radio show, and other public performances I saw in several of the central parks of Juchitán. Young people in Juchitán did not need to be encouraged to attend these events, they simply turned up.

Like Toledo himself, these hip-hop events were associated with both international and local reference points, simultaneously. By appropriating hip-hop styles to express *Istmeño* realities through Spanish and Zapotec, these rappers created a space for new forms of expression. One of the founding members of Juchirap, Cosijopi Ruiz López articulated this powerfully in a social media post:

> *A todos los que dicen que mesclar dos culturas, (hip hop, y zapoteco) esta mal, o no deberíamos hacer esto, o e inclusive no les gusta escuchar el zapoteco en una rola de rap, les quiero decir con todo respeto, "no tomare en cuenta eso" yo seguiré haciendo esto, como lo he estado haciendo, despierten!!!! ya nadie habla zapoteco, ya nadie usa carreta, ya nadie usa huaraches, les propongo algo!! rescatemos nuestro juchitan! hablemos zapoteco, rescatemos las tradiciones! saludos, y bendiciones!*

> To everyone who says that mixing two cultures (hip hop, and zapotec) is bad, or we shouldn't do that, and or also those that don't like hearing Zapotec in a rap verse, I want to say something with all due respect, "I won't take that into account" I will continue doing that, as I have been doing it, wake up!!!! now no one speaks Zapotec, now no one

---

38 When Toledo passed away in September 2019 the enormous outpourings of mourning and appreciation from all corners of society included graffiti art in his honor.

uses carts, now no one uses sandals,[39] I am offering you something!! let's recuperate our juchitan! let's speak Zapotec, let's recuperate the traditions! greetings, and blessings!

(May 2014, reproduced with permission as posted)

Rejecting a purist orientation to language and culture, Cosijopi encouraged listeners to "wake up" to the changes occurring in society and to accept what he and other younger artists are offering. They know that following the same lifestyle that their grandparents did is not a possibility, whether they want it to be or not, and they are making sense of the world they find themselves in now.

Groups such as Juchirap which 'mix two cultures' have arguably been very successful in their efforts. In the years following their founding in 2014, Juchirap has made multiple music videos which they post on their social media sites, and have been the subject of multiple news stories and video shorts, gaining a wider audience and renown within the Isthmus and well beyond. Many of the news stories about them have highlighted the fact that they rap in an Indigenous language, with titles and tag-lines like '*Con rap buscan jóvenes conservar el zapoteco del Istmo*' [With rap youth aim to conserve Isthmus Zapotec] (Cha'ca 2015) and '*Estos jóvenes rapean en zapoteco para preservar su lengua*' [These youth rap in Zapotec to preserve their language] (Plumas Atómicas 2019) appearing in local and national news channels. They performed as part of the 2019 Guelaguetza, a high-profile yearly event held in Oaxaca City which showcases music and *baile folklórico* [folk dance] from different Indigenous communities in Oaxaca. They were also one of the groups invited to perform in a Septermber 2019 concert alongside well-established artists to commemorate the anniversary of the massive earthquakes that caused extensive damage in the Isthmus in September 2017. The concert was entitled *Dxi guni' xu en Juchitán* [The day the earthquake spoke in Juchitán], and was sponsored by the national government through the Ministry of Culture. These performances place them in the company of well-recognized Indigenous artists locally and nationally. From organizing their own events and grassroots performance spaces, they have been invited into officially endorsed cultural spaces and reached a wider audience.

The hip-hop events in the Isthmus attract mainly men, although some women also perform, and many women are fans. While it is not uniquely a masculine space, there is a clear gender trend within this activist community. Women are also active in redefining popular culture spaces in a variety of ways, as explored in the next section.

---

39 Horse or donkey-drawn carts and hand-made leather sandals are symbols of the traditional Isthmus agricultural lifestyle, both of which are still in use, but now by fewer and fewer members of society.

7.2.2 The granddaughters of the *Binnigula'za*: Feminist events and representations

A feminist collective has been active organizing events and spaces of expression in the Isthmus, hosting a yearly *Encuentro de mujeres poetas del Istmo* [Gathering of female poets of the Isthmus] since 2014, and a 'Festival of Female Artists in the Isthmus' entitled *Gunaa Ruzaani* [Shining woman/ Woman who gives light] in 2018. One of the organizers, Aurora Cobon, explained in an interview in January 2018 that these initiatives were organized and facilitated by a collective of around 20 women, most in their 20s and 30s, and were designed to give a space to the many female writers and artists in the Isthmus who are lesser known than their male counterparts. Through the strategy of creating events, this collective has supported connections and networks among female artists. Furthermore, they have contributed to representations of *Istmeña* women, which, similar to the representations produced by the rappers, are a vibrant mixture of tradition and contemporary realities.

Many of their promotional materials evidence their local-global orientation, as well as their critical focus on the current moment as a product of colonial histories. For example, the poster for the 2018 Festival of Female Artists (Figure 21) takes an image from the classic European art canon, the armless Venus de Milo at the top, giving it first arms in the middle image, and then brown arms holding a paintbrush in a strong pose in the bottom image. A yellow circle initially highlights the head and upper torso of the armless woman in the top two images, and then moves to highlight her hand and paintbrush in the bottom image, shifting from a focus on a helpless female body to the action and authorship of the woman. This symbolic empowerment of Venus through gaining brown arms and a means of expression is coherent with the aims and vision of the collective which seeks to shine light on the skills of female creators in the Isthmus. They represent *Istmeña* artists as part of an international art milieu, their strong arms helping to change the gender imbalance not only locally, but internationally by lending a hand to the helpless white Venus.

With bright colors and asymmetrical geometric shapes, the poster also presents a youthful, irreverent aesthetic. The organizers are listed towards the bottom of the poster, and the symbols of the organizers and collaborating hosts are aligned along the foot of the page. One of the organizers is named *Las nietas de lxs Binnigula'za* [The granddaughters of the [male and female] Zapotec Ancestors]. This name combines standard Spanish (the granddaughters of) with a gender neutral 3rd person determiner (*lxs*) which has been popularized by gender activists throughout the global Spanish-speaking community as a way to avoid the standard practice of defaulting to a masculine form whenever both

Figure 21: Poster for the '1st Festival of Female Artists in the Isthmus of Tehuantepec "*Gunaa Ruzaani*"' 3–5 April 2018.

males and females are present (in this case standard Spanish would require the male determiner *los*). The final word, *binnigula'za*, is Diidxazá, and means roughly Zapotec ancestors or figures that are significant in pre-colonial mythology and spirituality. These young activists demonstrate their ownership of both Spanish and Diidxazá, and signal their explicit feminist stance through this name. They skillfully represent themselves as the descendants and inheritors of an ancient tradition, who are also intent on commenting on and improving today's unequal gender practices.

Although the patriarchal dominance which these young women resist is perpetuated on multiple fronts, the religions imposed through European colonization and the racial hierarchy which persists through coloniality in the Americas are central factors (Lugones 2016; Mendoza 2016). The feminist agenda is therefore also a decolonial agenda in many ways. While none of the young women in the collectives believe that the precolonial past was free of gender hierarchies, there is a widespread perception that Isthmus Zapotec society has been, and to some extent still is, matriarchal, with more respect granted to women than the norm of mestizo Mexican society (Poniatowska 1993; Taylor 2006). As Campbell noted, there is a "rich community oral tradition and national mythology about 'matriarchal' Zapotecs that continues to shape both local and external perceptions of Isthmus women" (Campbell 1993:89), a stereotype which I observed clearly several decades later. Additionally, Diidxazá does not distinguish between male and female gender; humans, animals and things are distinguished grammatically, requiring different determiners and verb agreement, but there are no sub-categories within the class of humans. In comparison to Spanish, which distinguishes not only between male and female humans, but assigns all objects a gender of male or female, Diidxazá allows for much more gender neutral communication practices. The fluidity of gender categories in Zapotec culture is also illustrated by the presence, and more-or-less mainstream acceptance, of *muxes*, or men who prefer female tasks, clothing, and male partners.[40] It is therefore not surprising that local language and culture are given value and taken up as part of the struggle for gender equality by *Istmeñas*. Language reclamation is not their central goal, but the promotion of Isthmus Zapotec poetry, music, and visual motifs is central in their projects and it is not a coincidence that Isthmus Zapotec names were chosen for several of the collectives and for the festival itself. In this way this group has contributed to a positive, contemporary image of Isthmus Zapotec language, linking it to a

---

[40] Gender in the Isthmus is a complex topic which cannot be fully explored here, but has been taken up elsewhere (e.g. Royce 1991; Miano Borruso 2002; Taylor 2006).

youth-led feminist movement and aspirations for gender equality. More importantly, they contribute to representations of *Istmeñas* as authors and artists, and help to create spaces for expression and exchange.

All of the organizers and hosts of the 2018 festival were Isthmus-based, volunteer-run organizations.[41] Each engages in their own creative endeavors, but they also showed solidarity with the feminist groups spearheading the festival, providing space and assisting with activities. This kind of collective support of large-scale events – whether the yearly saints' *Velas*, or a wedding or birthday – is common, so much so that multiple terms exist for it. Collaborative labor was often described as *tequio* or *trueque* (terms for voluntary collaborative work which are used across Mexico) or occasionally as *guendalisaa* (an Isthmus Zapotec term for the action of doing relationality/ solidarity/ kinship) by the people I spent time with in the Isthmus. While local groups would not necessarily be opposed to support from larger organizations outside the Isthmus, they generally do not need such support in order to mobilize a considerable amount of resources and people. All of the workshops and performances throughout the 3 days of the festival, including workshops in visual art and creative writing, and a rap workshop led by Oaxaca City-based rapper Mare Advertencia Lirika, were free for participants and female participants were given first priority to attend.

The participatory events organized by the hip-hop and feminist communities attract the attention of adults and younger people in the Isthmus. They are both driven largely by young adults, although they seek and appreciate recognition and support from pre-existing organizations and networks where possible. By positioning themselves as simultaneously traditional and modern, local and global, they have achieved a successful, convivial form of activism. Collaboration or *guendalisaa* has been central to these endeavors, building on local social networks for material and intangible forms of support. The circulation of images, music and text through mass media and social media is also central to the practices of the groups described above, as they seek to promote and invite participants to their events, and reach wider audiences through on-line networks. In the following section I examine the role that digital spaces play in facilitating language activism in the Isthmus.

---

41 The other organizers are *Colectivas Bacuzaguí* (Firefly collectives) and *Mujeres Poetas* (Female poets), who were supported and given physical space for the festival by *Colectivo Bicu Yuba* (Mad/ rabid dog collective), *Casa El Ocote* (a cultural center named after a Mexican pine tree) and the *Bibliotheca popular Víctor Yodo* (Víctor Yodo people's library, a library established and maintained by the family of a well-known Juchitán Indigenous rights activist who was disappeared in 1978 during the COCEI movement (see chapter 2)).

7.2.3 Creating virtual resources and spaces of negotiation

The virtual space of social media and digital communication is a significant part of most people's lives in the Isthmus, and numerous language activists have engaged in strategic use of these resources to promote Diidxazá. "Digital activism" has been a topic of investigation and admiration in multiple Indigenous communities (Coronel-Molina 2019). The use of technology in service of Indigenous activism builds on a well-established tradition of Indigenous language radio in the Americas dating back several decades. Isthmus Zapotec radio has been active since the 1970s (Campbell 1989) and several radio stations continue to produce substantial programming in Diidxazá. Radio Totopo, based in the southern 7th section of Juchitán, broadcasts only in Diidxazá and has also served as a base for political activism around community rights, in particular resistance to the wind farm developments (Sánchez Miguel 2016). Coronel-Molina (2019) notes that considering the achievements of Indigenous language radio, the use of Indigenous languages in the mass media is not new. However, he argues that "media and technology are contributing to the creation of new hybrid, heteroglossic cultural and linguistic forms through complex interplays between virtual and real communities in contemporary times. Virtual spaces are multilingual, pluricultural, multiethnic, translingual, transcultural and translocal" (95). This contrasts with the communication produced by radio stations such as Radio Totopo, which is entirely in Diidxazá. Coronel-Molina (2019) points out that there are important asymmetries and hierarchies within these multilingual virtual spaces, which minority language activists must attempt to address.

Digital language activism includes trying to address virtual hierarchies and the so-called digital divide by making more information available in Indigenous languages, as well as providing infrastructure for people to use Indigenous languages in the media that are part of their everyday communication practices. In relation to the former, there have been several initiatives to create on-line as well as app-based vocabulary lists and translation resources for Isthmus Zapotec, including an on-line audio vocabulary of Juchitán Zapotec created by the non-profit group *Fundación Historico Cultural Juchitán*[42] [Historical Cultural Foundation of Juchitán]. This group, another volunteer-driven collective, was founded in 2003 by elder men from Juchitán with the aim to "*preservar y fortalecer nuestra identidad histórico-cultural*" [preserve and strengthen our historical cultural identity] (*Fundación Historico Cultural Juchitán* website). The website that they created presents a clear historical aesthetic, with a parchment-style

---

42 www.zapotecoteco.org.mx

background and a logo that represents a pre-colonial sculpture found in the Isthmus which is now on display in the National Museum of Anthropology in Mexico City. Aside from a Spanish-Zapotec translation function and audio samples of words in Juchitán Zapotec, the site also contains "*Homenajes*" [Homages] giving biographies and images of 10 men from Juchitán who they view as having made a mark in politics or in the cultural sphere. The site also contains multimedia (historical photographs, music, and documents), and the group has created several YouTube videos. One of the founders, retired educator David Ruíz Martínez, discussed the importance of representing Zapotec on a par with other languages, noting that many young people have been socialized to have "*ese complejo de creer que ser indígena es ser tonto, ser torpe, ser mediocre*" [that complex of believing that to be Indigenous is to be stupid, to be clumsy, to be mediocre] (Interview April 2014). He and the other members of the group are committed to countering these stereotypes through highlighting the history behind the language and the participation of *Istmeños* in high status social domains such as politics, science and culture. He argued that Zapotec needs to be used more in higher education, and saw the website as a small contribution towards representing Zapotec as a language of literature, science and philosophy. As language and cultural activists, this group had a strong focus on the past, but by choosing to develop digital resources they illustrated their desire to engage with a wide audience in the present and to bridge from the traditions that they grew up with to the society around them today.

This was an apt choice; people (especially young people) who want to gain more knowledge about Isthmus Zapotec often turn to the internet as a source of information and authority. On-line dictionaries, translation apps, and thesaurus have become the resource of choice for many writers. A young adult university student commented on how useful some of the Zapotec resources are for her:

> *A mí me gusta publicar también en Facebook cosas en zapoteco entonces no podía estar llamando a mi mamá cada que yo quisiera [subir algo en zapoteco] entonces cuando me surgen dudas así voy al buscador de google que es el más bueno y busco cosas nuevas. Entonces en esa búsqueda encontré un diccionario en línea de español a zapoteco, no hay de zapoteco a español, pero sí de español a zapoteco. Entonces escribes lo que quieres saber y te aparece la pronunciación. También en YouTube hay lecciones de zapoteco es un usuario que se llama Tehuanos76 algo así pero ya tiene muchos videos tiene como ciento y tantos videos de. . . zapoteco.*

> I like to publish things in Zapotec on Facebook also, so I couldn't be calling my mom every time I would want to [post something in Zapotec], so when I have doubts like that, I go to the Google search that is the best and I look for new things. So in that search I found a Spanish to Zapotec on-line dictionary, there isn't one from Zapotec to Spanish, but yes Spanish to Zapotec. So you write what you want to know and the pronunciation appears for you. Also

in YouTube there are Zapotec lessons, it's a user that is called Tehuanos76, something like that, there are many videos, there are like a hundred or so videos of. . . Zapotec.

(Interview October 2013)

For some people, such as this young adult, the use of Zapotec in texting or social media posts is a natural thing, representing the significant place of Zapotec in their communicative repertoire. Depending on their interests and abilities, some turn to on-line resources as a way to find new words, to check their spelling, or even to learn pronunciation through video and audio resources. The somewhat static resources such as word lists and videos are thus directly linked to and supportive of more communicative and fluid use of Zapotec, such as social media posts and conversations. While not everyone who uses Zapotec in social media does so with an activist agenda, their practices help to make up the language ecology in the Isthmus and thus carry a political significance. Some people choose to post in Zapotec due to their stance in support of the language, while others may choose their language(s) for practical, aesthetic or semantic motivations. Resources that can enable these multimedia communication practices are important supports for the normalization of Isthmus Zapotec in the contemporary communicative landscape.

As discussed in previous chapters (2, 4, 6), most *Istmeños* have not had the opportunity to learn the Isthmus Zapotec popular alphabet, and instead they write drawing upon their Spanish literacy. Some people are not concerned with following a writing norm, while others express a desire to improve their ability to write in Zapotec. Perhaps exacerbated by this, there is a considerable amount of meta-commentary about Diidxazá, Diidxazá competence, and *Istmeño* culture that occurs on social media, such as the meme shown in Figure 13, section 5.1. Negotiating competence through discussions of spellings and translations can occur in public and private conversations, and multiple pages and profiles exist in social media to disseminate information about the language or culture. One example of this kind of activist social media site is a Facebook group called *Guca'nu jneza diidxazá* [Let's write good Diidxazá] that was founded in March 2014. This initiative was started by León Medellín, a young man from Union Hidalgo in the Isthmus, who spent many of his formative years outside the region due to his family's economic migration. He was motivated to learn Isthmus Zapotec spelling norms himself, and to engage others in discussion and awareness-raising about the writing practices in the region. Discussing writing practices, he argued:

Hay que unificarlo porque yo al rato escribo un libro en zapoteco, y fulanito escribe otro, y al rato se va a hacer una antología de escritos en zapoteco. Y si no hacemos todos el mismo esfuerzo del mismo lado, pues a la hora que nuestros nietos, nuestros bisnietos y tataranietos quieran agarrar esa información, pues se van a ver en un mar de complicaciones [. . .] Entonces esa es la finalidad del, de la ortografía, ¿no? Que pueda, se pueda este, conservar. Conservar la literatura y conservar la lengua, ¿no?

It must be unified because in a bit I'll write a book in Zapotec, and so-and-so writes another, and in a bit an anthology of writing in Zapotec is going to be made. And if we don't all make the same effort from the same side, well when our grandchildren, our great-grandchildren and great-great-grandchildren want to get a hold of that information, well they will find themselves in a sea of complications [. . .] So that is the final goal of, of orthography, right? That one can, one can, um, conserve. Conserve the literature and conserve the language, right? (Interview May 2014)

When asked about the possible paradox between conserving the diversity present within the Zapotec speech community (such as the dialect variants) and unifying the writing system (which would mean less diverse writing practices and potentially disadvantage for some dialects), he responded that the variation was not so great, and a common writing system was the most important goal, allowing Zapotec to be read in the future in the way that Greek texts are still read today. His intention was to both present a unified view of Isthmus Zapotec orthography, and to assist in the production of writers (of a standard variety).

León considered an open social media group to be an appropriate way to achieve his goals, explaining:

> León   *Hice ese grupo principalmente para que a la gente que le interese escribir en zapoteco pueda este, pueda ir enseñando. Y además es abierto, ¿no? Es abierto para que cualquiera publique, como foro de discusión. Es decir, bueno, "yo lo escribo así porque aquí dice que así se escribe." "No, pero yo pienso que"– así y ahora viene esta nueva norma que se va a escribir así. "Ah, bueno. ¿Entonces cómo va a quedar?"*
>
> HDK   *Hum.*
>
> León   *Como un foro de discusión. Sin embargo, no ha tenido tanta repercusión como he querido, pero, pero sí lo hago y yo publico mucho en ese lugar sobre [. . .] las grafías del zapoteco. Para que la gente también se entere cómo es.*
>
> León   I made that group principally so that people who are interested in writing in Zapotec could um, could be teaching. And additionally it's open, right? It's open so that anyone can publish, as a form of discussion. That's to say, right "I write it like this because here they say that it's written like this." "No, but I think that it's like this" and now comes this new norm that it's going to be written like this. "Ah, OK. So how is it going to turn out?"
>
> HDK   Hmm.

> León Like a discussion forum. However, it hasn't had as much repercussion as I had wanted, but, but yes I do it and I post a lot in that place about [. . .] the Zapotec graphemes. So that people also find out how it is. (Interview May 2014)

This Diidxazá activist imagined the homogenization of Zapotec writing as a necessary goal which he hoped to achieve through convivial interactions and discussions. He attempted to foster a community of practice among people who are voluntarily interested in Zapotec writing norms. The public participation was not as lively as he had hoped in the beginning, and the group has not always remained tightly focused on writing, but has rather become a space of general interest in the language, including sharing texts, news articles, and events relevant to Isthmus Zapotec (as of November 2020 there are 1,731 members). Representations of Diidxazá as a language (not a *dialecto*) and pan-Zapotec ethnic pride have also been common on the page. Considering the kinds of posts and discussions on the page, most members seem more (or at least equally) interested in language use, history and culture, than they are in discussing language norms.

Another way in which meta-commentary about Zapotec circulates in cyberspace is through humorous memes and comics produced by both individuals and by group pages. Memes often recycle images and texts from one context to another (Wiggins and Bowers 2015), creating the kind of juxtaposition and recontextualization which can lead to new perceptions as discussed by Bauman and Briggs (1990) and Pietikäinen (2018). There are several Facebook pages where Isthmus-specific memes are posted and often recirculated. One example is the public page *Nanixhe & Guendanayahui* [*Sabroso & [hacer] chistoso*, delicious and being funny] which publishes a wide range of memes and commentaries in relation to many aspects of life in the Isthmus, the vast majority with humorous content. This page (founded in 2014, with over 9,000 followers as of November 2020) does not have the explicit pedagogical approach present in the *Guca'nu jneza diidxazá* [Let's write good Diidxazá] page. However, the moderators of the page were motivated to post an explicit encouragement to people who are making memes that they should use the popular alphabet, and the pedagogical grammar and vocabulary produced by SIL (based on the work of Velma Pickett and her collaborators, see also chapter 3). They provide links to these resources and state that meme-makers should avoid fragmenting the language. They take a light, but direct tone, writing *"Invitamos a todos aquellos que hacen memes, que aman y hablan la lengua zapoteca a que hagamos un pequeño esfuerzo, -además, nadie quiere decirle víbora a su hermana-."* [We invite everyone who makes memes, who loves and speaks the Zapotec language to all make a small effort,- additionally, no one wants to call their sister a viper-.]⁴³ (June 2019).

Language ideologies are present in some of the memes that are circulated as well. Figure 22 shows a meme which was produced by a different page, *Memes Idiomas UABJO* [Memes for/ from the UABJO Faculty of Languages] and reposted on *Nanixhe & Guendanayahui* in November 2018, which represents different languages as superheroes fighting over superiority. The first frame shows a blue character with a head-band saying in Spanish and (globalized) Japanese *"¡Japonés es la lengua más kawai! ¡Muere, baka!"* [Japanese is the most *kawai* [adorable] language! Die *baka* [stupid]!]. In the second frame a green character with a mohawk lunges forward yelling in French-accented Spanish *"¡No, Fgancés es la mejog! ¡Muege!"* [No, French is the best! Die!]. In the third frame a significantly more powerful character has impaled both of the fighters on swords, while yelling

Figure 22: Meme from the page *Memes Idiomas UABJO*, 2018.

---

43 This refers to a minimal pair (or trio) in Diidxazá, the words for *benda'* (my sister), *beenda'* (snake/ viper), and *benda* (fish).

in Isthmus Zapotec and Spanish *"¡Padiuxhi, perros!"* [Hello, dogs!]. The comic meme implies that Zapotec is infinitely superior to both Japanese and French, a message that many are likely to understand as the greeting '*Padiuxhi*' is often recognized also by people who do not speak Isthmus Zapotec.

The examples of pedagogical and social uses of Diidxazá in multimedia channels discussed here are only a glimpse of the variety of initiatives and practices which digital language activists have created. On one hand these social media practices reflect and reproduce Zapotec communication among those who already use it in their daily lives. For example, the blending of different languages, or translanguaging, as illustrated in the meme in Figure 22, is common both in face to face conversation and in digital forms of communication. On the other hand, these practices are also often intended to bring about change in the speech community, for example through the (positive) ways that Indigenous languages are represented, the new resources made available, and/ or the norms that are modelled and encouraged.

7.3 Summary: Characteristics of popular culture activism

The people who participate in the fluid spaces of popular culture initiatives are deeply engaged in the politics of language and identity in the Isthmus, albeit in many different ways. Like community-based education activists, popular culture activists have extensive scope to imagine new ways of being. The strategies which these activists employ range from the promotion of a pure, prestigious variety of Diidxazá, to recontextualizing Diidxazá for the purposes of humor and commentary. Some activists use the language and culture as a tool to critique socio-economic, racial, and gender inequalities – as well as linguistic inequalities. Popular culture activism is characterized by a high level of open *participation*, whether in the *tequio* needed to produce local events or in the creation and recirculation of information and images on-line. The voluntary collaborations within the hip-hop community, the feminist collectives, and the digital activists all illustrate the value placed on *convivencia* and participation by language activists in the Isthmus. Like the Indigenous activists described by Pietikäinen (2018), their strategies combine "resistance and compassion in an attempt to develop creative, alternative and critical considerations to existing, powerful and often ideologically fixed views on identity and its categories" (193).

Some of the key activism strategies in popular culture spaces are illustrated in Table 6. The young musicians, poets and meme-makers are engaged in creating events and spaces where there is place for their local-global identities. Their acts of linguistic citizenship (Stroud 2018) go beyond promotion of language, to include understandings of identity and the contemporary community. Popular culture spaces largely represent multilingual, pluralist communication practices as a norm, although these spaces can also be used to open debates about norms and standards, as discussed above. In most cases, popular culture activism ties together different ends of the strategy characteristic scales, drawing on local and global references and forms of support, and linking the past with the present. A majority of initiatives are also oriented towards pluralist or syncretic language use, although there are expections. In all of these initiatives, a relatively high degree of open participation is present and explicitly recognized by the initiators as a key to the success of the endeavor.

Table 6: Key language activism strategies in popular culture initiatives.

Actions →	Goals →	Examples
– Creating	– Events – Spaces/ Structures	– Performances and festivals which focus on local participation and draw on multilingual repertoires – Radio shows, yearly events, social media pages
– Representing	– People/ Identities	– Local-global and traditional-modern identities – Anti-colonial and anti-patriarchal identities – High status local artists and intellectuals
– Representing	– Communication practices	– Promotion of pluralist, multilingual communication as a norm – Promotion of standard writing norms

Additionally, popular culture initiatives often emerge and evolve at a speed and with a fluidity that many of the institution-based forms of activism cannot match. Organizing an event or festival, or writing a new song, are likely to take a substantial amount of time, but sharing images and music after the fact, recirculating memes, and engaging in digital language politics can happen very rapidly. This speed and flexibility allows for adaptation and sensitivity to context, as well as building on the contributions of participants. At the same time, not all of the popular culture initiatives that emerge in the Isthmus achieve longevity– some do not aim to do so. The shorter, faster timeframe of popular cultural activism may lead to it being overlooked, or its results being harder to ascertain that the slower, more explicit forms of change in educational institutions. However, the potentially wide reach of the messages and content created by popular cultural activists make them of undeniable importance. Ways of representing Diidxazá in memes, websites or songs tend to be fairly visible or accessible and rapid in comparison with other strategies, such as representing the language in a classroom or institution. This does not mean that such representations are ephemeral, however, as they may build up over time and help to establish new ways of thinking and viewing the world.

New perspectives emerge from the recontextualizations in the music, art, and digital media that popular cultural activists create. These "chains of decentering and recentering" (Bauman and Briggs 1990: 78) create links beween history and the present, and between the local and the global. David Ruíz Martínez, one of the founders of the *Fundación Historico Cultural Juchitán*, was hopeful that new links between the local context of the Isthmus and the language ideologies present in other parts of the world are supporting a change in attitude and in cultural norms. He commented:

> *Pero ahora está surgiendo como--- [. . .] una neoculturación zapoteca. Como que está habiendo una--- un despertar de nuestra niñez, de nuestra juventud, de nuestra--- de nuestros adolescentes. Porque han visto que al llegar a otras universidades, a otras instituciones de educación superior, no solamente del país sino de otros países, donde se valoran muchísimo las lenguas originales. Y en ese momento se quedan. . . ¡sorprendidos! [. . .] 'Bueno, entonces. . . no es tonto el que habla el zapoteco, es un hombre sabio, ¿verdad?' Porque prueba de ello ahí está, Chico Toledo, un gran pintor.*
>
> But now there is like--- [. . .] a Zapotec neo-enculturation emerging. Like there is happening a--- an awakening of our children, of our youth, of our—of our adolescents. Because they have seen, when arriving at other universities, other higher education institutions, not only in this country but in other countries, where original [Indigenous] languages are greatly valued. And in that moment they stop and feel. . .Surprised! [. . .] 'Alright, so . . . he who speaks Zapotec isn't stupid, he's a wise man, right?' Because a proof of it is there, Chico Toledo,[44] a great painter. (Interview April 2014)

Referring to Francisco Toledo as an example of a speaker of Zapotec who has gained international renown, Ruíz Martínez observed that more young people seemed to see Zapotec as a sophisticated language with an illustrious history and which is respected globally. Representing role-models such as this in a globally accessible digital space is one of the strategies that he and his collaborators use to promote positive representations of Isthmus Zapotec language and speakers.

---

44 Chico is the nickname or shortened version of Francisco.

The female poets, artists, and hip-hop musicians in the Isthmus today are quickly becoming role-models for the generations that are growing up under them. The messages broadcast by the young rappers and feminist collectives have also valorized local language and identity within global frames of reference, albeit with a different tone and style. Members of these groups all articulate the need to recognize and deal with the changes and inequalities which they see around them, one of which is the prejudices against Indigenous language speakers. They often reference their predecessors with respect, and gesture towards the literary and artistic lineage that they are building upon, for example in citing deceased poets and labelling themselves the 'granddaughters of the Zapotec ancestors'. At the same time, they do not hesitate to make their own marks that are unique to the contemporary moment, to recirculate and recontextualize everything from memes and images to words and identity categories. As Aurora Cobon, one of the organizers of the feminist collective, commented *"Otras generaciones se organizarón en su tiempo, ahora es de nosotras"* (Other generations organized themselves in their time, now is for us) (Interview January 2018).

Chapter 8
Developing a repertoire of activism strategies

Lenia Toledo Rasgado attended the very first *Camino de la Iguana* literacy workshop that occurred in 2012 in Juchitán when she was in her late teens. A cousin from Mexico City was visiting and was interested in going, so she and her sister went along too. Growing up in the center of La Ventosa, a village 15 minutes outside of Juchitán, her parents had discouraged her from speaking Zapotec. She had never used Zapotec in school, and they had been forbidden to use it when she attended primary school in La Ventosa. Over the years she had picked up a lot nonetheless, and as a young adult she felt she could more or less get by, although she was more comfortable in Spanish. When she was in secondary school in Juchitán a member of the collective *Comité Melendre* had given a presentation about Zapotec history in her class, which had inspired her interest and desire to learn more. She admired Zapotec poets and cultural activists, especially the female writers Natalia Toledo and Irma Pineda.

After participating in the 2012 *Camino de la Iguana* workshop she began writing poetry but felt that she did not know the writing system well enough, and when the *Camino de la Iguana* was offered in La Ventosa in the fall of 2013 she attended again. I was also attending and joined her and the other students in the activities and the final *convivio*, or closing celebration. The workshop was held in the brand new "*Bacusa gui*" (firefly) cultural center (during the workshop participants learned that it should be spelled "*bacuza gui*" in the popular alphabet, although this didn't motivate anyone to repaint the sign). The cultural center had been completed just a few months before as a corporate social responsibility project by a Spanish-owned wind farm whose windmills had come to fill the horizon on all sides of La Ventosa over the previous seven years. Some residents of La Ventosa had benefited economically from this development through employment or leasing land, and now had houses as big and freshly painted as the cultural center. Other residents had not benefited, and remained in one or two-room cinderblock or adobe brick houses, but with the same view of the forest of white windmill towers.

The following winter I participated in planning a language and botany-themed workshop for children in La Ventosa as part of the Smithsonian-funded project to document ethnobotanical knowledge, and I asked if Lenia would be willing to participate in it by teaching some language activities. When she readily agreed we talked about some games she could play to help children learn to use simple, daily phrases. We initially planned to conduct the workshop in one group, facilitated by Gibrán Morales, a visual artist from Oaxaca City who was

 Open Access. © 2021 Haley De Korne, published by De Gruyter. This work is licensed under the Creative Commons Attribution-NonCommercial-NoDerivatives 4.0 International License.
https://doi.org/10.1515/9781501511561-008

the photographer for the Smithsonian team, myself, Lenia, her sister Citlalli, and José López de la Cruz, a senior male member of a cultural committee in La Ventosa. José had long wanted to teach Zapotec workshops for children, although he did not have pedagogical experience and his full-time job with the wind farm left him little spare time. I visited the local (monolingual) primary schools to promote the workshop. In one school the director escorted me to each classroom where he added his own words of encouragement for the children to attend the workshop after I had issued the invitation. In one classroom there were some words in English on the chalkboard that the teacher had been teaching the class as part of the 'additional language' subject in primary school. Another school director told me that he was glad that children could do something other than sit in front of the television, where they spent much of their time nowadays in his opinion.

On the first day of the 2-day workshop children poured through the door of the cultural center, and we realized we would have to split the 60 participants into two alternating groups. As I went in and out of the rooms, dealing with logistics, I saw that Lenia used a few games, and also followed form-focused teaching practices that she had experienced in the *Camino de la Iguana*; she wrote the 3 kinds of Zapotec vowels on a whiteboard and had children copy them, followed by drilling consonants, color-words and numbers. The children participated with enthusiasm in both the games and the drills. The younger children, 10 and below, appeared to understand very little Zapotec, while the older children knew considerably more, although none were conversant. Three young sisters who I had seen hanging around the cultural center on previous occasions were among the children who recognized and offered the most words. They were also among the children wearing the most worn-out clothing. The youngest stood out due to her wide grin, showing off a mouth of black baby teeth.

The next time I saw the sisters in the cultural center was a month later, and the older one approached and bragged to me that she knew how to count in Zapotec (a topic covered in the workshop, although she might have known it before). Great, I responded, how? She rattled off the numbers up to 10 fluently. Then she wanted to know, how are the numbers in English? The fact that foreigners like myself were interested in Zapotec had made an impression on her, but the link between foreigners and English, and the status of English in mass media and in school, were also clearly in her mind. As on many other occasions, I wondered whether the benefits gained from the presence and practices of foreign language activists, such as myself, outweighed the risks of reproducing aspects of Eurocentrism and coloniality, such as the status, privilege and mobility of Euro-descended languages and people. And, as on other occasions,

I continued to seek ways to support local activism initiatives and to disrupt the Eurocentric logics that my presence might evoke, hoping that the benefits did outweigh the harm.

The sisters continued to attend subsequent Diidxazá workshops that were facilitated by a team of La Ventosa residents on a near-monthly basis, following from the success of the first workshop. The workshops were sponsored initially by the Smithsonian through project-leader Gabriela Pérez Báez, and eventually by donors of a crowd-funding campaign that Gabriela and I ran when the initial grant money was exhausted. The core team included Lenia and José, who had volunteered in the first workshop, and several other residents of La Ventosa who had worked in the ethnobotany project and were interested in engaging in outreach (see also Pérez Báez 2018; Purkarthofer and De Korne 2020).[45] In a discussion with Lenia and team-member Reyna López López in 2017, they commented on how other members of the community had come to see them as language experts during the years that the workshops had been running; children would come to them outside of the workshop if they had questions about Diidxazá. Reyna had become a confident writer of Diidxazá prior to participating in the workshops during the years she worked as an assistant to several linguists conducting language documentation in the region. She had enjoyed developing confidence to teach these skills to children through the workshops. Several of the senior members of the workshop team noted that teaching and presenting in Zapotec was initially difficult and made them nervous, but they had come to feel comfortable using Zapotec in public and pedagogical ways. Over several years of facilitating workshops, Lenia also became more confident in both writing and speaking Diidxazá. Some of the senior members of the workshop team commented on how her competence had improved; they had gone from viewing her as a marginal speaker to a fully accepted speaker. This represented a meaningful identity shift for Lenia, whose generation and class were widely expected to be Spanish-speaking. Figure 23 shows Lenia and Reyna in the bustle prior to a *calenda* [traditional procession] that they organized to mark the conclusion of the workshops in April 2017. They are holding a bunch of firecrackers to be shot off as the procession of children wound through the village. Like the participating children, they wore traditional embroidered *huipil* blouses, or *bidaani*, skirts and flowers, with formal white shirts, black trousers and red bandanas for the boys. With festive clothing, music and even firecrackers, they turned the conclusion of

---

45 The team consisted of Reyna López López, José López de la Cruz, Lenia Toledo Rasgado, Fernando Sánchez López, Rosaura López Cartas, and Velma Orozco Trujillo, with additional support from Gabriela Pérez Báez, Gibrán Morales Carranza, Kate Riestenberg, Kenia Velasco Gutiérrez, and myself.

Chapter 8 Developing a repertoire of activism strategies — 191

Figure 23: Lenia Toledo Rasgado and Reyna López López preparing a celebration for the end of their workshops in La Ventosa (photo April 2017).

the workshop into a full-fledged celebration that no one in La Ventosa could fail to notice. Participating children arrived early, talking together with excitement, as their parents waited on the outskirts, ready to watch.

The spaces, actors, practices and socio-political processes that make up the ecology of language in the Isthmus intertwine in countless ways, as illustrated in this description of some of the factors influencing the overlapping trajectories of a young adult Isthmus Zapotec speaker, and local and transnational language activism initiatives. The Spanish-only ideology of Lenia's parents and schooling led her to grow up more comfortable in Spanish, but encouragement from her peer group, local activists and her admiration for the literary heritage of Diidxazá helped motivate her to work towards biliteracy and bilingualism. The presence of the Smithsonian ethnobotany project in La Ventosa facilitated the creation of a workshop there, which was then supported by the existence of the cultural center (built by a foreign wind farm), money from mainly international sources, and most essentially by the interest of a few key local people, including Lenia, Reyna, and José. Motivated by my training as an educational linguist, I encouraged the facilitators to create a workshop focused on communicative language use. The interests and prior experiences of Lenia, and later the other facilitators, lead to the implementation of writing-centric approaches to teaching Zapotec, however, a choice which was aligned with the importance that writing has in determining language status in the Isthmus. The children remained enthusiastic and participative, and the presence of Zapotec in their linguistic repertoire was clear. However, interest in learning Zapotec in a fun, foreign-sponsored event, or locally run events and workshops, coexisted alongside an entrenched preference for Spanish (and English) in a region where Zapotec remains ideologically and materially associated with poverty and discrimination, and where meeting basic economic needs remains a pressing priority for some.

Language activism initiatives are always deeply entwined in contextual factors, and experienced differently by the various actors who initiate and participate in them. For this reason, my approach to language activism remains anti-prescriptivist and constructivist, as stated in chapter 1. The language activism framework, presented in chapter 1 and illustrated throughout this book, aims to show how some language activists have imagined and pursued positive social change through and around language use. While there is no one-size-fits-all strategy, I hope that the descriptions of language activism initiatives in schools, higher education, community-based workshops, and popular culture spaces in the Isthmus may resonate with other contexts. In previous chapters I teased apart some of the strategies employed in different contexts, discussing the characteristics of activism in each setting, and the diverse imaginaries of language equality which characterize different communities of practice. In this concluding chapter, I discuss some of the trends in relation to each strategy that may be relevant to language activism initiatives elsewhere. I also highlight how the strategies I observed more often than not flow across and among local, regional, national, and international domains, emphasizing how many language activists participate in multiple communities of practice and employ multiple intertwined strategies, as illustrated in the description of Lenia's participation in the Smithsonian-supported workshops above. For language activists in the Isthmus it is natural to develop a repertoire of strategies; some of which correspond to one area of their life, some to another.

The following section (8.1) provides a summary of the central actions and goals of the language activism strategy framework with examples from the cases described throughout the book, and a discussion of the importance of slow, local strategies as well as fast, transnational ones. I then turn to further discussion of how these strategies can lead to achieving positive social change (8.2), including the establishment of a multi-perspectival approach to 'language' and exploration of different theories of social change. I contrast problem-solving approaches to change with those which imagine a non-teleological, incremental social project, and consider the pros and cons of comparing and judging different forms of activism. In conclusion, I emphasize the importance of language activist networks within language politics, and the creative and contextualized strategies through which activists are shifting language politics in more inclusive, convivial and egalitarian directions (8.3).

8.1 Language activism strategies across contexts and scales

There are numerous ways that stakeholders in the Isthmus are working to counteract the processes of denigration that have indexed local ways of speaking and being with poverty and ignorance, and excluded them from social spaces such as education. I observed many different practices related to the teaching, learning, researching and promotion of Diidxazá, as discussed in previous chapters. My own practices and strategies as an activist were bound up in those of the people around me, although also influenced by my personal orientations, theories and priorities. As I observed, participated in and eventually initiated actions, I did not have analytical categories for what I was observing. I thought of my area of interest as activities relating to "Indigenous language promotion", and later "Indigenous language inclusion" or resistance to exclusion. Within an ethnographic monitoring paradigm, I aimed to understand what imaginaries of positive social change around language are present in the Isthmus, asking what changes do people want? What are their language imaginaries? Seeking to better understand the emic perspectives of stakeholders is the foundation of ethnographic monitoring, and is also a cornerstone of working as an ally or outside scholar (Antony-Stevens 2017). By focusing on these questions, it became clear that there are multiple perspectives and priorities to consider, whether one is looking at the scale of a primary school, a village, or a speech community spread across a region. An outsider's attempt to understand emic imaginaries can never be full nor comprehensive, but it can serve as the basis for engagement and collaboration where local stakeholders have a defining voice.

As I came to understand some of the multiple imaginaries of language, I also gained better insight into the different forms of social engagement around and through Isthmus Zapotec. In the analysis of my data, I came to look at this area as the politics of Zapotec activism, a material and discursive social project which negotiates Diidxazá use and education in various ways, and encompasses various conceptions of what Diidxazá is. The language activism strategy framework aims to capture some of the common features of this broad social project. Through this framework I aim to illustrate that possible strategies are wide-ranging and can be carried out by social actors with varying stances and access to resources. They may be fast or slow, visible or private, tightly planned and executed or loose and emergent. This broad perspective allows for insight into the possible alliances among activists working in different areas, as well as the importance of people who do not consider themselves to be activists but whose stances and actions do contribute to this social project. Scholar-activists cannot change the social status of minoritized languages alone. Educator-activists cannot change the social status of minoritized languages alone. Artist-activists cannot change the social status of minoritized languages alone. It is helpful for all of us to see our actions in relation to those of others, and to explore points of connection.

At least some of the examples of language activism in the Isthmus should resonate with efforts in other contexts; prying open spaces within formal education, preparing minoritized language teachers, addressing the insecurity of emergent speakers, and negotiating the opportunities and challenges of literacy are all common challenges in minoritized language promotion around the world. The ways these issues have been addressed in the Isthmus may not be appropriate in other contexts, but the effort to address these issues is hopefully one which other activists will recognize. The breadth of activism strategies, and the complex interrelations among actions, targets and characteristics are taken up in 8.1.1, 8.1.2, and 8.1.3. This discussion necessarily omits the details and dynamics of the individual activism strategies which are described more fully (although still much smaller-than-life) in chapters 3–7. In section 8.1.4, I analyze some of the trends in activism strategies across contexts, and discuss the importance of locally-grounded, slow strategies which sometimes receive less attention than faster, non-local initiatives.

8.1.1 Strategic creating

Ways of creating vary greatly depending on what is produced and the positionality of the creators. As laid out in the framework, language activists' creating is aimed at goals which include:
- *Resources*, such as the documentation and dictionaries created by researchers (chapter 3), the digital platforms created by individuals and civil society groups (chapter 7) or the didactic materials created by student teachers at the university (chapter 5).
- *Events*, such as the conference hosted by the Tehuantepec Faculty of Languages (chapter 3); the primary school flag ceremony (chapter 4); or the festivals of female writers and artists (chapter 7).

– *Spaces or structures*, such as the weekly hip-hop radio program (chapter 7), the series of workshops that emerged from the Smithsonian ethnobotany project (described in the opening of this chapter), or the university classes teaching Diidxazá as a subject and teaching about bilingual Indigenous literature (chapter 5).
– *People or identities*, such as new Diidxazá readers and writers (chapter 6); certified Indigenous language teachers (chapter 5); or Isthmus Zapotec women (chapter 7).
– *Communication practices*, such as young adults speaking or writing Diidxazá (chapters 5, 7 and the case of Lenia described above); the use of a specific writing norm (chapters 6 and 7); or the use of a multi-dialectal norm (chapters 5 and 6).

Each of these forms of creating is influenced by some or all of the strategy characteristics in the framework, as illustrated by representative examples in Table 7 in section 8.1.4. For example, the *location* of the activists clearly impacts the kinds of actions they can undertake, as well as the priorities they are likely to have. As noted in chapter 3, I observed non-local researchers to be especially focused on the creation of resources, a product which can often be produced and circulated across local and international scales. In contrast, all of the spaces or structures directly related to teaching and learning Zapotec that I observed were produced through local, regional, and occasionally state-level support, including classes in cultural centers, the Faculty of Languages, the *Camino de la Iguana*, and public schools working to implement the state-level PTEO policy. These spaces are developed over a slower *timeframe* than what it takes to produce learner materials, and are often less *visible* than a mobile phone app or an on-line dictionary when they occur within existing institutional structures and do not draw media attention. Additionally, the creation of a learning space necessitates the creation of Diidxazá teachers and learners as recognizable social categories or identities, a process which is also likely to be slow. The creation of learning spaces inevitably fosters increased Zapotec communicative practices within them as well, an occurrence that may be rapid and ephemeral or enduring if learners incorporate language use into their lives over time.

Activists' initiatives may have a *socio-historical orientation* towards the past, such as the website created by the *Fundación Historico-Cultural Juchitán*, or towards the present and future, such as the *Raptivismo* hip-hop radio show. Initiatives may follow an *orientation to diversity* which prioritizes what is perceived as more or less unitary or pure communicative and cultural practices, such as the *Guca'nu jneza diidxazá* [Let's write good Zapotec] social media page. In contrast, they may orient towards what is perceived as syncretism and hybridity, such as the feminist collective *Las nietas de lxs Binnigula'za* [The granddaughters of the [male and female] Zapotec ancestors], or they may slide between the poles of this continuum in relation to different issues. Finally, activists may aim to create a *participatory*, negotiated space, such as a social media site intended for discussion, or they may exert various levels of control over what is created, such as authorial and editorial choices made by scholars or artists.

Some targets can be created relatively rapidly by an individual or a small group, such as learning materials or an event. Other strategies take much more time and require a wide coalition, such as the creation of a structure, or a recognized identity. In the pursuit of creating these socially- and structurally- embedded changes, I observed the following strategies of connecting and representing to be especially significant.

8.1.2 Strategic connecting

While strategies that create something may often receive more attention due to greater tangibility and novelty, strategies of connecting are also of crucial importance in language activism. Strategic connecting seeks to change the way that existing actors, resources, spaces, identities and/ or communication practices relate to each other by building or strengthening networks and relationality. Examples of some of the strategic connections which Diidxazá language activists make include:

- *Resources* to other resources, to spaces and to people, such as the production of databases, dictionaries, and libraries (chapter 3) or the *Camino de la Iguana* teachers giving away books (chapter 6).
- *Events* to people, such as inviting participants to a conference on the radio (chapter 3) or inviting children to a workshop (as mentioned in the opening of this chapter).
- *Spaces and structures* to people and to communication practices, such as involving parents in primary school activities (chapter 4), and using Diidxazá in the university (chapter 5).
- *People and identities* to resources and to each other, such as taking student-teachers to a specialist library and introducing them to more experienced teachers (chapter 5), and encouraging people to discuss writing norms together in a social media space (chapter 7).
- *Communication practices* to people, such as speaking Diidxazá to children as part of a workshop (as in the opening of this chapter) or providing an online translator with audio pronunciation for learners (chapter 7).

Ways of connecting can be rapid and of low visibility, such as an invitation or a personal introduction, or more longitudinal and higher visibility, such as the creation of an archive or coordinating an exchange between two institutions. For example, the teachers and director that invited families to participate in activities designed to valorize local culture in their primary school took an action that was fairly quick (the invitation) and resulted in raised visibility (chapter 4). The creation of the activities was obviously more time-consuming, but inviting parents to participate in the activities once they existed was a strategy that made the activities rapidly more inclusive and more convivial. A quick connection may be the first, necessary step in strengthening a network or community of practice. For example, an introduction between student-teachers and more experienced teachers made a contribution towards the development of Diidxazá classes in a university space where none previously existed, but actually solidifying this structural change is a much longer-term goal which requires many other supports along the way (chapter 5). Connections between members of different communities of practice can be advantageous in order to strengthen activist networks, such as between teachers in different contexts, or between transnational researchers and local activists (chapter 8).

Collecting resources or information, such as the creation of an archive, can also be viewed as a form of connecting. The creation of a collection or archive can serve to pool resources, and to connect people to these resources, especially when publicized on-line. Decisions about what to exclude are inevitable however, and the knowledge or objects to be archived typically go through considerable manipulation as they are prepared for conservation, making this generally a more closed form of activism. The Smithsonian ethnobotany project resulted in an archive and eventually a dictionary of plants which grow in the Isthmus along with their Spanish, Latin, and Diidxazá names, made accessible on-line through the Smithsonian National Herbarium. Which languages to use, including which plant name(s), was an editorial choice made by the research team. Use of both Spanish and Diidxazá was a priority in order to make the collection accessible to viewers in the Isthmus, and fortunately the on-line format allowed for a multilingual approach more readily than printed materials.

Static forms of connection, such as a collection, are dependent on access and visibility in order to result in social benefits, whereas human connections are perhaps less longitudinal, but can much more readily result in convivial interactions and actual communication practices. For example, by giving a book of Isthmus Zapotec texts to a library in Santa María Xadani I made them more widely available. By giving a copy of the book directly to a teacher trainee who was developing an extra-curricular program for elementary children, I had a much greater assurance that actual benefit might result from my action, as

I hoped that he would use the texts in support of his teaching and thus eventually the production of communication practices among his students. Connecting can thus be a way to resist current inequalities, such as lack of resources or access, or the marginalization of certain people and communication practices (such as Diidxazá-speaking parents) from important social spaces (such as school).

8.1.3 Strategic representing

Ways of representing– discursively framing something (or someone)– occur constantly in conjunction with other strategic actions, and are themselves an important contribution to language politics. Representations tend to be fairly rapid in comparison with other strategies, but may build up over time, leading to long-lasting impacts. Examples of the representations of language activists include:
- *Resources*, such as designing didactic materials to be attractive or sophisticated (chapter 3), or promoting Zapotec hip-hop as cool on the radio (chapter 7).
- *Events*, such as the posters and fliers that advertise workshops and events by depicting them as fun or in some way appealing (chapters 6 and 7).
- *Spaces or structures*, such as the representation of higher education as a site where local languages are valued (chapter 5), and the Isthmus region as space where Diidxazá literature is vibrant (chapter 6).
- *People or identities*, such as memes that praise or ridicule young Zapotec speakers (chapters 5 and 7), and teachers that show respect for students who speak Indigenous languages (chapters 4 and 5).
- *Communication practices*, such as promoting multilingual communication as legitimate (chapter 3) or promoting multiple dialect variants as legitimate (chapter 6).

While all Diidxazá activists engage in positive representations of Diidxazá speakers and/ or language use, there are differences in the discourses of locally-affiliated people versus non-locally affiliated advocates. In my observations, local advocates engaged in representations in more personal and specific ways, such as praising an individual writer, or telling a story about a *Juchiteco* who attended a bilingual school and went on to become a Doctor. Non-local advocates on the other hand were more likely to promote the benefits of multilingualism in general ways, or take up the "language as universal heritage" and "treasure" tropes cautioned against by Jane Hill (2002). The former focuses on the creation of positive representations in relation to Zapotec speakers, while the latter focuses on representing abstract phenomena– multilingualism, and the language itself– as valuable and desirable. The representations made by actors in positions of power at different social scales may be more visible or circulate more than others, such as when researchers are interviewed on the radio or their work is represented in the newspaper.

Orientations to history, diversity, and participation are often significant factors that shape the representations of activism initiatives. For example the social media page, *Guca'nu jneza diidxazá* [Let's write good Zapotec] orients towards a somewhat purist or normative view of Zapotec writing, while at the same time encouraging open participation and discussion through a public social media page. The teachers at the Tehuantepec Faculty of Languages attempted to represent multiple regional dialects as equal, but they were challenged by expectations (theirs and in some cases those of students) of a standard, unitary writing norm. The *Camino de la Iguana* teachers oriented towards the history of Diidxazá literature, while also including and promoting contemporary literature, including praising the hip-hop and feminist movements described in chapter 7. Finally, while many residents of the Isthmus represented Diidxazá as a communicative practice which did not include children nor recent migrants to the region, many activists resisted this and represented an inclusive and participatory Diidxazá speech community. Strategies of representation thus have an important role to play in influencing social imaginaries about legitimate language and identities in the Isthmus.

As discussed from chapter 1 onwards, my objective has not been to identify 'successful' strategies, or 'the best' technique, as I do not believe a one-size-fits-all solution is possible. I do wish to draw attention to the value of strategies which often receive less attention and praise, yet which I argue are also crucial pieces of the language politics puzzle. If activists hope to counter structural inequalities and exclusionary socio-political processes there is a need to design effective strategies to chip away at these inequalities in their context. In the following section I reflect on the characteristics of strategies from local to global scales, and the benefit of locally-grounded strategies. While one of the arguments of the language activism strategy framework is that all strategies are of value, in my observations some kinds of strategies and some theories of change receive more attention and recognition than others, and undeservedly so.

8.1.4 Characteristics across scales and activist positionality

In analyzing a range of activism strategies, I have highlighted aspects that I observe to be especially important in defining the nature and potential kind of impact of the strategy. These strategy characteristics are presented in chapter 1 (see Figure 2), and have been discussed in relation to specific initiatives throughout the book. Examples of activism strategies with different characteristics drawn from the chapters of this book are illustrated in Table 7 below. As argued multiple times, all of these characteristics have something to offer, and may be an effective choice for a particular moment. In some cases, the characteristic may be easy to shift; for example making a pedagogical grammar available in a digital as well as print version will increase the mobility and likely also the visibility of the resource. A workshop or learning resource drawing primarily on historical, past motifs can incorporate a more contemporary style relatively easily if the creators choose to do so. Additionally, the degree of participation in many ititiatives can be changed throughout the initiative by choosing to find ways to invite a wider range of stakeholders to have a role (such as crowd-sourcing approaches to language documentation, rather than a traditional linguist-speaker model), or choosing to narrow down the number of participants in order to move ahead and complete a project quickly (such as a small team of teachers producing a lesson plan after collecting input from an open group of parents and community members).

Table 7: Examples of language activism strategies with contrasting characteristics.

Characteristic	Scale
Location:	Local ↔ International
– E.g. Hip-hop events	Created through local networks, drawing on global culture
– E.g. Primary school class project	Local participants; some influence from national policies
Timeframe:	Slow ↔ Rapid
– E.g. Teacher education	Learning & practice over years
– E.g. 2-day seminar for teachers	Several months to plan; relatively rapid
Visibility & mobility:	Low ↔ High
– E.g. Social media posts	Fast, extensive circulation
– E.g. Pedagogical grammar in print	Limited copies & circulation
Socio-historical orientation:	Future ↔ Past
– E.g. Literacy workshop	Explicit ties to both past and present
– E.g. Website with archival/ historical content	Focus on past
Diversity orientation:	Syncretic ↔ Purist
– E.g. Univeristy language classes	Efforts to include multiple varieties Standard language ideologies remain influential

Table 7 (continued)

Characteristic	Scale	
Participation:	Open participation ↔	Controlled participation
– E.g. Cultural events	Open participation encouraged	
– E.g. Traditional language documentation		Expert linguist & elder speakers

One characteristic that is harder to adjust is the location and identity, or positionality of the person or people involved in the initiative, whether they have primarily local ties or primarily non-local ties. The actions of non-local activists in the Isthmus tended to focus on resources, including producing, publicizing (representing), and accumulating (connecting) texts, recordings, videos, and didactic games. They also engaged in producing and publicizing events. Events and resources are generally highly visible and lend themselves well to widely circulating positive representations, such as articles in online media. Some resources also lend themselves to geographic mobility, such as mobile phone apps and downloadable grammars and dictionaries. Considering that non-local advocates are by nature not, or at least less, embedded in local institutions and daily life than local Diidxazá advocates are, it is not surprising that their actions focus more around mobile and short-term targets such as resources and events.

The most common strategies of local activists, on the other hand, are indicative of their position within place-based networks and their potential for long-term engagement. Local actors engaged in representing, connecting and producing across all analyzed areas, but unlike non-local actors their actions most often targeted people, communication practices and spaces, with less attention to producing resources or one-off events. Some of these strategies have lower visibility, and thus may receive less praise and attention. A grandparent who chooses to use Diidxazá with their grandchildren at home, or a teacher who presents and praises the work of Zapotec writers to her class, are making important contributions to the kinds of communication practices and representations that children will grow up with. Likewise, a musician who chooses to make bilingual music and share it with their peers is influencing representations of language and culture. These kinds of strategies may seem limited in terms of the timeframe they occur in and how many people participate in them, and there may be little or no tangible evidence of the strategy after the fact. Yet in these ways local activists help to tackle persistent prejudices and reimagine the relationship between language and social status. As Mayoli García, the language activist and university student quoted in the opening of chapter 1 stated, "*Hasta que no crees una conciencia real en las personas, no va a haber eso*" [Until you create a real awareness in people, it won't happen]. Changing the status of Isthmus Zapotec speakers, and countering the marginalization of the language requires strategies with the intangible goal of creating a different social imaginary, as well as tangible goals such as creating more equal resources and structures.

During the course of my fieldwork in the Isthmus I often reflected on tangible versus intangible strategies, as well as when to speak up and offer an idea or initiative, and when to listen and observe. I gradually shifted away from my initial interest in producing resources, and towards a focus on supporting existing networks and spaces (see also chapter 3). During fieldwork I regularly wrote reflective memos on my own initiatives; in one memo entitled "Things and non-things" I recorded my on-going doubts:

> A focus on creating 'materials' is limited. It makes these things seem like the solution to much broader problems. Now that I've [. . .] gained a clearer focus on the limits of focusing on materials, I realize I often do the same thing– make it sound like the whole focus is the production of some 'thing'. Producing a 'thing' is the simplest way to demonstrate support though, so I'm not sure how to get around this. Much like the limitations of focusing on language as a 'thing', an object. We know it's not accurate, but it's hard to get out of that way of talking & thinking. (Memo December 2014)

Although I still asked people about materials or supports that they might be interested in having, I began to shift my focus towards strategies of connecting people and existing materials, and fostering learning spaces. I also started to question the assumption I had made that the production of material things is "the simplest way to demonstrate support", noticing that this focus on materialism was influenced in part by my cultural background as a settler-European American. As a scholar activist, the strategy of creating resources and providing the greater visibility that my social position allows me to contribute to a certain extent, does remain important to me. I have observed many positive impacts from the materials and events that other scholar activists have created, and I am confident this strategy will continue to be important in many minority language contexts. At the same time, I believe more energy could be invested in working with teachers and institutions (people and spaces, in the terminology of the framework) on issues of quality and sustainability, as experienced by the local educational community. Additionally, supporting the work of artist activists is crucial in the process of reimagining more equal futures for minoritized languages.

This work is slower, generally less visible, and more local in scale, but has the potential to create a meaningful change.

From attempting to inventory resources, to creating events for larger scale connection of people, and producing long-term learning spaces, I certainly never felt that I ran out of possible strategies to try while working in the Isthmus. As a scholar activist, the strategies outlined help me to better conceptualize my work in socially engaged ways, and to fulfill my goal of conducting ethnography in the service of critical reflection and social change within a constructivist paradigm. With the recognition that policy is performed and negotiated across social scales, the repertoire of strategies described in this study may be useful to actors seeking to participate effectively in the politics of minoritized language advocacy from varying positions of social power. The need to go beyond state-centric paradigms of policy and social change has been well established; the strategies discussed here are offered in contribution towards furthering participatory ways of understanding and undertaking language politics. Many actors are not in a position to frame their goals as state authorities would, and more importantly many may choose to avoid framing their goals in positivist or top-down ways. It is not necessary to be an insider to engage in contextualized, meaningful strategies; nor is it necessary to be internationally or politically connected to engage in impactful strategies. Language activists pursue different goals in relation to their social position, priorities, and the theory of social change that they hold. A social constructivist approach to engaging in language politics, as illustrated through examples of Diidxazá activism, requires flexible practices, creative reimaginings, and tenacious resistance from a variety of standpoints.

8.2 Engaging in social change through language

In the Isthmus, as in other multilingual contexts, there are varying views of what a desirable language ecology would look like, and inevitably varying imaginaries of what constitutes positive social change. While some parents are pleased to have Diidxazá increasingly taught in school, others oppose it. School directors or parents who use only Spanish with children in the Isthmus are pursuing a monolingual future they view to be better than their multilingual past and/or present, in which they hope that the new generation will not experience discrimination or material need. Engaging in language activism despite the multiplicity of evaluations or perspectives present among diverse stakeholders has many pitfalls; certain forms of engagement may be viewed positively by some actors and negatively by others.

The framework of language activism strategies in this book, aiming to include a wide range of actors across contexts, does not incorpate measures for judging or evaluating these strategies. This is intentional. In our own contexts we may observe that certain strategies seem to have a larger or more lasting effect, and that certain activists make what seem to be more powerful efforts, while others make efforts that seem less engaged. These differences do matter of course – a strategy such as liking a social media post in a minoritized language is not the same as a strategy of writing and publishing bilingual literature, or organizing an event. In activist communities of practice there are typically some people who are the charismatic core and leaders of initiatives (e.g. Hornberger 2017), and others who participate in more peripheral ways. By arguing for the importance of small, less visible forms of activism I do not want to draw attention away from the trailblazing work of dedicated leaders, which is indeed at the core of every minoritized language initiative I am familiar with, in the Isthmus and elsewhere. I encourage evaluation and reflection of one's own activism initiatives, and learning through observation of others, but I am not interested in attempting to judge or compare activism strategies out of context, nor in relation to a universal notion of what 'good' activism must be. These are important questions to ask and discussions to have *within* language activism initiatives.

For example, Johnson (2013) lays out concrete strategies for teachers and researchers aiming to promote multilingual education in public schools in the US, including building local coalitions and influencing key power-brokers through legal and media channels (188–214). In this context, it is valuable to have prescriptive guidelines about what kinds of letters to the editor might get published, and tips for putting pressure on politicians. Under some circumstances, activists may find it necessary to demand a certain level and kind of participation. However, Johnson also emphasizes the importance of open participation and different kinds of contributions to language politics. He argues for "changing participation frameworks to empower a diversity of language policy agents" (2013: 191), and a paradigmatic shift whereby researchers, teachers, and parents come to view themselves as language policy makers. In the context of scholar engagement in language revitalization, Whaley (2011) cautions against scholars trying to assume control of a revitalization initiative in the way they typically aim to control a research project. The more open or convivial the form of participation in the activism initiative is, the more likely that there is room for different kinds of contributions.

Based on my observations and participation in language activism in the Isthmus, I also argue the need to facilitate open participation and to make space for diverse imaginaries within language activism initiatives. How contrasting priorities and evaluations play out in activism initiatives, and the power dynamics among charismatic leaders and people who make up the wider networks of support are often a challenge, however. Many initiatives come to an end for these reasons. The encouragement to include different voices and potentially multiple priorities is in no way easy or straightforward. This is the case in all forms of activism, whether the focus is on inclusive language education or land rights. Further discussion of the struggles within initiatives and 'what not to do' could be beneficial to other language activists, however I believe an academic book is not the most useful place for that. Throughout this book I have chosen to focus on examples of relatively successful initiatives that I have observed, and to reserve critical reflection primarily for scholar-activist strategies (including my own). In the following sections I discuss what the activism strategies examined in this study have taught me about possible ways of working with multiple understandings of language (8.2.1) and multiple theories of social change (8.2.2).

8.2.1 Diidxazá as a deictic

As examined in chapter 1, and throughout this book, 'Diidxazá', and indeed all languages, have multiple meanings for the varied social actors who engage in language activism. Understanding the deictic or indexical nature of Diidxazá is helpful when engaging in activism initiatives. Linguistic anthropologist Michael Silverstein (1976) defined deictic shifters as words which gesture towards specific people, places, or times, having no independent referent out of context. Indexicality is likewise a useful framework for understanding how language is always intertextual and takes its meaning from other times and places (Bauman and Briggs 1990; Briggs and Bauman 1992). The deconstructivist tradition in the philosophy of language suggests that all words and speech, not just certain deictics, acquire meaning through indexicality with an absolute meaning indefinitely deferred (Derrida 1967). By discussing the ontology of Diidxazá (and named languages in general) as deictic I am not promoting extreme deconstruction of meaning nor a solipsistic framing; rather I locate the construction of mutually available meanings within different social groups or communities of practice, as part of their shared repertoire or social imaginary. This is one way to achieve the post-deconstructivist "reconstituting" discussed by Makoni and Pennycook (2007); by understanding minoritized languages as placeholders, windows, perhaps even magnifying glasses onto a variety of social phenomena and shared concerns.

Integrating an understanding of the inherently multiple ontologies of Diidxazá into language activism is helpful in considering diverse imaginaries of language use that are present in any one context. For example, the approach that *Istmeño* scholar-educator-activist Víctor Cata has developed in his work as co-facilitator of the literacy workshop *Camino de la Iguana* is based on his multi-level understanding of Diidxazá, as discussed in section 6.3.1. Although he promotes reclaiming the use of words and concepts which are not in common use today, in line with his appreciation of Diidxazá as a repository of cultural and historical knowledge, he also notes that for some speakers and learners Diidxazá is tied up with personal feelings of insecurity. With this understanding, his strategy as a teacher includes avoiding creating further negative feelings. As he commented (quoted in full in 6.3.1) *"si de por sí no habla y aparte les digo que no hablan bien . . . [. . .] mejor que hable, ya sobre la marcha ya aprende."* [if in fact someone doesn't speak and besides I tell them that they don't speak well . . . [. . .] it's better that they speak, then learn along the way]. I observed Víctor's ability and willingness to shift between his perspective as a linguist and historian, and his perspective as a teacher and member of the Zapotec-speaking community to be a valuable asset in his work as a language activist.

I aimed to apply a similar deictic perspective of Diidxazá in a presentation that I gave to a local audience in the Isthmus (one of several times that I gave public presentations as a way of sharing back my research and receiving feedback), where I analyzed the question *"¿Por qué parece "difícil" escribir en diidxazá?"* [Why does it seem to be 'hard' to write in Diidxazá?] (Field notes July 2015). On many occasions I have been told by *Istmeños* that they find writing Diidxazá to be hard; it is a source of pride and for many an important part of their aspirations and imaginaries of their future language use, and yet at the same time many find it daunting. In my analysis of this concern, I identified phonetics, phonology, schooling, and ideology as key domains that contribute to the perception and experience of difficulty. I began with a discussion of language attitudes and ideologies, asking the audience what makes a language 'useful', followed by a discussion of what makes a language 'difficult'. The goal was to highlight that 'difficult' is a social construction in some ways, just as 'useful' is, in a context where learning the foreign language English is not considered too difficult to attempt, despite a much less transparent orthography. In order to show how the perception of 'difficulty' is created, I turned to the level of linguistic features, discussing the relation between the phonemes of Isthmus Zapotec and how they are represented in the popular alphabet, and identifying contrasts with the phonemes of Spanish and their representations. I then discussed phonetic and phonological elements which are not represented in the popular alphabet (tone and stress), but which do play a role in meaning making (i.e. are contrastive features), and whose absence sometimes confuses beginning writers and readers in my observations. I then discussed the past and present schooling practices in the Isthmus, which have not only focused uniquely on Spanish as a language of reading and writing, but have also delegitimized and devalued Diidxazá through exclusion and punishment of speakers. I also mentioned that the popular alphabet is an unenforced and polynomic norm, yet the exposure to standard language attitudes in schooling makes many people apply prescriptivist expectations onto Zapotec writing. In conclusion, I argued that greater metalinguistic awareness of the features of Diidxazá and contrasts between Diidxazá and their current (Spanish) repertoire, as well as confidence and opportunity to appropriate Diidxazá writing, could considerably enhance the experience of Diidxazá learners and lower their perception of difficulty in the process of learning to write.

In order to bring together appropriate knowledge to tackle such problems, it is useful to adopt linguistic, social, educational, and ideological perspectives on Diidxazá, without the need to privilege any one perspective. When I began this study, I was interested in ways of bringing different actors with different perspectives into conversation, and finding shared perceptions and common denominators, such as the inclusion of minoritzed speakers. I am now less interested in forging common understandings across communities of practice, and more interested in normalizing a multi-perspectival or indexical approach to minoritized language activism. The way that a language is understood within a community of practice may be relatively coherent– as a medium of convivial interactions in the *Camino de la Iguana* classes, or as a valuable code and source of knowledge in documentation projects for example. One solution would be to limit the scope of an initiative and work only within an activism initiative where there is a shared social imaginary and goal. This approach could miss out on the possible coalitions and networks that I have observed to be so crucial among language activists however. It is worth working together, even if there will never be large-scale coherence across the different communities and disciplines engaging in issues around language. Perhaps I am returning to an inclination towards Whorfian worlds of thought which drew me to study language diversity many years ago, or I am simply becoming more realistic about the affordances and limits of interdisciplinary collaboration. Regardless, I expect that my perspective will continue to shift as I engage in future projects. At present I am hopeful that more awareness may develop around the plurality of perspectives among minoritized language activists in particular, which would be helpful in building future knowledge and strategies in this area.

In particular for scholar activists, engaging with different paradigms or ontologies of language is crucial if we are to avoid reproducing the coloniality of previous research practices. Scholar activists who are not members of the community they work in can take an "allied stance" and help to provide a platform for the perspectives and imaginaries of those who have been marginalized (Anthony-Stevens 2017). Problematizing and probing common concepts, such as 'language' and 'revitalization' is an important step in this direction

(Leonard 2017; Davis 2017). A constructivist research project that aims to contribute to positive socio-political change must adopt some reductionist concepts and/ or perspectives in order to identify positive potentials and communicate about them with a wider audience, while a pragmatic project that aims to contribute to change must take seriously the constantly-shifting, locally-specific place and people from whom change might emerge. As I hope to be able to have productive conversations in both local spaces and the centralist spaces of government and academia, I have found it useful to work towards a research repertoire that includes these different paradigms, their discourses, and their theories of social change.

8.2.2 'A grain of sand' theory of change

In addition to the concern of what positive change looks like, there are different understandings of how social change occurs. Is change produced through top-down government policy? Can individual actors incite change? Is it something that can be negotiated within a local community of practice? Is it primarily about resisting and tearing down the structures of inequality? Or about building and creating new structures? The focus on creation of materials and awareness-raising events and publicity that I observed among non-local scholar activists, including myself, aligns well the "theory of error correction" which has characterized the outreach activities of language scholars for decades (Lewis 2018). Within this theory of action or change, what is needed in order for Diidxazá to be transmitted are adequate learning or reference materials (acquisition and corpus planning, in the standardized nation-state tradition) and the presentation of sufficient scientific evidence as to the benefits of multilingualism and/ or the imminent loss of language and thus knowledge. The implied theory of action is that people's behavior will then logically shift when the right materials and the right argument have been presented to them. Correcting misinformation may indeed have some effects on peoples' perspectives, and improving the availability and access to materials is also a tangible step towards greater language equality. But none of these valuable contributions are in themselves a solution to the complex factors that perpetuate language-based inequalities.

On the other hand, local activists often described their efforts whether in teaching, learning, writing, performing, or otherwise promoting Diidxazá as the way they *"aportar su grano de arena"* [contribute their grain of sand] — not expecting to bring about a radical shift in the language ecology, but doing something that they feel has value. While proud of their work, many Zapotec activists are aware that it is not of interest to all of their neighbors. The creation of educational spaces, public use and valorization of Diidxazá, and modest expectations as to the outcomes of their work point to the influence of a more constructivist and non-teleological theory of change, where numerous contextual factors and others' agency will all influence the outcome of any attempt at social intervention. The strategies of these activists reflect a place-based understanding of the context they are working in; an environment that they experience as a complex whole, where incremental changes may be possible if lots of people get on board, but nothing will shift overnight.

Among local-oriented activists the use of conviviality is also a common factor, both through person-to-person interactions and more ritualized *convivio* events such as bestowing participant certificates, organizing public readings, or incorporating music and art into a conference. The ideologies and imaginaries that independent group members bring with them are inevitably crucial factors in how language practices and norms emerge in a community, but in a convivial paradigm they are negotiated among the group. For example, the interest of some Diidxazá students and teachers in conserving pre-Spanish words and ideas is present in education initiatives, while other students' interest in learning the repertoire of the modern market and appreciation for syncretic language use also has a place. Prescriptivism and purism do not need to disappear from the social imaginary of the group, as long as they are subjected to a process of convivial negotiation rather than being imposed as norms. In observing language activism initiatives in the Isthmus, practices of *convivencia* or conviviality emerged as a significant characteristic facilitating the positive outcomes of these social projects.

The underlying theories that influence the strategies of different actors are evident in the following vignette from the final day of a four-day linguistic workshop on tone in Diidxazá run by Gabriela Pérez Báez who was in the Isthmus on a research trip and was excited to facilitate an open workshop for interested participants.

> Throughout the 4 days of the workshop Gabriela has explained the phonology of Diidxazá with a focus on lexical tone. She uses examples and interactive exercises with a group of around 8–10 adult participants. Attendees are mainly teachers and retired teachers, plus Gabriela's colleagues Víctor Cata and myself. At the end of the final day, she shows them several different possible ways to represent lexical tone in writing, including the popular alphabet, which does not represent it consistently. She would like to represent it in the dictionary that she is preparing, but she wants speaker input in order to choose the approach that they prefer. At several points Gabriela and the participants discuss that "if in 100 years there are no speakers" this writing system should represent as much phonological detail as possible. She says she knows it has been a quick workshop, but she would

like to know if they think that tone should be represented, and if so how? Most participants have been fairly quiet throughout the workshop, and this question is also initially received with silence. Then Víctor jumps in: We need to practice, we need time to experiment with different approaches before deciding, he says. Others nod. Gabriela agrees, it would be helpful to try the styles with children and different potential users, and to use them on social media she notes. She wonders how to resolve this question in a timely manner though. A man comments that writing is so much harder than speaking– he only understood the vowel phonations for the first time yesterday (a characteristic much simpler than the tonal patterns that Gabriela has been explaining, and which is already represented consistently in the popular alphabet). In the end, everyone agrees to Víctor's suggestion that they should try using the different approaches for a while and come back with more input at a later time. (Field notes August 2013)

From activist linguists working to create a transparent representation of sound patterns for posterity, and local educators who want any new norms to be as accessible as possible, the perspectives and priorities of stakeholders in just one workshop event are clearly very diverse. Gabriela had initiated a participatory approach to getting input through the workshop, and Víctor built on this to propose further interaction and practice over an extended timeframe. The participatory solution proposed by Víctor and readily endorsed by Gabriela is an example of a convivial approach to language activism, where collaboration in decision-making and in processes of social change are promoted. The importance of participation and investment of the wider speech community in language activism initiatives has been established in other minoritized communities (Urla et al. 2017). This approach is also inevitably slower, and subject to many perspectives, and incremental contributions or 'grains of sand'. The social meanings of Diidxazá use will always be multiple, however among voluntary participants and activists the aim to resist structural inequalities and enact equality from the ground-up contributes to a social imaginary in which historical inequalities begin to lose some of their social meaning and hopefully also their impact.

This framing is in line with an interest in social projects as a scale where new spaces and practices may emerge in support of marginalized groups which resist homogenizing national and international governance (Povinelli 2011). It is also in line with social and political life in the Isthmus, where there is universal distrust of national and international government (and corporate) interventions, and intricately structured social networks. The backbone of social life in the Isthmus is the reciprocity performed among social networks, through voluntary labor (*guendaruchaa, guendalisaa, tequio* or *trueque*), attendance at parties, godfather/ mother (*compadrazgo*) duties at birth, school graduations, and weddings, among other forms of communality (see e.g. Mintz and Wolf 1950; Royce 1975, 2011, also chapters 2 and 7). In this setting, the most effective way to contribute to social improvements thus appears to be through collaboration and social networks, rather than structural or official interventions. As has been argued in relation to individual policy actors (Ricento and Hornberger 1996; Shohamy 2006), it is clear that social networks are also important mediators of language politics, especially in contexts like the Isthmus.

As discussed in chapter 1 and above, I am interested in strategies of engagement not just to describe and analyze this political phenomenon, but also from a practitioner perspective, viewing myself as a social actor with potential to participate in language and education politics, and aiming to do so in appropriate and creative ways. Traditional approaches and types of language policy have privileged the perspective of a state or government decision-making authority, with less insight into local language politics and ideological dimensions, a bias critiqued by Canagarajah (2005), Johnson (2013), and Davis and Phyak (2017), among others. Along with these scholars, I argue that a wide range of people are potential activists and agents in language politics. As such, we can learn from activists who are choosing to engage in language politics within different social spheres or communities of practice, and from attending to the underlying imaginaries and theories present in their activism strategies.

8.3 Summary: Convivial language activism

It is one thing to acknowledge that working towards positive social change in an intentional, strategic way requires adapting to multiple perspectives and not expecting a final solution— it is another to sustain the energy, motivation, and humor necessary to keep working at it without the possibility of ever achieving unanimous support or complete success. Minority language activism is no different from any other field of social activism in this respect. The politics of (Indigenous) language activism will inevitably remain a site of contention over group boundaries and other social ideals. Social imaginaries of language, identity, and education must be negotiated again and again across social scales, whether in policy documents, program models, classroom interactions, or popular culture spaces. From this point of view, language inequalities are problems that have no final resolution, a conceptualization that differs from the problem-solving orientation inherent in much language planning and educational development work. As such it is worth considering whether a problem-solution theory of social change is appropriate to work on Indigenous language activism, or whether it is more appropriate to view our improvements and interventions in another light, such as participating in the creative design of social futures (Cazden et al. 1996), supporting processes of decoloniality through linguistic self-determination

(Leonard 2017), or contributing grains of sand to a hill whose growth may only be visible many years from now.

Being an activist in language politics in today's local-global language ecologies requires ongoing creativity and adaptation of political strategies. With official recognition of Indigenous languages a reality for nearly two decades in Mexico, national policy has so far created few new ideological and implementational spaces of language equality, as discrimination and Spanish monolingualism remain the promoted norm. Policies of recognition ("language rights") in Mexico and elsewhere have not resulted in greater social equality, as minoritized communities continue to be denied necessary material rights and resources under neoliberal economic systems (Hale 2005; Muehlmann 2009; Overmyer-Velázquez 2010; Povinelli 2011). The effort to change inequalities on the ground must clearly go beyond state-generated, rights-oriented approaches to language planning and policy and the small spaces of opportunity that recognition policies do open up.

This book has aimed to show that there are many strategies that Zapotec language activists employ across diverse communities of practice. There are some common ways that activists engage in representing, connecting, and creating resources, events, spaces, people, and communicative practices, such as positive representations of Indigenous language speakers and communicative practices, and creation of learning spaces and/or materials. There are also differences shaped by contextual factors such as the social positioning of actors and the constraints and affordances of time and visibility. These include tendencies towards production of rapid, mobile resources, versus slow, place-based structures. Conceptual factors, such as the meanings that Diidxazá holds within different communities of practice and underlying theories of action, also influence how strategies are developed and employed, as advocates envision success to be different, and to be achieved in different ways. The valorization and inclusion of Diidxazá remain common goals however, whether through so-called expert planning and influence, or many small grains of sand– or both.

Throughout this book I have aimed to increase the visibility of some of the Diidxazá speakers, learners, and activists in the Isthmus, although it is inevitably a partial perspective and there are many brilliant activists whose work has not been mentioned here. As one young teacher, Carlos Antonio Celaya Gómez commented at the end of an interview when I asked if there was anything else he would like to say:

> Pues, que si alguien llega a escuchar eso que sea aquí de la región o de la universidad donde vas a presentar, que se animen a venir a visitar a la región o el estado, a conocer un poco más de esa cultura y de la lengua. Para que no solo escuchen "zapoteco, zapoteco, zapoteco" en tu investigación y en las documentaciones que hagan. Que realmente lo conozcan tal cual es, el contexto y todo eso.

Well, that if someone hears this that is from here in the region or in the university where you're going to present, that they should get motivated to visit the region or the state, to know more about this culture and the language. So that they won't just hear "Zapotec, Zapotec, Zapotec" in your research and in the documentation that's made. That they really get to know it how it is, the context and everything. (Interview July 2015)

I wholeheartedly echo Carlos' caveat to my (and all academic) work– and his suggestion to visit the region, made with the tone of pride with which residents of the Isthmus often describe their homeland as unique and a place worthy of note. At the same time, I view this comment as another example of the convivial norm typical of Diidxazá activists, where personal interaction and participation are prioritized. For those unable to take up the invitation, I hope that my observations and interpretations presented here offer a view of the dynamic sociolinguistic ecology of the Isthmus of Tehuantepec and the ways that language activists are charting paths towards linguistic equality through diverse strategies of resistance and reimagining.

Appendix A: Language activism strategy framework

The language activism strategy framework consists of 3 central actions targeted towards 5 goals. Actions may be influenced by any combination of 6 key characteristics. These characteristics are represented as scales, and different activism strategies can be described through their relative positions on these scales. This framework is intended to describe a range of strategic actions, and does not imply the superiority of strategies with certain targets nor certain characteristics. Each strategy is embedded in a specific language ecology which shapes and informs the who, what, and how of language activism, and enables or constrains the outcomes. Different strategies will thus be more or less possible and desirable depending on the context and the actors involved.

Actions	Goals
– Creating	– Resources
– Connecting	– Events
– Representing	– Spaces/ Structures
	– People/ Identities
	– Communication practices

Characteristic	Scale		
Location:	Local	↔	International
Timeframe:	Slow	↔	Rapid
Visibility & mobility:	Low	↔	High
Socio-historical orientation:	Future	↔	Past
Diversity orientation:	Syncretic	↔	Purist
Participation:	Open participation	↔	Controlled participation

Appendix B: Transcription conventions

Interviews were conducted in Spanish, all translations are mine. The translations attempt to stay close to the original spoken language, rather than revising to idiomatic English. In order to maintain confidentiality in some cases, I give the year and month of interviews throughout but not the exact date.
- /slashes/ are used to indicate overlapping speech between two speakers.
- . . . Three dots are used to indicate a pause.
- ---Dashes are used to indicate interrupted speech.
- [. . .] Brackets with three dots are used to indicate an omission of the original transcript.
- [brackets] are used to indicate an editorial or translation insertion, such as a word that is implied but not actually present in the transcript.

Appendix C: Glossary of common abbreviations, Diidxazá, and Spanish terms

Term/ abbreviation	Translation/ interpretation
alfabeto popular	Popular or people's alphabet (a de facto standard for Isthmus Zapotec developed in 1956)
Bidaani (Isthmus Zapotec); huipil (Spanish)	Sleeveless blouse typically decorated with embroidery and/or patterned stitching
Binnizá	Isthmus Zapotec people, often translated as people of the cloud (literally people (*binni*) cloud (*zá*))
Camino de la Iguana	The path of the iguana (a literacy workshop)
Casa de la Cultura	Cultural Center
castellanización	Process of spreading use of Spanish, literally Spanishization, begun under Spanish colonialism and continuing through the present
CEDELIO, Centro de Estudios y Desarrollo de Lenguas Indígenas de Oaxaca	Center for the Study and Development of Indigenous Languages of Oaxaca
CASA, Centro para las Artes San Agustín	Saint Augustine Center for the Arts
COCEI, Coalición Obrero-Campesino-Estundiantil del Istmo	Laborer-peasant-student coalition of the Isthmus
Convivio; convivencia	A social event or gathering; togetherness, pleasant social interaction
dialecto	Literally 'dialect'. Used as a low-status term for Indigenous languages in Mexico, in contrast to so-called *idiomas* (languages) such as Spanish and English. Not the same as the concept of dialect or variety in Linguistics, which does not carry prejudice.
diidxastia	Spanish, literally language of Castilla
diidxazá	Isthmus Zapotec, often translated as language of the clouds (literally 'word/ language' (*diidxa*) 'cloud' (*zá*)). Also referred to in this book as Diidxazá or Zapotec.
Guchachi' Reza	Sliced Iguana (a journal published by *Istmeños*)

(continued)

Term/ abbreviation	Translation/ interpretation
IIEPO, Instituto Estatal de Educación Pública de Oaxaca	Oaxacan State Public Education Institute
INALI, Instituto Nacional de Lenguas Indígenas	National Institute of Indigenous Languages (Mexico)
Istmeño; Istmeña	A person from the Isthmus (male; female)
Juchiteco (Teco); Juchiteca (Teca)	A person from Juchitán (male; female)
muxe	A gender category recognized in the Isthmus
Neza	The path (a journal published by Istmeños)
PTEO, Plan para la transformación de la educación en Oaxaca	Plan for the transformation of education in Oaxaca
SIL (ILV)	Summer Institute of Linguistics (Instituto Lingüístico de Verano)
UABJO, Universidad Autónoma Beníto Juárez de Oaxaca	Autonomous Benito Juarez University of Oaxaca
velas	A series of celebrations held annually in honor of different saints and churches, and forming a central part of the social calendar in the Isthmus

References

Acuña, René, ed. 1984. *Relaciones Geográficas del siglo XVI. Antequera*. Volume 1 & 2. Mexico City, Mexico: UNAM-IIA (Serie Antropología, 54, 58).
Agha, Asif. 2007. *Language and Social Relations*. Cambridge, UK: Cambridge University Press.
Aguilar Gil, Yasnaya Elena. 2016. "(Is There) An Indigenous Literature?" *Diálogo* 19 (1): 157–59.
Alexander, Neville. 2005. *Mother Tongue-Based Bilingual Education in Southern Africa: The Dynamics of Implementation*. Cape Town, South Africa: PRAESA.
Alim, H. Samy, Awad Ibrahim, and Alastair Pennycook, eds. 2008. *Global Linguistic Flows: Hip Hop Cultures, Youth Identities, and the Politics of Language*. New York & London: Routledge.
Anderson, Benedict. 1991. *Imagined Communities: Reflections on the Origin and Spread of Nationalism*. London: Verso.
Anthony-Stevens, Vanessa. 2017. "Cultivating Alliances: Reflections on the Role of Non-Indigenous Collaborators in Indigenous Educational Sovereignty." *Journal of American Indian Education* 56 (1): 81–104.
Anthony-Stevens, Vanessa, Philip Stevens, and Sheilah Nicholas. 2017. "Raiding and Alliances: Indigenous Educational Sovereignty as Social Justice." *Journal of Critical Thought and Praxis* 6 (1). https://www.iastatedigitalpress.com/jctp/article/id/545/.
Anzures Tapia, Aldo. 2015. "Evaluations in Mexico: Institutionalizing the Silence of Indigenous Populations." *Working Papers in Educational Linguistics* 30 (2): 27–46.
Augsburger, Deborah. 2004. "Language Socialization and Shift in an Isthmus Zapotec Community of Mexico." PhD Dissertation, University of Pennsylvania.
Bakhtin, Mikhail. 1986. *Speech Genres and Other Late Essays*. Austin, TX: University of Texas Press.
Ball, Jessica. 2010. "Educational Equity for Children from Diverse Language Backgrounds: Mother Tongue-Based Bilingual or Multilingual Education in the Early Years." Paris: UNESCO.
Barabas, Alicia M., and Miguel A. Bartolomé, eds. 1999. *Configuaraciones Étnicas En Oaxaca: Perspectivas Etnográficas Para Las Autonomías (Vol. 1)*. México, D.F.: Instituto Nacional de Antropología e Historia.
Barton, David, and Karin Tusting. 2005. "Introduction: Beyond Communities of Practice: Language, Power, and Social Context." In *Beyond Communities of Practice: Language, Power, and Social Context*, edited by David Barton and Karin Tusting, 1–13. Cambridge, UK: Cambridge University Press.
Battiste, Marie. 2013. *Decolonizing Education: Nourishing the Learning Spirit*. Saskatoon, AB: Purich Publishing Ltd.
Bauman, Richard, and Charles L. Briggs. 1990. "Poetics and Performance as Critical Perspectives on Language and Social Life." *Annual Review of Anthropology* 19: 59–88.
Benson, Carol. 2004. "The Importance of L1-Based Schooling for Educational Quality." Paris: UNESCO.
Bhabha, Homi. 1994. *The Location of Culture*. London: Routledge.
Blackledge, Adrian, and Angela Creese. 2010. *Multilingualism*. London: Continuum.
Blair, Heather A., Linda Pelly, and Rochelle Starr. 2018. "Connecting Indigenous Languages Policy, Programs, and Practices." In *Promising Practices in Indignous Teacher Education*, edited by Paul Whitinui, Maria del Carmen Rodríguez de France, and Onowa McIvor, 119–30. Singapore: Springer Nature.

Blommaert, Jan. 2010. *The Sociolinguistics of Globalization*. Cambridge, UK: Cambridge University Press.
Blommaert, Jan, and Dong Jie. 2010. *Ethnographic Fieldwork*. Bristol, UK: Multilingual Matters.
Blommaert, Jan, and Jef Verschueren. 1998. *Debating Diversity: Analysing the Discourse of Tolerance*. London: Routledge.
Boaz, Franz. 1911. *Handbook of American Indian Languages*. Washington, D.C.: Smithsonian Institution, Bureau of American Ethnology.
Bourdieu, Pierre. 1984. *Distinction : A Social Critique of the Judgement of Taste*. London: Routledge & Kegan Paul.
Bourdieu, Pierre. 1991. *Language and Symbolic Power*. Cambridge, MA: Harvard University Press.
Bourdieu, Pierre, and Jean-Claude Passeron. 1970. *La Reproduction : Éléments d'une Théorie Du Système d'enseignement*. Paris: Minuit.
Bowern, Claire. 2015. *Linguistic Fieldwork: A Practical Guide*. 2nd Edition. Basingstoke & New York: Palgrave MacMillan.
Brayboy, Bryan M. J., Heather R. Gough, Beth Leonard, Roy F. Roehl II, and Jessica A. Solyom. 2012. "Reclaiming Scholarship: Critical Indigenous Research Methodologies." In *Qualitative Research: An Introduction to Methods and Design*, edited by Stephen D. Lapan, MaryLynn T. Quartaroli, and Frances J. Reimer, 423–50. San Francisco, CA: John Wiley.
Briggs, Charles L., and Richard Bauman. 1992. "Genre, Intertextuality, and Social Power." *Journal of Linguistic Anthropology* 2 (2): 131–72.
Burns, Anne. 2005. "Action Research: An Evolving Paradigm?" *Language Teaching* 38 (02): 57–74.
Busch, Brigitta. 2012. "The Linguistic Repertoire Revisited." *Applied Linguistics* 335: 503–23.
Byram, Michael. 1997. *Teaching and Assessing Intercultural Communicative Competence*. Clevedon, UK: Multilingual Matters.
Cajete, Gregory. 1994. *Look to the Mountain: An Ecology of Indigenous Education*. Durango, CO: Kivaki Press.
Calvet, Louis-Jean. 1974. *Linguistique et Colonialisme: Petit Traité de Glottophagie*. Paris: Payot.
Cameron, Deborah. 2007. "Language Endangerment and Verbal Hygiene: History, Morality and Politics." In *Discourses of Endangerment: Ideology and Interest in the Defense of Languages*, edited by Alexandre Duchêne and Monica Heller, 268–85. London: Continuum.
Cameron, Deborah, Elizabeth Frazer, Penelope Harvey, Ben Rampton, and Kay Richardson. 1992. *Researching Language: Issues of Power and Method*. New York: Routledge.
Cameron, Deborah, Elizabeth Frazer, Penelope Harvey, Ben Rampton, and Kay Richardson. 1993. "Ethics, Advocacy and Empowerment: Issues of Method in Researching Language." *Language & Communication* 13 (2): 81–94.
Campbell, Howard. 1989. "Juchitán: The Politics of Cultural Revivalism in an Isthmus Zapotec Community." *The Latin American Anthropology Review* 2 (2): 47–55.
Campbell, Howard. 1993. "Tradition and the New Social Movements: The Politics of Isthmus Zapotec Culture." *Latin American Perspectives* 20 (3): 83–97.
Campbell, Howard. 1994. *Zapotec Renaissance: Ethnic Politics and Cultural Revivalism in Southern Mexico*. Albuquerque, NM: University of New Mexico.
Canagarajah, Suresh, ed. 2005. *Reclaiming the Local in Language Policy and Practice*. Mahwah, NJ: Lawrence Erlbaum Associates.
"Carpeta Regional Istmo: Información Estadística y Geográfica Básica." 2012. http://www.bieoaxaca.org/sistema/pdfs/ciedd/carp_istmo.pdf.
Cata, Víctor. 2003. "Tehuantepec: Las Últimas Voces." *Guiña Ndaga (Baúl Rústico)* 1 (1): 1–22.
Cata, Víctor. 2012. *Libana*. Oaxaca de Juarez.

Cazden, Courtney, Bill Cope, Norman Fairclough, Jim Gee, Mary Kalantzis, Gunther Kress, Allen Luke, Carmen Luke, Sarah Michaels, and Martin Nakata. 1996. "A Pedagogy of Multiliteracies: Designing Social Futures." *Harvard Educational Review* 66 (1): 60–92.

Cha'ca, Roselia. 2013. "Crean La Primera Lotería En Zapoteco de La Flora Del Istmo." *Agencia Quadratín*, October 21, 2013. http://oaxaca.quadratin.com.mx/Crean-la-primera-Loteria-en-zapoteco-de-la-flora-del-Istmo/.

Cha'ca, Roselia. 2015. "Con rap buscan jóvenes conservar el zapoteco del Istmo." *Agencia Quadratín*, 21 February 2015. https://oaxaca.quadratin.com.mx/Con-rap-buscan-jovenes-conservar-el-zapoteco-del-Istmo/

Chomsky, Noam. 1965. *Aspects of the Theory of Syntax*. Cambridge, MA: MIT Press.

Cochran-Smith, Marilyn, and Susan Lytle. 2009. *Inquiry as Stance: Practitioner Research for the next Generation*. New York: Teachers College Press.

Comaroff, John L., and Jean Comaroff. 2009. *Ethnicity, Inc.* Chicago, IL: Chicago University Press.

Cooke, Bill, and Uma Kothari, eds. 2001. *Participation: The New Tyranny?* New York: Zed Books.

Cooper, Robert. 1989. *Language Planning and Social Change*. Cambridge, UK: Cambridge University Press.

Cope, Lida, and Susan Penfield. 2011. "'Applied Linguist Needed': Cross-Disciplinary Networking for Revitalization and Education in Endangered Language Contexts." *Language and Education* 25 (4): 267–71.

Coronado Suzán, Gabriela. 1992. "Educación Bilingüe En México: Propósitos y Realidades." *International Journal of the Sociology of Language* 96: 53–70.

Coronel-Molina, Serafín M. 2015. *Language Ideolgoy, Policy and Planning in Peru*. Bristol, UK: Multilingual Matters.

Coronel-Molina, Serafín M. 2019. "Media and Technology: Revitalizing Latin American Indigenous Languages in Cyberspace." In *A World of Indigenous Languages: Politics, Pedagogies and Prospects for Language Reclamation*, edited by Teresa L. McCarty, Sheilah E. Nicholas, and Gillian Wigglesworth, 91–114. Bristol, UK: Mulitlingual Matters.

Costa, James. 2015. "New Speakers, New Language: On Being a Legitimate Speaker of a Minority Language in Provence." *International Journal of the Sociology of Language* (231): 127–45.

Costa, James, Haley De Korne, and Pia Lane. 2017. "Standardising Minority Languages: Reinventing Peripheral Languages in the 21st Century." In *Standardizing Minority Languages: Competing Ideologies of Authority and Authenticity in the Global Periphery*, edited by Pia Lane, James Costa, and Haley De Korne, 1–23. London: Routledge.

Covarrubias, Miguel. 1946. *Mexico South*. New York: Alfred A. Knopf.

Cru, Josep. 2017. "Bilingual Rapping in Yucatán, Mexico: Strategic Choices for Maya Language Legitimation and Revitalisation." *International Journal of Bilingual Education and Bilingualism* 20 (5): 481–96.

Crúz, Wilfrido C. 1935. *El Tonalamatl Zapoteco: Ensayo Sobre Su Interpretación Lingüística*. Oaxaca, Mexico: Imprenta del Gobierno del Estado Oaxaca de Juárez.

Cummins, James. 2009. "Fundamental Psycolinguistic and Sociological Principles Underlying Education Success for Linguistic Minority Students." In *Social Justice through Multilingual Education*, edited by Tove Skutnabb-Kangas, Robert Phillipson, Ajit K. Mohanty, and Minati Panda, 19–35. Bristol, UK: Multilingual Matters.

Czaykowska-Higgins, Ewa. 2009. "Research Models, Community Engagement, and Linguistic Fieldwork: Reflections on Working within Canadian Indigenous Communities." *Language Documentation and Conservation* 3 (1): 15–50.

Czaykowska-Higgins, Ewa, Strang Burton, Onowa McIvor, and Aliki Marinakis. 2017. "Supporting Indigenous language revitalisation through collaborative post-secondary proficiency-building curriculum." *Language Documentation and Description* 14: 136–159. http://www.elpublishing.org/docs/1/14/ldd14_07.pdf

Dalton-Puffer, Christiane. 2007. *Discourse in Content and Language Integrated Learning (CLIL) Classrooms*. Philadelphia, PA: John Benjamins Publishing Company.

Davis, Jenny L. 2017. "Resisting Rhetorics of Language Endangerment: Reclamation through Indigenous Language Survivance." *Language Documentation and Description* 14: 37–58. http://www.elpublishing.org.

Davis, Jenny L. 2019. *Talking Indian: Identity and Language Revitalization in the Chickasaw Renaissance*. Tucson, AZ: University of Arizona Press.

Davis, Kathryn A. and Prem Phyak. 2017. *Engaged Language Plolicy and Practices*. London & New York: Routledge.

De Korne, Haley. 2010. "Indigenous Language Education Policy: Supporting Community-Controlled Immersion in Canada and the US." *Language Policy* 9 (2): 115–41.

De Korne, Haley. 2017a. "'A Treasure' and 'a Legacy': Individual and Communal (Re)Valuing of Isthmus Zapotec in Multilingual Mexico." In *Language, Education and Neoliberalism: Critical Studies in Sociolinguistics*, edited by Mi-Cha Flubacher and Alfonso Del Percio, 37–61. Bristol, UK: Multilingual Matters.

De Korne, Haley. 2017b. "'That's Too Much to Learn': Writing, Longevity, and Urgency in the Isthmus Zapotec Speech Community." In *Standardizing Minority Languages: Competing Ideologies of Authority and Authenticity in the Global Periphery*, edited by Pia Lane, James Costa, and Haley De Korne, 222–41. London: Routledge.

De Korne, Haley. 2017c. "The Multilingual Realities of Language Reclamation: Working with Language Contact, Diversity, and Change in Endangered Language Education." *Language Documentation and Description* 14: 111–35. http://www.elpublishing.org.

De Korne, Haley, and Nancy H. Hornberger. 2017. "Countering Unequal Multilingualism through Ethnographic Monitoring." In *Researching Multilingualism: Critical and Ethnographic Perspectives*, edited by Marilyn Martin-Jones and Dierdre Martin, 247–58. London: Routledge.

De Korne, Haley, Mario E. López Gopar, and Kiara Ríos Ríos. 2019. "Changing Ideological and Implementational Spaces for Minoritised Languages in Higher Education: *Zapotequización* of Language Education in Mexico." *Journal of Multilingual and Multicultural Development* 40 (6): 504–517.

De Korne, Haley, and The Burt Lake Band of Ottawa and Chippewa Indians. 2009. "The Pedagogical Potential of Multimedia Dictionaries Lessons from a Community Dictionary Project." In *Indigenous Language Revitalization: Encouragement, Guidance, and Lessons Learned*, edited by Jon Reyhner and Louise Lockard, 141–53. Flagstaff, AZ: Northern Arizona University.

De Korne, Haley, and Miranda Weinberg. 2021. "'I Learned That My Name Is Spelled Wrong': Lessons from Mexico and Nepal on Teaching Literacy for Indigenous Language Reclamation." *Comparative Education Review*, 65 (2): 288–309.

de la Cruz, Víctor. 1993. "Brothers or Citizens: Two Languages, Two Political Projects in the Isthmus." In *Zapotec Struggles: Histories, Politics, and Representations from Juchitán*,

Oaxaca, edited by Howard Campbell, Leigh Binford, Miguel Bartolomé, and Alicia Barabas, 241–48. Washington, D.C.: Smithsonian Institution Press.
de la Cruz, Víctor. 2008. *Mapas Genealógicos Del Istmo Oaxaqueño*. Oaxaca, Mexico: Culturas Populares, CONACULTA.
Dekker, Diane, and Catherine Young. 2005. "Bridging the Gap: The Development of Appropriate Educational Strategies for Minority Language Communities in the Philippines." *Current Issues in Language Planning* 6 (2): 182–199.
Derrida, Jacques. 1967. *De La Grammatologie*. Paris: Minuit.
Doane, Molly. 2005. "The Resilience of Nationalism in a Global Era: Megaprojects in Mexico's South." In *Social Movements: An Anthropological Reader*, edited by Julie Nash, 187–202. Malden, MA: Blackwell Publishing.
Dobrin, Lise, Peter Austin, and David Nathan. 2009. "Dying to Be Counted: The Commodification of Endangered Languages in Documentary Linguistics." *Language Documentation and Description* 6: 37–52.
Douglas Fir Group, The. 2016. "A Transdisciplinary Framework for SLA in a Multilingual World." *The Modern Language Journal* 100 (S1): 19–47.
Duchêne, Alexandre and Monica Heller, eds. 2007. *Discourses of Endangerment: Sociolinguistics, Globalization and Social Order*. London: Continuum.
Dunlap, Alexander. (2019). *Renewing Destruction: Wind Energy, Conflict and Resistance in a Latin American Context*. New York & London: Rowman and Littlefield International.
Edelman, Murray. 1995. *From Art to Politics: How Artistic Creations Shape Political Conceptions*. Chicago, IL: University of Chicago Press.
Eriks-Brophy, Alice, and Martha Crago. 1994. "Transforming Classroom Discourse: An Innuit Example." *Language and Education* 8: 105–22.
Errington, Joseph. 2001. "Colonial Linguistics." *Annual Review of Anthropology* 30 (1): 19–39.
Escobar, Arturo, and Sonia Alvarez. 1992. "Theory and Protest in Latin America Today." In *The Making of Social Movements in Latin America: Identity, Strategy, and Democracy*, edited by Arturo Escobar and Sonia Alvarez, 1–15. Boulder, CO: Westview Press.
Fairclough, Norman. 2003. *Analysing Discourse: Textual Analysis for Social Research*. London: Routledge.
Faudree, Paja. 2013. *Singing for the Dead: The Politics of Indigenous Revival in Mexico*. Durham, NC: Duke University Press.
Faudree, Paja. 2015. "Singing for the Dead, on and off Line: Diversity, Migration, and Scale in Mexican Muertos Music." *Language & Communication* 44: 31–43.
Ferguson, Charles. 1959. "Diglossia." *Word* 15: 325–40.
Ferguson, Jenanne. 2010. "*Shäwthän Dän, Shäwthän Kwänjè* : Good People, Good Words: Creating a Dän k'è Speech Community in an Elementary School." *Current Issues in Language Planning* 11 (2): 152–72.
Ferguson, Jenanne. 2019. *Words like birds: Sakha Language Discourses and Practices in the City*. Lincoln, NE: University of Nebraska Press.
Fill, Alwin, and Peter Muhlhausler. 2001. *Ecolinguistics Reader: Language, Ecology and Environment*. New York: Continuum.
Firth, Alan, and Johannes Wagner. 1997. "On Discourse, Communication, and (Some) Fundamental Concepts in SLA Research." *The Modern Language Journal* 81 (3): 285–300.
Fishman, Joshua. 1989. *Language and Ethnicity in Minority Sociolinguistic Perspective*. Clevedon, UK: Multilingual Matters.

Fishman, Joshua. 1991. *Reversing Language Shift: Theoretical and Empirical Foundations of Assistance to Threatened Languages*. Clevedon, UK: Multilingual Matters.

Flores Farfán, José Antonio. 2002. "The Use of Multimedia and the Arts in Language Revitalization, Maintenance and Development: The Case of the Balsas Nahuas of Guerrero, Mexico." In *Indigenous Languages Across the Community*, edited by Barbara Burnaby and Jon Reyhner, 225–236. Flagstaff, AZ: Northern Arizona University.

Flores, Nelson. 2013. "The unexamined relationship between neoliberalism and plurilingualism: A cautionary tale." *TESOL Quarterly*, 47 (3), 500–520.

Flores, Nelson, and Hugo Baetens Beardsmore. 2015. "Programs and Structures in Bilingual and Multilingual Education." In *Handbook of Bilingual and Multilingual Education*, edited by Wayne Wright, Sovicheth Boun, and Ofelia García, 205–222. Hoboken, NJ: Wiley Blackwell.

Flores, Nelson, and Sofia Chaparro. 2018. "What Counts as Language Education Policy? Developing a Materialist Anti-Racist Approach to Language Activism." *Language Policy* 17 (3): 365–84.

Foucault, Michel. 1980. *Power/Knowledge: Selected Interviews and Other Writings 1972–1977*. New York: Pantheon Books.

Francis, Norbert, and Jon Reyhner. 2002. *Language and Literacy Teaching for Indigenous Education*. Bristol, UK: Multilingual Matters.

Fraser, Nancy. 1992. "Rethinking the Public Sphere: A Contribution to the Critique of Actually Existing Democracy." In *Habermas and the Public Sphere*, edited by Craig Calhoun, 109–141. Cambridge, MA: MIT Press.

Freire, Paulo. 1969. *La Educación Como Práctica de La Libertad*. Mexico, D.F.: Siglo XXI Editores.

Freire, Paulo. 1970. *Pedagogy of the Oppressed*. New York: Continuum.

Friede, Stephanie, and Rosa Lehmann. 2016. "*Consultas*, Corporations, and Governance in Tehuantepec, Mexico." *Peace Review* 28 (1): 84–92.

Gal, Susan. 2006. "Contradictions of Standard Language in Europe: Implications for the Study of Practices and Publics." *Social Anthropology* 14 (2): 163–81.

Gal, Susan, and Kathryn A Woolard, eds. 2001. *Languages and Publics: The Making of Authority*. Manchester, UK & Northampton, MA: St. Jerome Publishing.

García, Maria Elena. 2005. *Making Indigenous Citizens: Identities, Education, and Multicultural Development in Peru*. Stanford, CA: Stanford University Press.

García, Mónica Esteva. 2020. "El Diidxaza En Los Procesos Comunicativos y Las Dinámicas Sociales En Guizii, Istmo de Tehuantepec." *Ciencia y Mar* 24 (71): 83–109.

García, Ofelia. 2009a. *Bilingual Education in the 21st Century: A Global Perspective*. New York: Wiley Blackwell.

García, Ofelia. 2009b. "En/Countering Indigenous Bilingualism." *Journal of Language, Identity & Education* 8 (5): 376–80.

García, Ofelia, and Patricia Velasco. 2012. "Insufficient Language Education Policy: Intercultural Bilingual Education in Chiapas." *Diaspora, Indigenous, and Minority Education* 6 (1): 1–18.

Goffman, Erving. 1967. *Interaction Ritual*. New York: Anchor/ Doubleday.

Goffman, Erving. 1981. *Forms of Talk*. Philadelphia, PA: University of Pennsylvania Press.

Gosling, Maureen, and Ellen Osborne. 2000. *Rama Del Fuego (Blossoms of Fire)*. https://www.imdb.com/title/tt0259219/.

Greenwood, Davydd J., and Morten Levin. 1998. *Introduction to Action Research: Social Research for Social Change*. Thousand Oaks, London, New Delhi: SAGE Publications.

Grenoble, Lenore, and Lindsay Whaley. 2006. *Saving Languages: An Introduction to Language Revitalization*. Cambridge, UK: Cambridge University Press.

Grinevald, Colette, and Michel Bert. 2012. "Langues En Danger, Idéologies, Revitalisation." *Langues de France, Langues En Danger: Aménagement et Rôle Des Linguistes*, 15–32. Toulouse, France: Editions Privat.

Gumperz, John. 1964. "Linguistic and Social Interaction in Two Communities." *American Anthropologist* 66: 137–54.

Gumperz, John. 1968. "The Speech Community." In *International Encyclopedia of the Social Sciences*, 381–86. New York: Macmillan.

Guzman, Estefania S. de. 2005. "Is the Medium of Instruction Debate in the Philippines Closing In?" In *Visions for Education: Essays on Philippine Education in Honor of Br. Andrew Gonzalez*, edited by Allan Bernardo and Roberto Borromeo, 127–51. Manila, the Philippines: De La Salle University.

Hagège, Claude. 2000. *Halte à La Mort Des Langues*. Paris: Odile Jacob.

Hale, Charles R. 2005. "Neoliberal Multiculturalism : The Remaking of Cultural Rights and Racial Dominance in Central America." *Political and Legal Anthropology Review* 28 (1): 10–28.

Hale, Ken, Michael Krauss, Lucille J. Watahomigie, Akira Y. Yamamoto, Collette Craig, Laverne Masayesva Jeanne, and Nora C. England. 1992. "Endangered Languages." *Language* 68 (1): 1–42.

Hamel, Rainer Enrique. 2008a. "Bilingual Education for Indigenous Communities in Mexico." In *Encyclopedia of Language and Education, Volume 5: Bilingual Education*, edited by James Cummins and Nancy H. Hornberger, 2nd Edition, 5: 311–22. New York: Springer.

Hamel, Rainer Enrique. 2008b. "Indigenous Language Policy and Education in Mexico." In *Encyclopedia of Language and Education, Volume 1: Language Policy and Political Issues in Education*, edited by Stephen May and Nancy H. Hornberger, 2nd Edition, 1: 301–13. New York: Springer.

Harrison, K. David. 2010. *The Last Speakers: The Quest to Save the World's Most Endangered Languages*. Washington, D.C.: National Geographic Books.

Haugen, Einar. 1972. *The Ecology of Language*. Stanford, CA: Stanford University Press.

Haugen, Einar. 1973. "The Curse of Babel." *Daedalus* 102 (3): 47–57.

Heath, Shirley Brice. 1972. *Telling Tongues: Language Policy in Mexico, Colony to Nation*. New York: Teachers College Press.

Heller, Monica. 1999. *Linguistic Minorities and Modernity: A Sociolinguistic Ethnography*. London: Longman.

Heller, Monica. 2007. *Bilingualism: A Social Approach*. Basingstoke, UK: Palgrave Macmillan.

Heller, Monica. 2011. *Paths to Post-nationalism: A Critical Ethnography of Language and Identity*. Oxford, UK: Oxford University Press.

Heller, Monica, and Marilyn Martin-Jones. 2001. "Introduction: Symbolic Domination, Education and Linguistic Difference." In *Voices of Authority : Education and Linguistic Difference*, edited by Monica Heller and Marilyn Martin-Jones, 1–28. London: Ablex.

Henestrosa, Andrés. 2009 [1929]. *Los Hombres Que Dispersó La Danza*. Second edition. Mexico, D.F.: Miguel Ángel Porrúa.

Henne-Ochoa, Richard, Emma Elliott-Groves, Barbra Meek, and Barbara Rogoff. 2020. "Pathways Forward for Indigenous Language Reclamation: Engaging Indigenous Epistemology and Learning by Observing and Pitching in to Family and Community Endeavors." *The Modern Language Journal* 104 (2): 481–93.

Hermes, Mary, Megan Bang, and Amanda Marin. 2012. "Designing Indigenous Language Revitalization." *Harvard Educational Review* 82 (3): 381–403.
Hermes, Mary, and Mel M. Engman. 2017. "Resounding the Clarion Call: Indigenous Language Learners and Documentation." *Language Documentation and Description* 14: 59–87.
Hernández Ruiz, Samael. Forthcoming. "Un Sol Se Oculta." In *Ensayos Sobre La Cultura Zapoteca Por Wilfrido C. Crúz*, 2–7. Espinal, Mexico: Municipio de Espinal, Oaxaca.
Hill, Jane H. 1998. "Don Francisco Márquez Survives: A Meditation on Monolingualism." *International Journal of the Sociology of Language* 132 (1): 167–82.
Hill, Jane H. 2002. "'Expert Rhetorics' in Advocacy for Endangered Languages: Who Is Listening, and What Do They Hear?" *Journal of Linguistic Anthropology* 12 (2): 119–33.
Hill, Jane H., and Kenneth Hill. 1986. *Speaking Mexicano: Dynamics of Syncretic Language in Central Mexico*. Tucson, AZ: University of Arizona Press.
Hinton, Leanne. 2013. *Bringing Our Languages Home: Language Revitalization for Families*. Berkeley, CA: Heyday Books.
Hinton, Leanne, and Ken Hale. 2001. *The Green Book of Language Revitalization in Practice*. San Diego, CA: Academic Press.
Hornberger, Nancy H. 1989. "Continua of Biliteracy." *Review of Education Research* 59 (3): 271–96.
Hornberger, Nancy H. 1991. "Extending Enrichment Bilingual Education: Revisiting Typologies and Redirecting Policy." In *Bilingual Education: Focusschrift in Honor of Joshua A. Fishman. Volume 1*, edited by Ofelia García, 215–34. Philadelphia, PA: John Benjamins Publishing Company.
Hornberger, Nancy H. 1993. "The First Workshop on Quechua and Aymara Writing." In *The Earliest Stage of Language Planning: The "First Congress" Phenomenon*, edited by Joshua A. Fishman, 233–56. Berlin: Mouton de Gruyter.
Hornberger, Nancy H. 1998. "Language Policy, Language Education, Language Rights: Indigenous, Immigrant, and International Perspectives." *Language in Society* 27 (4): 439–58.
Hornberger, Nancy H. 2002. "Multilingual Language Policies and the Continua of Biliteracy: An Ecological Approach." *Language Policy* 1 (1): 27–51.
Hornberger, Nancy H. 2003. *Continua of Biliteracy*. Bristol, UK: Multilingual Matters.
Hornberger, Nancy H. 2005. "Heritage / Community Language Education : US and Australian Perspectives" *International Journal of Bilingual Education and Bilingualism* 8 (2): 101–8.
Hornberger, Nancy H., ed. 2008. *Can Schools Save Indigenous Languages?* New York: Palgrave Macmillan.
Hornberger, Nancy H. 2009. "Multilingual Education Policy and Practice: Ten Certainties (Grounded in Indigenous Experience)." *Language Teaching* 42 (2): 197–211.
Hornberger, Nancy H. 2013a. "Negotiating Methodological Rich Points in the Ethnography of Language Policy." *International Journal of the Sociology of Language*, 219: 101–22.
Hornberger, Nancy H. 2013b. "On Not Taking Language Inequality for Granted: Hymesian Traces in Ethnographic Monitoring of South Africa's Multilingual Language Policy." *Working Papers in Educational Linguistics* 28 (1): 1–21.

Hornberger, Nancy H. 2017. "Portraits of three language activists in Indigenous language reclamation." *Language Documentation and Description*, 14, 160–175. http://www.elpublishing.org/PID/156

Hornberger, Nancy H., Haley De Korne, and Miranda Weinberg. 2016. "Ways of Talking (and Acting) About Language Reclamation: An Ethnographic Perspective on Learning Lenape in Pennsylvania." *Journal of Language, Identity & Education* 15 (1): 44–58.

Hornberger, Nancy H., and Francis M. Hult. 2008. "Ecological Language Education Policy." In *The Handbook of Educational Linguistics*, edited by Bernard Spolsky and Francis M. Hult, 280–96. Oxford, UK: Blackwell.

Hornberger, Nancy H., and David Cassels Johnson. 2007. "Slicing the Onion Ethnographically : Layers and Spaces in Multilingual Language Education Policy and Practice." *TESOL Quarterly* 41 (3): 509–32.

Hornberger, Nancy H., and Kendall A. King. 1996. "Language Revitalisation in the Andes: Can the Schools Reverse Language Shift?" *Journal of Multilingual and Multicultural Development* 17 (6): 427–41.

Hornberger, Nancy H., and Holly Link. 2012. "Translanguaging and Transnational Literacies in Multilingual Classrooms: A Biliteracy Lens." *International Journal of Bilingual Education and Bilingualism* 15 (3): 261–78.

Huesca-Pérez, María Elena, Claudia Sheinbaum-Pardo, and Johann Köppel. 2016. "Social Implications of Siting Wind Energy in a Disadvantaged Region – The Case of the Isthmus of Tehuantepec, Mexico." *Renewable and Sustainable Energy Reviews* 58 (May): 952–65.

Hult, Francis M. 2010. "Analysis of Language Policy Discourses across the Scales of Space and Time." *International Journal of the Sociology of Language* 202: 7–24.

Hymes, Dell. 1968. "The Ethnography of Speaking." In *Readings in the Sociology of Language*, edited by Joshua Fishman, 99–138. The Hague, the Netherlands: Mouton.

Hymes, Dell. 1980. "Ethnographic Monitoring." In *Language in Education: Ethnolinguistic Essays*, 104–18. Washington, D.C.: Center for Applied Linguistics.

Illich, Ivan. 1970. *Deschooling Society*. London: Marion Boyers Publishers.

Illich, Ivan. 1973. *Tools for Conviviality*. New York: Harper & Row.

INEE. 2018. "Planea: Resultados Nacionales 2017." Mexico, D.F.

Ingram, S. 2010. "UNICEF Helps Children Overcome Language Barriers at Schools in Lao PDR." http://www.unicef.org/education/laopdr_52881.html.

Instituto Nacional de Lenguas Indígenas (INALI). 2008. "Catalogo de Las Lenguas Indígenas Nacionales: Variantes Lingüísticas de México Con Sus Autodenominaciones y Referencias Geoestadísticas." http://www.inali.gob.mx/clin-inali/.

International Labour Organization. 1989. *Convention 169*. http://www.ilo.org/indigenous/Con ventions/no169/lang-en/index.htm.

Irvine, Judith, and Susan Gal. 2000. "Language Ideology and Linguistic Differentiation." In *Regimes of Language: Ideologies, Polities, and Identities*, edited by Paul V. Kroskrity, 35–84. Santa Fe, NM: School of American Research Press.

Jaffe, Alexandra. 2009. "Stance in a Corsican School: Institutional and Ideological Orders and the Production of Bilingual Subjects." In *Stance: Sociolinguistic Perspectives*, edited by Alexandra Jaffe. Oxford, UK: Oxford University Press.

Janks, Hilary. 2000. "Domination, Access, Diversity and Design: A Synthesis for Critical Literacy Education." *Educational Review* 52 (2): 175–86.

Jiménez Moreno, Wigberto. 1942. "Fr. Juan de Cordova y La Lengua Zapoteca." In *Vocabulario Castellano-Zapoteco*, 7–21. Mexico, D.F.: Biblioteca Lingüística Mexicana.

Johansen, Åse Mette. 2010. "Fra dobbelt stigma til dobbel stolthet." *NOA – Norsk Som Andrespråk*, 26 (1), 7–29.

Johnson, David Cassels. 2012. "Positioning the Language Policy Arbiter: Governmentality and Footing in the School District of Philadelphia." In *Language Policies in Education: Critical Issues*, edited by James W. Tollefson, 128–48. New York: Routledge.

Johnson, David Cassels. 2013. *Language Policy*. Basingstoke & New York: Palgrave MacMillan.

Johnson, David Cassels, and Eric J. Johnson. 2015. "Power and Agency in Language Policy Appropriation." *Language Policy* 14 (3): 221–43.

Kamanā, Kauanoe, and William H. Wilson. 2001. "'*Mai Loko Mai o Ka 'I'ini*: Proceeding from a Dream': The 'Aha Punana Leo Connection in Hawaiian Language Revitalization." In *The Green Book of Language Revitalization in Practice*, edited by Leanne Hinton and Ken Hale, 147–76. San Diego, CA: Academic Press.

King, Kendall A. 2016. "Who and What Is the Field of Applied Linguistics Overlooking?: Why This Matters and How Educational Linguistics Can Help." *Working Papers in Educational Linguistics* 31 (2): 1–18.

Kipp, Darrell R. 2000. "Guidance, Insights, and Lessons Learned for Native Language Activists Developing Their Own Tribal Language Programs." Browning, MT: Piegan Institute.

Krashen, Stephen. 1982. *Principles and Practice in Second Language Acquisition*. Oxford, UK: Pergamon Press.

Kress, Gunther. 2000. "Multimodality." In *Multiliteracies: Literacy Learning and the Design of Social Futures*, edited by Bill Cope and Mary Kalantzis, 182–202. London: Routledge.

Kroskrity, Paul. 2009. "Language Renewal as Sites of Language Ideological Struggle: The Need for 'Ideological Clarification.'" In *Indigenous Language Revitalization: Encouragement, Guidance and Lessons Learned*, edited by Jon Reyhner and Louise Lockard, 71–83. Flagstaff, AZ: Northern Arizona University.

Kroskrity, Paul. 2014. "Borders Traversed, Boundaries Erected: Creating Discursive Identities and Language Communities in the Village of Tewa." *Language & Communication* 38: 8–17.

Kroskrity, Paul. 2018. "On Recognizing Persistence in the Indigenous Language Ideologies of Multilingualism in Two Native American Communities." *Language & Communication* 62: 133–44.

Kroskrity, Paul, and Margaret Field, eds. 2009. *Native American Language Ideologies: Beliefs, Practices, and Struggles in Indian Country*. Tucson, AZ: University of Arizona Press.

Kumaravadivelu, B. 2016. "The Decolonial Option in English Teaching: Can the Subaltern Act?" *TESOL Quarterly*, 50 (1), 66–85.

Labov, William. 1970. *The Study of Language in Its Social Context*. New York: Springer.

Labov, William. 2008. "Unendangered Dialects, Endangered People." In *Sustaining Linguistic Diversity: Endangered and Minority Languages and Varieties*, edited by Kendall A. King, Natalie Schilling-Estes, Jia Jackie Lou, Lyn Fogle, and Barbara Soukup, 219–37. Washington, D.C.: Georgetown University Press.

Lado, Robert. 1959. *Linguistics across Cultures*. Ann Arbor, MI: University of Michigan Press.

Ladson-Billings, Gloria. 1995. "Toward a Theory of Culturally Relevant Pedagogy." *American Educational Research Journal* 32 (3): 465–91.

Lambert, Wallace. 1975. "Culture and Language as Factors in Learning and Education." In *Education of Immigrant Children*, edited by Aaron Wolfgang. Toronto, ON: Ontario Institute for Studies in Education.

Larsen-Freeman, Diane, and Lynne Cameron. 2008. *Complex Systems and Applied Linguistics*. Oxford, UK: Oxford University Press.

Lave, Jean, and E. Wenger. 1991. *Situated Learning: Legitimate Peripheral Participation*. Cambridge, UK: Cambridge University Press.

Leonard, Wesley Y. 2017. "Producing Language Reclamation by Decolonizing 'Language.'" *Language Documentation and Description* 14: 15–36.

Leonard, Wesley Y. 2012. "Framing Language Reclamation Programmes for Everybody's Empowerment." *Gender and Language* 6 (2): 339–67.

Leonard, Wesley Y., and Erin Haynes. 2010. "Making 'Collaboration' Collaborative: An Examination of Perspectives That Frame Linguistic Field Research." *Language Documentation & Conservation* 4: 269–93. http://scholarspace.manoa.hawaii.edu/handle/10125/4482.

Levinson, Bradley A., Douglas E. Foley, and Dorothy C. Holland, eds. 1996. *The Cultural Production of the Educated Person: Critical Ethnographies of Schooling and Local Practice*. Albany, NY: State University of New York Press.

Lewin, Kurt. 1946. "Action Research and Minority Problems." *Journal of Social Issues* 2: 34–46.

Lewis, M. Paul, Gary F. Simons, and Charles D. Fennig. 2015. "Zapotec." In *Ethnologue: Languages of the World, Eighteenth Edition*. Dallas, TX: SIL International. http://www.ethnologue.com/language/zap.

Lewis, Mark C. 2018. "A Critique of the Principle of Error Correction as a Theory of Social Change." *Language in Society* 47 (3): 325–46.

Ley General de Derechos Lingüísticos de Los Pueblos Indígenas. 2003. Mexico. http://www.diputados.gob.mx/LeyesBiblio/pdf/257.pdf.

Lillehaugen, Brook. 2016. "Why Write in a Language That (Almost) No One Can Read? Twitter and the Development of Written Literature." *Language Documentation and Conservation* 10: 356–93. https://scholarspace.manoa.hawaii.edu/handle/10125/24702.

Lim, Lisa, Christopher Stroud, and Lionel Wee, eds. 2018. *The Multilingual Citizen : Towards a Politics of Language for Agency and Change*. Bristol, UK: Multilingual Matters.

Limerick, Nicholas. 2018. "Kichwa or Quichua? Competing Alphabets, Political Histories, and Complicated Reading in Indigenous Languages." *Comparative Education Review* 62 (1): 103–24.

López Bárecenas, Francisco. 2009. *Autonomías y Derechos Indígenas En México*. Mexico, D.F.: MC Editores.

López Chiñas, Gabriel. 1971. *Guendaxheela*. Mexico, D.F.

López Gopar, Mario E. 2007. "El Alfabeto Marginante En La Educación Indígena: El Potencial de Las Multilectoescrituras." *Lectura y Vida* 28 (3): 48–57.

López Gopar, Mario. 2009. "'What Makes Children Different Is What Makes Them Better': Teaching Mexican Children 'English' to Foster Multilingual, Multiliteracies, and Intercultural Practices." PhD Dissertation, University of Toronto.

López Gopar, Mario. 2016. *Decolonizing Primary English Language Teaching*. Bristol, UK: Multilingual Matters.

López Gopar, Mario E., Narcedalia Jiménez Morales, and Arcadio Delgado Jiménez. 2014. "Critical Classroom Practices: Using 'English' to Foster Minoritized Languages and Cultures in Oaxaca, Mexico." In *Minority Languages and Multilingual Education*, edited by Dirk Gorter, Victoria Zenotz, and Jasone Cenoz, 177–99. Dordrecht, the Netherlands: Springer.

López Gopar, Mario E., Omar Núñez-Méndez, William Sughrua, and Angeles Clemente. 2013. "In Pursuit of Multilingual Practices: Ethnographic Accounts of Teaching 'English' to Mexican Children." *International Journal of Multilingualism* 10 (3): 273–91.

Lüdi, Georges. 2004. "Pour Une Linguistique de La Compétence Du Locuteur Plurilingue." *Revue Française de Linguistique Appliquée* 9: 125–35.

Lugones, Maria. 2016. "The Coloniality of Gender." In *The Palgrave Handbook of Gender and Development*, edited by Wendy Harcourt, 13–33. London: Palgrave Macmillan UK.

Maffi, Luisa. 2001. *On Biocultural Diversity: Linking Language, Knowledge, and the Environment*. Washington, D.C.: Smithsonian Institution Press.

Makoni, Sinfree, and Alastair Pennycook, eds. 2007. *Disinventing and Reconstituting Languages*. Bristol, UK: Multilingual Matters.

Maldonado Alvarado, Benjamín. 2002. *Los Indios En Las Aulas: Dinamica de Dominación y Resistencia En Oaxaca*. Mexico, D.F.: Instituto Nacional de Antropología e Historia.

Marcellesi, Jean-Baptiste. 1983. "Identité Linguistique, Exclamatives et Subordonnées: Un Modèle Syntaxique Spécifique En Corse." *Études Corses* 20–21:399–424.

Marcial Cerqueda, Vicente. 2014. "Plan de Acción Para El Impulso de La Lengua Zapoteca En El Programa de Gobierno Municipal 2014–2016." Juchitán, Oaxaca.

Martin-Jones, Marilyn, and Kathryn E. Jones, eds. 2001. *Multilingual Literacies: Reading and Writing Different Worlds*. Amsterdam: John Benjamins Publishing Company.

Martínez Vásquez, Víctor Raúl. 2004. *La Educación En Oaxaca*. Oaxaca de Juarez, Mexico: IISUABJO.

Maurial, Mahia, and Moisés Suxo. 2011. "Does Intercultural Bilingual Education Open Spaces for Inclusion at Higher Education?" In *Social Justice Language Teacher Education*, edited by Margaret Hawkins, 49–62. Bristol, UK: Multilingual Matters.

May, Stephen. 2006. "Language Policy and Minority Rights." In *An Introduction to Language Policy: Theory and Method*, edited by Thomas Ricento, 255–272. Malden, MA: Blackwell.

May, Stephen. 2013. *The Multilingual Turn : Implications for SLA, TESOL and Bilingual Education*. New York & London: Routledge.

May, Stephen, and Sheila Aikman. 2003. "Indigenous Education: Addressing Current Issues and Developments." *Comparative Education* 39 (2): 139–45.

McCarty, Teresa. 1997. "American Indian, Alaska Native and Native Hawaiin Bilingual Education." In *Encyclopedia of Language and Education, Volume 5: Bilingual Education*, edited by James Cummins and David Corson. London: Kluwer Academic Publishers.

McCarty, Teresa. 2013. *Language Policy and Planning in Native America: History, Theory, Praxis*. Bristol, UK: Multilingual Matters.

McCarty, Teresa. 2017. "Commentary: Beyond Endangerment in Indigenous Language Reclamation." *Language Documentation and Description* 14: 176–84. http://www.elpub lishing.org/PID/157.

McComsey, Melanie. 2015. "Bilingual Spaces: Approaches to Linguistic Relativity in Bilingual Mexico." PhD Dissertation, University of California San Diego.

McGroarty, Mary E. 2010. "Language and Ideologies." In *Sociolinguistics and Language Education*, edited by Nancy H. Hornberger and Sandra McKay, 3–39. Bristol, UK: Multilingual Matters.

McHoul, Alexander. 1978. "The Organization of Turns at Formal Talk in the Classroom." *Language in Society* 7: 183–213.

McIntyre, Alice. 2008. *Participatory Action Research*. Thousand Oaks, CA: Sage.

McIvor, Onowa. 2005. "Building the Nests : Indigenous Language Revitalization in Canada through Early Childhood Immersion Programs." MA Thesis, University of Victoria.

McKenzie, James. 2020. "Approaching from Many Angles: Seeing the Connections for Our Languages to Live." *The Modern Language Journal* 104 (2): 501–6.
Meek, Barbra. 2010. *We Are Our Language: An Ethnography of Language Revitalization in a Northern Athabaskan Community.* Tucson, AZ: University of Arizona Press.
Mendoza, Breny. 2016. "Coloniality of Gender and Power: From Postcoloniality to Decoloniality." In *Oxford Handbook of Feminist Theory*, edited by Linda Disch and Mary Hawkesworth, 100–121. Oxford, UK: Oxford University Press.
Menken, Kate, and Ofelia García. 2010. *Negotiating Language Policies in Schools: Educators as Policy Makers.* New York: Routledge.
Messing, Jacqueline. 2007. "Multiple Ideologies and Competing Discourses: Language Shift in Tlaxcala, Mexico." *Language in Society* 36 (4): 555–77.
Meyer, Lois M. 2018. "'Carrying on the Word That I Know': Teacher-Community Language Revitalization Collaborations in Indigenous Oaxaca, Mexico." In *The Routledge Handbook of Language Revitalization*, edited by Leanne Hinton, Leena Huss, and Gerald Roche, 384–94. London: Routledge.
Miano Borruso, Marinella. 2002. *Hombre, Mujer y Muxe' en el Istmo de Tehuantepec.* Mexico, D.F.: INAH.
Milroy, James, and Lesley Milroy. 1999. *Authority in Language: Investigating Standard English.* London: Routledge.
Mintz, Sidney, and Eric Wolf. 1950. "An Analysis of Ritual Co-Parenthood (*Compadrazgo*)." *Southwestern Journal of Anthropology* 6 (4): 341–68.
Moll, Luis C, Cathy Amanti, Deborah Neff, and Norma Gonzalez. 1992. "Funds of Knowledge for Teaching: Using a Qualitative Approach to Connect Homes and Classrooms." *Theory into Practice* 31 (2): 132–41.
Montemayor, Carlos. 2004. "Past and Present Writing in Indigenous Languages." In *Words of the True Peoples: Anthology of Contemporary Mexican Indigenous-Language Writers*, edited by Carlos Montemayor and Donald Frischmann, Volume 1, 1–8. Austin, TX: University of Texas Press.
Moore, Robert. 2000. "Endangered." *Journal of Linguistic Anthropology* 9 (1–2): 65–68.
Moore, Robert. 2012. "'Taking up Speech' in an Endangered Language: Bilingual Discourse in a Heritage Language Classroom." *Working Papers in Educational Linguistics* 27 (2): 57–78.
Moore, Robert, Sari Pietikainen, and Jan Blommaert. 2010. "Counting the Losses: Numbers as the Language of Language Endangerment." *Sociolinguistic Studies* 4 (1): 1–26.
Morales Henestrosa, Bernabé. 1935. "Zapotequización." *Neza* 1 (2).
Morgan, Marcyliena. 2004. "Speech Community." In *A Companion to Linguistic Anthropology*, edited by Alessandro Duranti, 3–22. Malden, MA: Blackwell.
Moriarty, Máiréad, and Sari Pietikäinen. 2011. "Micro-Level Language-Planning and Grass-Root Initiatives : A Case Study of Irish Language Comedy and Inari Sámi Rap." *Current Issues in Language Planning* 12 (3): 363–79.
Mosley-Howard, G. Susan, Daryl Baldwin, George Ironstrack, Kate Rousmaniere, and Bobbe Burke. 2016. "Niila Myaamia (I Am Miami)." *Journal of College Student Retention: Research, Theory & Practice* 17 (4): 437–61.
Muehlmann, Shaylih. 2008. "'Spread Your Ass Cheeks': And Other Things That Should Not Be Said in Indigenous Languages." *American Ethnologist* 35 (1): 34–48.
Muehlmann, Shaylih. 2009. "How Do Real Indians Fish? Neoliberal Multiculturalism and Contested Indigeneities in the Colorado Delta." *American Anthropologist* 111 (4): 468–79.

Muehlmann, Shaylih. 2012. "Von Humboldt's Parrot and the Countdown of Last Speakers in the Colorado Delta." *Language & Communication* 32 (2): 160–68.
Munro, Pamela, Brook Danielle Lillehaugen, and Felipe H Lopez. 2007. *Cali Chiu? A Course in Valley Zapotec*. Lulu.com.
National Indian Brotherhood. 1972. "Indian Control of Indian Education." Ottawa, Canada.
Nevins, M. Eleanor. 2004. "Learning to Listen : Confronting Two Meanings of Language Loss in the Contemporary White Mountain Apache Speech Community." *Journal of Linguistic Anthropology* 14 (2): 269–88.
Nicholas, Sheilah E. 2019. "Without the Language, How Hopi Are You?: Hopi Cultural and Linguistic Identity Construction in Contemporary Linguistic Ecologies." In *A World of Indigenous Languages: Politics, Pedagogies and Prospects for Language Reclamation*, edited by Teresa L. McCarty, Sheilah Nicholas, and Gillian Wigglesworth, 173–93. Bristol, UK: Mulitlingual Matters.
Noriega Sánchez, Julia. 2012. "Las Maestras y el Sindicato." In *Para Que No Se Olviden: Mujeres en el Movimiento Popular, Oaxaca 2006*, edited by Maria Romero Frizzi and Margarita Dalton, 23–36. Oaxaca, Mexico: Secretaría de de las Culturas y Artes de Oaxaca.
Norton, Bonny. 2000. *Identity and Language Learning: Gender, Ethnicity and Educational Change*. Harlow, UK: Longman.
Ochs, Elinor, and Bambi Schieffelin. 1984. "Language Acquisition and Socialization: Three Developmental Stories and Their Implications." In *Culture Theory: Essays on Mind, Self, and Emotion*, edited by Richard Shweder and Robert LeVine, 276–320. Cambridge, UK: Cambridge University Press.
Osborne, A. Barry. 1996. "Practice into Theory into Practice: Culturally Relevant Pedagogy for Students We Have Marginalized and Normalized." *Anthropology & Education Quarterly* 27 (3): 285–314.
Outakoski, Hanna. 2015. "Multilingual Literacy Among Young Learners of North Sámi : Contexts, Complexity and Writing in Sápmi." PhD Dissertation, Umeå University, Sweden.
Overmyer-Velázquez, Rebecca. 2010. *Folkloric Poverty: Neoliberal Multiculturalism in Mexico*. University Park, PA: Pennsylvania State University Press.
Paris, Django. 2012. "Culturally Sustaining Pedagogy." *Educational Researcher* 41 (3): 93–97.
Paris, Django, and H. Samy Alim, eds. 2017. *Culturally Sustaining Pedagogies : Teaching and Learning for Justice in a Changing World*. New York: Teachers College Press.
Pennycook, Alastair. 2001. *Critical Applied Linguistics*. Mahwah, NJ: Lawrence Erlbaum Associates Publishers.
Pennycook, Alastair. 2006. "Postmodernism in Language Policy." In *An Introduction to Language Policy: Theory and Method*, edited by Thomas Ricento, 60–76. Malden, MA: Blackwell.
Pennycook, Alastair. 2010. *Language as a Local Practice*. London: Routledge.
Pennycook, Alastair. 2018. "Posthumanist Applied Linguistics." *Applied Linguistics*, 39 (4): 445–461.
Pérez Báez, Gabriela. 2005. "Language Shift Reversal for a Non-Standardized Language: San Lucas Quiaviní Zapotec." *Proceedings from the Annual Meeting of the Chicago Linguistic Society*.
Pérez Báez, Gabriela. 2011. "Semantics of Body Part Terms in Juchiteco Locative Descriptions." *Language Sciences* 33 (6): 943–60.

Pérez Báez, Gabriela. 2015. *Cuaderno de Lectoescritura Del Zapoteco Del Istmo*. Washington, D.C.: Smithsonian Institution Press.
Pérez Báez, Gabriela. 2016. "Addressing the Gap between Community Beliefs and Priorities and Researchers' Language Maintenance Interests." In *Language Documentation and Revitalization: Latin American Contexts*, edited by Gabriela Pérez Báez, Chris Rogers, and Jorge Emilio Rosés Labrada, 165–94. Berlin: Mouton de Gruyter.
Pérez Báez, Gabriela. 2018. "'Slowly, Slowly Said the Jaguar': Collaborations as a Goal of Linguistic Field Research over Time." In *Insights from Practices in Community-Based Research: From Theory To Practice Around The Globe*, edited by Shannon Bischoff and Carmen Jany, 112–31. Amsterdam: De Gruyter Mouton.
Pérez Báez, Gabriela, Victor Cata, and Juan José Bueno Holle. 2015. "Xneza Diidxazá: Retos En La Escritura Del Zapteco Del Istmo Vistos Desde El Texto Teria." *Tlalocan* XX: 135–72.
Pérez Báez, Gabriela, and Terrence Kaufman. 2016. "Verb Classes in Juchitán Zapotec." *Anthropological Linguistics* 58 (3): 217–57.
Pérez Díaz, Fidel. 2008. "El Bachillerato Integral Comunitario, Un Modelo Educativo de Nivel Medio Superior de Los Pueblos Originarios En Oaxaca, México: Un Análisis Curricular." Instituto Latinoamericano de la Comunicación Educativa.
Philips, Susan. 1972. "Participant Structures and Communicative Competence : Warm Springs Children in Community and Classroom." In *Bilingualism and Language Contact: Anthropological, Linguistic, Psychological and Social Aspects – Acquisition of Rules for Appropriate Speech Usage*, edited by James Alatis, 77–101. Washington, D.C.: Georgetown University Press.
Pica, Teresa. 1997. "Second Language Teaching and Research Relationships: A North American View." *Language Teaching Research* 1 (1): 48–72.
Pickett, Velma B. 1993. "Reflexiones Históricas Sobre La Ortografía Del Zapoteco Del Istmo." *Guchachi Reza* 42: 27–30.
Pickett, Velma B., Cheryl Black, and Vincente Marcial Cerqueda. 2001. *Gramatica Popular Del Zapoteco Del Istmo*. 2nd Edition. Instituto Linguistico de Verano. www.sil.org/mexico/za poteca/istmo/G023a-GramaticaZapIstmo-ZAI.htm.
Pietikäinen, Sari. 2018. "Investing in Indigenous Multilingualism in the Arctic." *Language & Communication* 62: 184–95.
Piller, Ingrid. 2016. *Linguistic Diversity and Social Justice : An Introduction to Applied Sociolinguistics*. Oxford, UK: Oxford University Press.
Pineda, Irma. 2014. "Oralidad y Literatura de los Binnizá." In *Oralidad y Escritura: Experiencias desde la Literatura Indígena*, edited by Luz María Lepe Lira, 55–71. Mexico City: PRODICI.
Pinnock, Helen. 2011. "Reflecting Language Diversity in Children's Schooling: Moving from 'Why Multilingual Education' to 'How?" Save the Children & CfBT Education Trust. https://www.educationdevelopmenttrust.com/EducationDevelopmentTrust/files/05/05d323c2-615e-469c-94f2-b0901dd3675b.pdf.
Plüddemann, Peter. 2010. "Home-Language Based Bilingual Education: Towards a Learner-Centred Language Typology of Primary Schools in South Africa." *PRAESA Occasional Papers* 32 (65).
Plumas atómicas. 2019. "Estos jóvenes rapean en zapoteco para preservar su lengua." Video news report 3 December 2019. Retrieved from https://twitter.com/plumasatomicas/status/1201939157523681507
Poniatowska, Elena. 1993. "Juchitán, a Town of Women." In *Zapotec Struggles: Histories, Politics, and Representations from Juchitán, Oaxaca*, edited by Howard Campbell, Leigh

Binford, Miguel Bartolomé, and Alicia Barabas, 133–35. Washington, D.C.: Smithsonian Institution Press.

Povinelli, Elizabeth A. 2011. *Economies of Abandonment: Social Belonging and Endurance in Late Liberalism*. Durham, NC: Duke University Press.

Premsrirat, Suwilai, and Uniansasmita Samoh. 2012. "Patani Malay – Thai MTB BE/MLE In Southern Thailand." *MLE Network*.

Purkarthofer, Judith and Haley De Korne. 2020. "Learning Language Regimes: Children's Representations of Minority Language Education." *Journal of Sociolinguistics* 24(2), 165–184.

Quijano, Aníbal. 2000. "Coloniality of Power and Eurocentrism in Latin America." *International Sociology* 15 (2): 215–32.

Rampton, M.B.H. 1990. "Displacing the 'Native Speaker': Expertise, Affiliation, and Inheritance." *ELT Journal* 44 (2): 97–101.

Ravitch, Sharon M., and Matthew Riggan. 2012. *Reason and Rigor: How Conceptual Frameworks Guide Research*. Los Angeles, CA: Sage Publications.

Rebelledo, Nicanor. 2008. "Learning with Differences: Strengthening Hñahño and Bilingual Teaching in an Elementary School in Mexico City." In *Can Schools Save Indigenous Languages? Policy and Practice on Four Continents*, edited by Nancy H. Hornberger, 99–122. New York: Palgrave Macmillan.

Rebolledo, Nicanor. 2010. "Indigenismo, Bilingüismo y Educación Bilingüe En México: 1939–2009." In *Construcción de Políticas Educativas Interculturales En México: Debates, Tendencias, Problemas, Desafíos*, edited by Saul Velasco Cruz and Aleksandra Jablonska Zaborowska, 113–57. México, D.F.: Universidad Pedagógica Nacional.

Reisigl, Martin, and Ruth Wodak. 2009. "The Discourse Historical Approach (DHA)." In *Methods of Critical Discourse Analysis*, edited by Ruth Wodak and Michael Meyer. London: Sage.

Ricento, Thomas, and Nancy H. Hornberger. 1996. "Unpeeling the Onion: Language Planning and Policy and the ELT Professional." *TESOL Quarterly* 30 (3): 401–27.

Riestenberg, Kate, and Ari Sherris. 2018. "Task-Based Teaching of Indigenous Languages: Investment and Methodological Principles in Macuiltianguis Zapotec and Salish Qlispe Revitalization." *Canadian Modern Language Review* 74 (3): 434–59.

Robles, Martha. 1977. *Educación y Sociedad En La Historia de México*. Mexico, D.F.: Siglo XXI Editores.

Rockwell, Elsie. 2005. "Indigenous Acounts of Dealing with Writing." In *Language, Literacy, and Power in Schooling*, edited by Teresa McCarty, 5–26. Mahwah, NJ: Lawrence Erlbaum Associates.

Romero Frizzi, María de los Angeles. 2003. *Escritura Zapoteca: 2500 Años de Historia*. Mexico, D.F.: INAH CONACULTA.

Rouvier, Ruth. 2017. "The Role of Elder Speakers in Language Revitalisation." *Language Documentation and Description* 14: 88–110.

Royce, Anya Peterson. 1975. *Prestigio y Afiliacion En Una Comunidad Urbana: Juchitán, Oaxaca*. Mexico, D.F.: Instituto Nacional Indigenista.

Royce, Anya Peterson. 1991. "Music, Dance, and Fiesta: Definitions of Isthmus Zapotec Community." *Latin American Anthropology Review* 3 (2): 51–60.

Royce, Anya Peterson. 2011. *Becoming an Ancestor: The Isthmus Zapotec Way of Death*. Albany, NY: State University of New York Press.

Rubin, Jeffrey W. 1994. "COCEI in Juchitan : Grassroots Radicalism and Regional History." *Journal of Latin American Studies* 26 (1): 109–36.

Ruíz Martínez, David. 2013. *Faro Inextinguible de La Niñez: 75 Aniversario de La Escuela Primaria Matutina Centro Escolar Juchitán*. Oaxaca, Mexico: IEEPO.
Ruiz, Richard. 1984. "Orientations in Language Planning." *NABE* 8 (2): 15–34.
Rymes, Betsy. 2010. "Classroom Discourse Analysis: A Focus on Communicative Repertoires." In *Sociolinguistics and Language Education*, edited by Nancy H. Hornberger and Sandra Lee McKay, 528–48. Bristol, UK: Multilingual Matters.
Rymes, Betsy. 2014. *Communicating Beyond Language: Everyday Encounters with Diversity*. New York: Routledge.
Salinas Pedraza, Jesús. 1996. "Saving and Strengthening Indigenous Mexican Languages: The CELIAC Experience." In *Indigenous Literacies in the Americas: Language Planning from the Bottom Up*, edited by Nancy H. Hornberger, 171–87. Berlin: Mouton de Gruyter.
Sallabank, Julia. 2010. "Standardisation, Prescription and Polynomie : Can Guernsey Follow the Corsican Model ?" *Current Issues in Language Planning* 11 (4): 311–30.
Sánchez Miguel, Griselda. 2016. *Aire No Te Vendas: La Lucha Por El Territorio Desde Las Ondas*. Oaxaca, Mexico: International Working Group for Indigenous Affairs. https://www.iwgia.org/es/recursos/publicaciones/317-libros/3231-aire-no-te-vendas-la-lucha-por-el-territorio-desde-las-ondas.
Santos, Boaventura de Sousa. 2007. *Another Knowledge Is Possible*. London: Verso.
Santos, Boaventura de Sousa. 2014. *Epistemologies of the South: Justice against Epistemicide*. New York: Routledge.
Schieffelin, Bambi, Kathryn Woolard, and Paul Kroskrity. 1998. *Language Ideologies: Practice and Theory*. Oxford, UK: Oxford University Press.
Schreyer, Christine. 2017. "Reflections on the Kala Biŋatuwā, a Three Year Old Alphabet, from Papua New Guinea." In *Creating Orthographies for Endangered Languages*, edited by Mari C. Jones and Damien Mooney, 126–41. Cambridge, UK: Cambridge University Press.
Schwab-Cartas, Joshua. 2018. "Keeping Up with the Sun: Revitalizing Isthmus Zapotec and Ancestral Practices through Cellphilms." *Canadian Modern Language Review* 74 (3): 363–87.
Schwartz, Saul. 2018. "Writing Chiwere: Orthography, Literacy, and Language Revitalization." *Language & Communication* 61: 75–87.
Selinker, Larry. 1971. "Interlanguage." *International Review of Applied Linguistics* 10: 209–31.
Shohamy, Elana. 2006. *Language Policy: Hidden Agendas and New Approaches*. London: Routledge.
Sicoli, Mark A. 2011. "Agency and Ideology in Language Shift and Language Maintenance." In *Ethnographic Contributions to the Study of Endangered Languages*, edited by Tania Granadillo and Heidi A. Orcutt-Gachiri, 161–76. Tucson, AZ: University of Arizona Press.
Silverstein, Michael. 1976. "Shifters, Linguistic Categories and Cultural Description." In *Meaning in Anthropology*, edited by Keith Basso and Henry Selby, 11–55. Albuquerque, NM: University of New Mexico.
Skutnabb-Kangas, Tove. 2009. "Multilingual Education for Global Justice: Issues, Approaches, Opportunities." In *Social Justice through Multilingual Education*, edited by Tove Skutnabb-Kangas, Robert Phillipson, Ajit Mohanty, and Minati Panda, 32–62. Bristol, UK: Multilingual Matters.
Skutnabb-Kangas, Tove. 2018. "Language Rights and Revitalization." In *The Routledge Handbook of Language Revitalization*, edited by Leanne Hinton, Leena Huss, and Gerald Roche, 13–21. London: Routledge.

Skutnabb-Kangas, Tove, and R. Phillipson. 1994. *Linguistic Human Rights: Overcoming Linguistic Discrimination*. Berlin: Mouton de Gruyter.
Smith, Linda Tuhiwai. 1999. *Decolonizing Methodologies: Research and Indigenous Peoples*. London: Zed Books.
Smith, Linda Tuhiwai. 2005. "Building a Research Agenda for Indigenous Epistemologies and Education." *Anthropology & Education Quarterly* 36 (1): 93–95.
Sociedad Pro-Planeación del Istmo, La. 1956. "Alfabeto Popular Para La Escritura de Zapoteco Del Istmo." Mexico, D.F. http://www.sil.org/system/files/reapdata/18/46/28/18462852663139743177456296293165996711/L073_AlfPopZapIstmoFacs_zai.pdf.
Speed, Shannon. 2005. "Dangerous Discourses : Human Rights and Multiculturalism in Neoliberal Mexico." *Political and Legal Anthropology Review* 28 (1): 29–51.
Spivak, Gayatri. 1996. "Subaltern Studies: Deconstructing Historiography." In *Selected Works of Gayatri Chakravorty Spivak*, edited by Donna Landry and Gerald MacLean, 203–35. London: Routledge.
Stebbins, Tonya N. 2012. "On Being a Linguist and Doing Linguistics : Negotiating Ideology through Performativity." *Language Documentation and Conservation* 6: 292–317.
Stephen, Lynn. 2002. "Sexualities and Genders in Zapotec Oaxaca." *Latin American Perspectives* 29 (2): 41–59.
Street, Brian V. 1984. *Literacy in Theory and Practice*. Cambridge, UK: Cambridge University Press.
Street, Brian V. 2011. "Literacy Inequalities in Theory and Practice: The Power to Name and Define." *International Journal of Educational Development* 31 (6): 580–86.
Stroud, Christopher. 2018. "Introduction." In *The Multilingual Citizen : Towards a Politics of Language for Agency and Change*, edited by Lisa Lim, Christopher Stroud, and Lionel Wee, 1–14. Bristol, UK: Mulitlingual Matters.
Stroud, Christopher, and Kathleen Heugh. 2004. "Linguistic Human Rights and Linguistic Citizenship." In *Language Rights and Language Survival: A Sociolinguistic Exploration*, edited by Donna Patrick and Jane Freeland, 191–218. Manchester: St. Jerome Publishing.
Suslak, Daniel F. 2009. "The Sociolinguistic Problem of Generations." *Language and Communication* 29 (3): 199–209.
Swinehart, Karl. 2012. "Tupac in Their Veins : Hip-Hop Alteño and the Semiotics of Urban Indigeneity." *Arizona Journal of Hispanic Cultural Studies* 16: 79–96.
Taylor, Analisa. 2006. "Malinche and Matriarchal Utopia: Gendered Visions of Indigeneity in Mexico." *Signs: Journal of Women in Culture and Society* 31 (3): 815–40.
Taylor, Charles. 2002. "Modern Social Imaginaries." *Public Culture* 14 (1): 91–124.
Taylor, Charles. 2004. *Modern Social Imaginaries*. Durham, NC: Duke University Press.
Thomas, Wayne, and Virgina Collier. 1997. "School Effectiveness for Language Minority Students." NCBE Resource Collection Series, No. 9. Washington, D.C.
Tollefson, James. 1991. *Planning Language, Planning Inequality*. London: Longman.
Tollefson, James, and Amy B. M. Tsui, eds. 2004. *Medium of Instruction Policies: Which Agenda? Whose Agenda?* Mahwah, NJ: Lawrence Erlbaum Associates.
Tuck, Eve, and K. Wayne Yang. 2012. "Decolonization Is Not a Metaphor." *Decolonization: Indigeneity, Education & Society* 1 (1): 1–40.
Tutino, John. 1993. "Ethnic Resistance: Juchitán in Mexican History." In *Zapotec struggles: Histories, Politics, and Representations from Juchitán, Oaxaca*, edited by Howard Campbell, Leigh Binford, Miguel Bartolomé, and Alicia Barabas, 41–61. Washington, D.C.: Smithsonian Institution Press.

UNESCO. 1953. "The Use of Vernacular Languages in Education." Paris.
UNESCO. 2003. "Education in a Multilingual World." Paris.
United Nations. 2007. *Declaration on the Rights of Indigenous Peoples.* http://www.un.org/esa/socdev/unpfii/documents/DRIPS_en.pdf.
Urcid, Javier. 2005. "Zapotec Writing: Knowledge, Power and Memory in Ancient Oaxaca." http://www.famsi.org/zapotecwriting/zapotec_text.pdf.
Urla, Jacqueline. 2012. *Reclaiming Basque: Language, Nation and Cultural Activism.* Reno & Las Vegas, NV: Nevada University Press.
Urla, Jacqueline, Estibaliz Amorrortu, Ane Ortega, and Jone Goirigolzarri. 2017. "Basque Standardization and the New Speaker: Political Praxis and the Shifting Dynamics of Authority and Value." In *Standardizing Minority Languages: Competing Ideologies of Authority and Authenticity in the Global Periphery*, edited by Pia Lane, James Costa, and Haley De Korne, 24–46. London: Routledge.
Valdés, Guadalupe. 2005. "Bilingualism, Heritage Language Learners, and SLA Research: Opportunities Lost or Seized?" *The Modern Language Journal* 89 (3): 410–26.
Van der Aa, Jeff, and Jan Blommaert. 2011. "Ethnographic Monitoring : Hymes's Unfinished Business in Educational Research." *Anthropology & Education Quarterly* 42 (4): 319–34.
Velasco Cruz, Saul. 2010. "Políticas (y Propuestas) de Educación Intercultural En Contraste." In *Construcción de Políticas Educativas Interculturales En México: Debates, Tendencias, Problemas, Desafíos*, edited by Saul Velaso Cruz and Aleksandra Jablonska Zaborowska, 63–112. Mexico, D.F.: Universidad Pedagógica Nacional.
Walter, Stephen, and Diane Dekker. 2008. "The Lubuagan Mother Tongue Education Experiement (FLC): A Report of Comparative Test Results." The Philippines: SIL.
Warner, Michael. 2002. *Publics and Counterpublics.* New York: Zone.
Warriner, Doris S., and Martha Bigelow, eds. 2019. *Critical Reflections on Research Methods: Power and Equity in Complex Multilingual Contexts.* Bristol, UK: Multilingual Matters.
Watahomigie, Lucille J, and Teresa McCarty. 1996. "Literacy for What? Hualapai Literacy and Language Maintenance." In *Indigenous Literacies in the Americas: Language Planning from the Bottom Up*, edited by Nancy H. Hornberger, 95–113. Berlin: Mouton de Gruyter.
Weber, Jean-Jacques. 2009. "Constructing Lusobourgish Ethnicities: Implications for Language-in-Education Policy." *Language Problems & Language Planning* 33 (2): 132–52.
Weber, Jean-Jacques. 2014. *Flexible Multilingual Education: Putting Children's Needs First.* Bristol, UK: Multilingual Matters.
Webster, Anthony K. 2010. "On Intimate Grammars: With Examples from Navajo English, Navlish, and Navajo." *Journal of Anthropological Research* 66: 187–208.
Wee, Lionel. 2018. "Essentialism and Language Rights." In *The Multilingual Citizen : Towards a Politics of Language for Agency and Change*, edited by Lisa Lim, Christopher Stroud, and Lionel Wee, 40–64. Bristol, UK: Mulitlingual Matters.
Weinberg, Miranda. 2021. "Scale-Making, Power and Agency in Arbitrating School-Level Language Planning Decisions." *Current Issues in Language Planning* 22 (1–2), 59–78.
Weinberg, Miranda, and Haley De Korne. 2016. "Who Can Speak Lenape in Pennsylvania? Authentication and Language Learning in an Endangered Language Community of Practice." *Language & Communication* 47: 124–34.
Wenger, Etienne. 1998. *Communities of Practice: Learning, Meaning, Identity.* Cambridge, UK: Cambridge University Press.
Wenger, Etienne. 2000. "Communities of Practice and Social Learning Systems." *Organization* 7 (2): 225–46.

Weth, Constanze, and Kasper Juffermans. 2018. "Introduction: The Tyranny of Writing in Language and Society." In *The Tyranny of Writing: Ideologies of the Written Word*, edited by Constanze Weth and Kasper Juffermans, 1–17. London: Bloomsbury Academic.

Whaley, Lindsay. 2011. "Some Ways to Endanger an Endangered Language Project." *Language and Education* 25 (4), 339–348.

Whitinui, Paul, Maria del Carmen Rodríguez de France, and Onowa McIvor, eds. 2018. *Promising Practices in Indigenous Teacher Education*. Singapore: Springer Nature.

Wiggins, Bradley E., and G. Bret Bowers. 2015. "Memes as Genre: A Structurational Analysis of the Memescape." *New Media and Society* 17 (11): 1886–1906.

Williams, Cen. 1994. *Arfarniad o Ddulliau Dysgu Ac Addysgu Yng Nghyd-Destun Addysg Uwchradd Ddwyieithog, [An Evaluation of Teaching and Learning Methods in the Context of Bilingual Secondary Education]*. PhD Dissertation, University of Wales, Bangor.

Williams, Quentin Emmanuel. 2017. *Remix Multilingualism: Hip-Hop, Ethnography, and Performing Marginalized Voices*. London: Bloomsbury.

Williams, Quentin Emmanuel, and Christopher Stroud. 2013. "Multilingualism in Transformative Spaces: Contact and Conviviality." *Language Policy* 12 (4): 289–311.

Wilson, Shawn. 2008. *Research Is Ceremony: Indigenous Research Methods*. Halifax, NS & Winnipeg, MB: Fernwood publishing.

Woolard, Kathryn A. 2008. "Language and Identity Choice in Catalonia : The Interplay of Contrasting Ideologies of Linguistic Authority." In *Lengua, Nación e Identidad: La Regulación Del Plurilingüismo En España y América Latina*, edited by Kirsten Süselbeck, Ulrike Mühlschlegel, and Peter Masson, 303–23. Frankfurt am Main & Madrid: Vervuert & Iberoamericana.

Wortham, Stanton. 2005. *Learning Identity: The Joint Emergence of Social Identification and Academic Learning*. Cambridge, UK: Cambridge University Press.

Wyman, Leisy Thornton. 2012. *Youth Culture, Language Endangerment and Linguistic Survivance*. Bristol, UK: Multilingual Matters.

Yamada, Racquel-Maria. 2007. "Collaborative Linguistic Fieldwork: Practical Application of the Empowerment Model." *Language Documentation & Conservation* 1 (2): 257–82. http://scholarspace.manoa.hawaii.edu/handle/10125/1717.

Zavala, Virginia. 2014. "An Ancestral Language to Speak with the 'Other': Closing down Ideological Spaces of a Language Policy in the Peruvian Andes." *Language Policy* 13 (1): 1–20.

Zentella, Ana Celia. 1997. *Growing up Bilingual : Puerto Rican Children in New York*. Malden, MA: Blackwell Publishers.

Zepeda, Ofelia. 1995. "The Continuum of Literacy in American Indian Communities." *Bilingual Research Journal* 19 (1): 5–15.

Zúñiga, Víctor, and Edmund T. Hamann. 2015. "Going to a Home You Have Never Been to: The Return Migration of Mexican and American-Mexican Children." *Children's Geographies* 13 (6): 643–55.

Index

activism, definition 1–2
- change in activism strategies 84–85, 102–103, 126, 148, 192, 200–203, 210–211

Álvaro Obregon 29, 45, 48–49, 96

art (see music; literature; visual art)

campaigns promoting language 6, 98, 143

Casa de la Cultura 38, 43, 59, 143, 146, 169, 172

civic/ non-government organizations, role of 42–44, 53–55, 58, 130, 137–138, 142–145, 155, 169–179, 186, 188–191

coloniality 6, 16, 37–38, 70, 84, 97, 118, 189
- resisting coloniality 37, 40, 42, 70, 84, 125, 174, 176, 207

Comitancillo 48, 100

communication practices
- digital communication practices 50–52, 54, 60, 115, 131, 178–179
- purist communication practices 21, 49, 52, 130, 133, 149–150, 180–182, 195, 199, 209
- syncretic communication practices 8, 21, 52, 129–130, 133, 163, 172–174, 185, 195, 209

community of practice 15–16, 61, 63, 94, 134, 163, 182, 217

conviviality 15, 21, 86–87, 90, 102, 107–108, 129, 142, 158–164, 168–169, 177, 182, 197, 204, 209–213

dialect (see varieties)

digital communication (see communication practices)

earthquake 42, 54, 98, 103, 142–143, 161, 173

economic inequality/ poverty 40, 43, 52, 98, 188–189, 192

education systems
- bilingual education 39–41, 73, 76, 91–99, 106, 135, 198
- community-based education 24, 29–30, 82, 103, 137–161, 168–170, 177, 188–192
- higher education 23, 60, 78–79, 109–136, 168, 179, 186, 194–196
- lack of enrollment in classes 118, 124, 134
- Mexican education policies 39, 41, 88, 94–99, 106
- public schooling 23, 31, 39–42, 66–67, 86–108, 109–110, 142–143, 165, 188–189, 195, 197, 203–204, 206–207

emotion/ affect 30, 52, 69, 79, 103, 109–110, 114–115, 127–128, 150, 157–158, 186, 190, 206, 208–209

English, role of 31, 40, 53, 98, 108–109, 112, 117–118, 120, 124, 134, 171, 189, 206

Espinal 47, 57, 96

ethnographic monitoring (see research)

evangelical groups 37, 50, 58, 61, 67, 143
- Summer Institute of Linguistics 58–61, 67, 143, 145–146

family language practices 30, 44–47, 97, 113–115, 121–122, 160

gender 2, 47, 113, 173–174, 176

government, role of 29, 38–42, 94–98, 106, 143, 210

hip-hop (see music)

ideology (see language ideologies)

identity 8–10, 13, 23–24, 27, 42–43, 53, 68–69, 89, 91–92, 112–119, 131–132, 135–136, 139, 146, 155, 165–169, 178–179, 184–187, 190, 195–196, 211

imaginaries (see social imaginary)

insider-outsider dynamics 2, 27, 53–54, 61, 68, 70–74, 81–85, 189–190, 193, 201, 207

Instituto Nacional de Lenguas Indígenas (INALI) 32, 41–42, 54, 143

Ixtaltepec 48

Ixtepec 48

Juchitán de Zaragoza 26, 29–30, 36–37, 43, 45–46, 58, 87, 99, 103–104, 114, 122, 137, 145, 148–149, 153, 156, 165, 170, 172–173, 178

La Mata 47, 109
La Ventosa 30, 45, 47, 51, 96, 188, 190
language documentation 37, 57, 59, 154
language ecology 9, 21–22, 53–55, 63, 78, 84, 111, 113, 134, 167, 180, 191–192, 208
– definition 31–32
language ideologies
– definition 5–6
– Eurocentric ideologies 6, 9, 16, 37–40, 70, 88, 112, 140, 189–190
– language ideological assemblage 6–7, 9–11, 52, 114
– monolingual ideologies 30, 52, 57, 60, 77, 112, 115–117, 191, 203
– negative ideologies about Indigenous languages 6, 52, 23, 88, 112–114, 119, 135, 179, 192, 206–207
– positive ideologies about Indigenous languages 6, 52, 56, 78, 100, 106, 162, 164, 183
– pluralist ideologies 4, 8–9, 15, 60, 77, 79, 166, 173, 185
– standard ideologies 9, 116–117, 119, 123, 130, 132–133, 140, 149, 163, 181–183
language ontology 7–11, 56–57, 60, 67, 69–70, 84–85, 103–104, 205–208
language policy
– arbiters 106–107, 128, 135
– field of language policy and planning 13, 63, 211
– Mexican Law on the Linguistic Rights of Indigenous Peoples 29, 94
language shift and endangerment 9, 11, 30–31, 45–47, 56, 79–80, 156–157
legitimation of
– Indigenous languages 6, 78–80, 99–105, 117, 123–126, 131–132, 183–184, 198–199
– Isthmus Zapotec identity 103, 117, 145–146, 166, 179, 184–187

– Isthmus Zapotec speakers 104, 106–107, 109–110, 131–132, 135–136, 179, 190, 198–199
– learners 106, 117, 131, 150, 153–154, 162–164, 171, 190, 194
linguistic citizenship 14, 18, 184
linguistic human rights 12–14, 67
linguistic insecurity
– with Isthmus Zapotec 11, 44, 113–116, 131, 206
– with Spanish 30, 115
– with teaching 82, 97, 104, 129–130, 190
– with writing 29, 97, 130, 188, 206
linguistic landscape 49, 100, 103, 189
literacy education 24, 29–31, 37, 39, 43, 52, 59–60, 66–67, 76, 87, 91, 98, 100, 103–106, 129–130, 137–164, 180, 188, 206
literature/ literacy, Isthmus Zapotec 29, 35, 42, 57–58, 104, 125, 130–131, 137, 142–146, 188
– *Neza* 42, 58, 66, 142, 169, 220
– *Guchachi' Reza* 43, 59, 138, 142–143, 169, 219
– poetry 26, 29, 43–44, 58, 106, 125, 143, 145–146, 155, 171, 176, 188
– writing competitions 29, 146, 155, 171–172

minority language, definition of 4
music, role of 9, 52, 104, 129, 142, 147, 153, 165, 201
– hip-hop 26, 147, 155, 165, 170, 177

orthography 43, 52, 60, 76, 143, 148, 163, 180, 182, 207, 209
– polynomic writing norm 149, 163, 207

participation in network/ collective, role of 14, 82, 103, 107, 130, 135, 166, 172, 177, 181, 184, 191, 201, 204, 207, 209–211
pedagogy (see teachers and teaching)
policy (see language policy)
political movements 41, 43–44, 97–98, 172, 177
polynomic writing norm (see orthography)

radio, use of 165, 178
research 17, 25–28
– data collection and analysis 26–28, 73–74
– ethnographic monitoring 72–74, 85, 193
– scholar-activist reflection 26–28, 68–70, 73–74, 83–85, 189–190, 193, 205–208

Salina Cruz 37, 45–46
San Blas Atempa 47–49, 51, 57, 76, 122–123, 126, 129, 137
Santa María Xadani 47–49
scales 14, 31, 53–54, 63, 192, 203
social imaginary
– definition 5
– conflicting imaginaries/ priorities 9–12, 84, 97, 107–108, 134, 203, 207
– multiple imaginaries 18, 60, 69, 108, 205–207, 210
– new imaginaries 132, 161, 173–174, 202

teachers and teaching
– creating materials and curriculum 82, 86–89, 99–108, 124–126, 129–131, 146–147
– lack of teachers 126, 134
– pedagogical approaches 76–77, 82, 86–87, 91–94, 100–108, 122–126, 129–131, 148–164, 188–192
– teacher education (and lack thereof) 29, 78–79, 82, 99, 107, 111, 126, 130–136
– teachers as policy arbiters 86–89, 106–108, 117, 128, 132, 135–136
teachers' union 88–89, 94–95, 97, 99–100
– PTEO 88–89, 94–95, 100, 102–104, 195, 220
Tehuantepec 36–37, 40, 43, 46–47, 109, 111, 117–118, 120–123, 125, 129, 148
theories of social change 11–17, 71, 87, 192, 203, 208–211

Union Hidalgo 47, 103, 170, 180

varieties or dialects of Isthmus Zapotec 47
– role in education 122–123, 129–130, 162
visual arts 43, 87, 105, 153, 166, 171–172, 174

wind farms 26, 40, 178, 188
writing (see literacy education; literature; orthography)

www.ingramcontent.com/pod-product-compliance
Lightning Source LLC
Chambersburg PA
CBHW071738150426
43191CB00010B/1618